CALIFORNIA: STATE OF COLLUSION

POWER, CONSPIRACY, AND COVER-UPS IN A FAILED CRIMINAL JUSTICE SYSTEM

JOSEPH TULLY

California: State of Collusion is published by Sutton Hart Press, llc
Vancouver, Washington

Inquiries: Inquiries@SuttonHart.com
Website: www.suttonhart.com
Author Website: www.josephtully.com
First Printing: February, 2018

ISBN: 978-1-947779-05-1
Library of Congress Number: Pending

Printed in the United States of America
Media and Reviewer Contact: maggie@platformstrategy.com
Cover Design: Lorraine Elias
Copy Editor: Veronica Pamoukaghlian
Layout Design: Jason Enterline

To every human being who has yearned and striven for greater justice on this beautiful planet that we all share in common.

—Joseph Tully

TABLE OF CONTENTS

FOREWORD BY NORM PATTIS

Trial Lawyer & Author of *Taking Back the Courts*

I've got two words for you if you ever find yourself charged with a crime in California: Joseph Tully.

I'd sound irreverent if I were to say this young lawyer has brass balls, so let me play it safe: Tully is a ferocious warrior. He's a trial lawyer in an era of vanishing trials, a gunslinger among paper-pushers, he's the sort of guy who might laugh in a confessional and then ask the priest if he wanted absolution.

And he writes.

In this, his second book, Tully talks some bold talk. He takes aim at psychopathic prosecutors, treasonous judges, and the preening politicians who make the words "all rise" in a courtroom sound more like foreplay than an invocation to show Lady Justice respect.

The book's subtitle is "*State of Collusion*." Its focus is California. That's a shame, really, because as I read this volume I kept thinking of my own home state of Connecticut, and what I have seen in courtrooms across the country: cops, judges, prosecutors, and lawmakers whirling madcap around a Maypole, all giddy at the prospect of doing the people's work, but heedless about the persons they maim in the name of justice.

Tully fights this mad dance.

"I fight an imbalance in a justice system run by psychopaths in government, law enforcement, and presiding over our courts," he writes. "This is the California that has created a system that ensures you are screwed from before you get arrested through your life as an ex-con." Like

Charon guiding people over the River Styx, Tully remains calm, steadfast even, as he surveils the California courts.

Take a broader aim, Joe, I muttered as I read the book. This is an era where claims of "fake news" and fact-checking have drawn battle lines coast to coast. We all say we read the same Constitution, but the meanings we attach to the document diverge and sometimes never meet.

The country has the feel of seventeenth century England before the English Civil War pitted Roundheads against Cavaliers; they read the same Bible but drew different meanings from a common text.

Tully's righteous fury reflects the crisis of legitimacy that made the new political landscape possible. Don't ask about the election, ask what sort of conditions made that sort of election possible. What I'm saying is this: the new administration is the canary in the mineshaft of American politics. If you think 2016 was raucous and wild, just you wait until 2020. Chaos is just around the corner.

So, too, in our courts.

Joseph Tully is a trial lawyer's trial lawyer. He fights, and wins. Why does he win? Because he can hear the beating heart of a people betrayed by their leaders and institutions.

Plenty of lawyers can talk the talk. The blawgosphere is filled with the chatter of keyboard warriors with plenty to say about everything. Not many of these wizbangs can walk the walk, though. Joseph Tully can and does.

You don't need to read this book. You can sit snugly in the web of illusion and pretend that all is well in this the best of all possible worlds. But if you read this book, and I encourage you to do so, you might just awaken to the reality the 2016 election made clear: there's plenty in the country that is broken just now.

Tully shows you the darker truths about California's criminal justice system. Read this book and weep. And then remember the two words worth recalling: Joseph Tully. When a twisted lawman sporting a badge snatches you or a loved one off the street, you'll want Joe standing beside you in court.

Norm Pattis

New Haven, Connecticut

CHAPTER ONE

WHY WE FIGHT

"Truly, I tell you, whatever you did for one of the least of these brothers and sisters of mine, you did for me." Matthew 25:40

Everyone deserves a fair trial. That is what I and other criminal defense attorneys remind ourselves when we get down, or when a case is a drain on the psyche. The wretched, despicable, vile, and even the evil have a right to legal representation. But it is not for the benefit of those villains that we pursue and excel in this area of practice. We fight for their rights because we are defending the rights of *all of us*[1].

The sad truth is that before you are arrested in California, you are already screwed. More likely than not, the system, the state, and the players, have all colluded to rig the machine and ruin your life before you are even booked. I hope that by exposing the corruption and the collusion, perhaps we can avoid the traps awaiting everyone, or help change the status quo, so others are not deprived of their rights. Let's fight together to fix the system and make it fair for everyone.

By exposing the corruption and evil lurking within the system, I hope to give a voice to the truly good law enforcement officer, prosecutor, and judge, who are treated as unwelcome outsiders in a fraternity from hell. I want to empower them to stand up to their peers, who will bend the laws

1 As Robert Kennedy put it in one of his first speeches as Attorney General in 1961, "We know that if one man's rights are denied, the rights of all of us are in danger."

to their wicked ways, rather than strive for Justice.

I grew up in the East Bay town of Martinez, California, in the San Francisco Bay Area. It is a small suburban town in the shadow of Berkeley and Oakland, a tunnel and a bridge away from San Francisco. The state's capital, Sacramento, is just an hour's drive Northeast.

In the '70s, I was a kid. In the '80s, I was a teen, and in the '90s, I was a young adult out on my own, learning the law. These formative years were turbulent for California, though my young life was quite stable. Hippies, protests, and riots were in the news. Back then, the City of Berkeley, led primarily by the students of UC Berkeley, actually protested for the right of free speech and against the violence of war. Throughout the same period, both the state and the people were transformed by technology, gentrification, immigration, and housing-boom growth. It was all very exciting for a young man—all this opened my eyes to the possibilities of the world ahead of me.

I didn't always want to be an attorney, but I was inspired by superheroes. My dad was a firefighter until he retired. My mom stayed home and raised my two older sisters and me, and later worked for the school district as we got older. I was raised with a sense of fair play and civic engagement. My childhood hero was Spider-Man, who balanced crime-fighting with the awkward social and professional life of his alter ego, Peter Parker. In high school, I didn't battle Doctor Octopus, but I did juggle things just like Peter Parker: athletics, school, student government, music, family, and the chance to date a girl.

Growing up, I learned that there are multiple Californias. As a Bay Area native who went to the University of California Davis in the agricultural heartland, visited metropolitan LA in the summers, camped in the Sierras, surfed in San Diego after college, attended law school in San Francisco, and had his first law job in the heart of the Central Valley in Fresno, I have seen quite a few of them. California is not as progressive and touchy-feely as the rest of the country envisions. Sure, we are pretty cool, blessed with great climate and geography, and we have strong, diverse economies. But Northern California is as different from Southern as coastal is from inland. We have big cities, huge suburbs, and vast tracts of agricultural land and wilderness.

Consider that the state hosting liberal enclaves like Berkeley, Hollywood, and San Francisco, once outlawed gay marriage with Prop. 8 in the year 2008. The culture that created the Grateful Dead, Cheech & Chong, and Snoop Dogg, still has very restrictive cannabis laws. We sent Nixon and Reagan to the White House, and we made celebrities of Jane Fonda and Sean Penn.

I see similar dichotomies as a lawyer. California is tough on crime but sensitive to prisoner rights, compassionate to cannabis use, yet refuses to fully legalize it. It is anti-gun-ownership, yet mostly okay with citizens defending themselves with a firearm.

These rich contrasts in our culture contribute to both confusion and collusion in California law. There are so many people and ideologies, that sometimes they all get represented simultaneously. Laws are proposed by attention-seeking politicians or well-intended activists, or made by committee with articles to appease. Specific verbiage is then crafted to placate, and it's all mottled and whittled until it gets passed by a majority. In the books, you can find a local law that is counter to state law, yet complies with federal law. A law could have a nice sentiment behind it, yet be so weakly written that people who obey it can still get prosecuted for a crime, based on some prosecutor's own subjective interpretation.

After law school, I followed my passion for law—and a girl I was dating—to Fresno. My love of the law was still nascent, but it was my chosen career path. This was during the tech boom, and I thought I'd become a high-tech, dot-com attorney and cash in. Well, there was no chance of that in Fresno. I got a job, like many freshly hatched lawyers, working for a County Court, the Public Defender's Office of Fresno County.

The moment I was truly called to criminal defense, my 'Saul of Tarsus' moment, was in Fresno. Away from my family and friends in the Bay Area, I threw myself into work. A Public Defender's office is understaffed and overworked, and there is always more to do for the cases you have, and more cases coming in the next day. Fresno County is typically cited as having the largest caseload of any Public Defender's office in the state. So, there were plenty of cases to immerse myself in. It is here, in the Public Defender's Office that "The Law" became real for me, with real people and faces tied to charges, courts, and decisions that would impact the rest of their lives.

I recall a case where I was called to defend a black man accused of a racist hate crime against a white man. Apprehensive, I met my client in jail, in a small room, secluded from any security. He turned out to be extremely pleasant and cordial, a really nice, decent guy. He didn't hate me, or white people. He might have been angry, he might have even hated the guy he was brawling with while the altercation lasted. He might have said some things he shouldn't, but he did not exhibit an ounce of dislike or unease around me. However, the official dialog from the cops and the DA was that he was a 'black menace to society.' The reality was that he was just a black guy who got into a fight with a white guy in Fresno.

Defendants are just people, like you and me. Bad timing or a bad situation, one bad decision, and they end up in cuffs. I have represented famous rappers from Oakland and former child stars in Los Angeles, and they are just people too. The phrase, "There, but for the grace of God, go I[2]." has real meaning to me now.

I learned quickly that when people are arrested and accused of crimes, they face the awesome power of the state. Police, prosecutors, and judges are backed by badges, authority, and taxpayer wealth. I saw firsthand how they colluded to jail the accused, with only a novice, overworked public defender—me—ready to protect their rights. In response to these overwhelming odds, I was determined to fight for justice and fair play.

Any Public Defender's office is a crucible that forges great criminal defense attorneys. Many lawyers wash out, overwhelmed, stressed, and depressed, and divert to other areas of practice. But a few are annealed by the experience and emerge as hardened weapons for justice. Worse yet for the collusion in power: they become warriors ready to fight injustice.

You will find that, contrary to what you see on TV, it is passion and humanity that separate defense attorneys from most prosecutors. Prosecutors generally fall into two categories: government time-clock punchers and political psychopaths. On the other hand, once the passion is ignited in a defender, we fight with a righteous zeal to protect the rights of our clients and of society.

Illegal search? Entrapment? Rough arrest? These are not just about the individual we represent, they are strikes against all of our liberties. Every aspect of each case is viewed through a lens that ultimately invokes the U.S. Constitution. This isn't a crutch to help us sleep at night whilst defending murderers; it becomes a part of our personality, a drive to protect *your rights*.

---

2 A phrase attributed to the English evangelical preacher and martyr John Bradford (circa 1510–1555), meaning, in witnessing another one's suffering through injustice, I understand the same could happen to me. Bradford is said to have coined the phrase while watching a line of people walking towards their execution. The grace of God did not protect him for too long, as he was burnt at the stake in 1555.

The hours and workload in the Public Defender's office were like Hamburg for the Beatles, or 924 Gilman Street[3] for Green Day. I received a lot of real-world practice and experience in a short amount of time. In the Fresno Public Defender's Office, I was exposed to more cases, crimes, and prosecutors than I would have encountered in private practice. I was also mentored by some of the greatest attorneys I have ever met. In fact, I met my current law firm partner Jack Weiss late one Saturday evening coming down the elevator. I could tell he was curious about this young kid leaving the office late on a Saturday night. We hit it off then and there, and we still run our practice together today.

I dove in deep. The usual track for a novice public defender, and even for a prosecutor is to spend a year on misdemeanors, a year in juvenile court, a year doing preliminary hearings or writing motions, and then you finally get elevated to the felony trial team after three, four, or even five years. In my case, I was lucky enough to earn a spot on a felony trial team in just eight months, a crucible indeed.

Careers with power and authority attract psychopaths bent on imposing their will on others. In criminal justice, a cohort of masochistic bullies can dominate the vulnerable. Some bully as bad cops, some love to destroy lives as prosecutors, using every advantage, legal and illegal, to throw the book at a defendant. But perhaps the worst of the worst are the evil ones in the black robes who impose their twisted views on—and systematically demean—our laws and Constitution.

In California, the forces of government and law enforcement collude against you for their own psychopathic goals. Collusion is the heart of the problem within the criminal justice system. Multiple parties: police,

3 Address of the non-profit music club in Berkeley that became a springboard for the punk revival band.

prosecutors, judges, and politicians, all work in concert to control and convict people. Unfortunately, these professions are highly attractive to psychopaths, who get pleasure from inflicting their will on others. Give a cop a badge, a prosecutor a podium, a judge a gavel, and a politician a pen, and they can do more harm to society than a horde of Huns.

In all my cases and trials, I have only encountered one truly evil defendant. On the flip side, I have encountered many, many cops, prosecutors, and judges who spewed evil unabashedly. They are the prime movers in this 'State of Collusion' that we live in.

Under the guise of being "tough on crime", they wage a "war on drugs." They ban "assault weapons" for you and me, yet arm cops with machine guns and tanks. They give you the "right to remain silent," and then eavesdrop to gain incriminating evidence. There is "zero tolerance" for consensual 'crimes' with no victim. Those in power use 'terrorism' as a catch-all for crimes involving drugs, civil protest, and free speech. Homeland Security pushes widespread domestic surveillance violating our Fourth Amendment rights. The language of a politician running on a 'Get tough on crime' platform drips with words intended to demonize a wide spectrum of acts, both legal and illegal; the mundane as well as the dangerous.

Lawmakers, police, district attorneys, and judges all have more to gain by making a criminal of you and criminalizing more behaviors. The crooked cop increases his or her arrest rate, their chances of promotion, and their twisted sense of self-esteem by bending laws to bring people in. The prosecutors and judges are motivated by 'winning,' rather than by justice. Further, since prosecutors and their frequent cohorts, judges, supposedly represent "The Law," they feel they can bend and twist it to get those wins; the ends justify the means.

Conveniently, a win equates to career headway and political advancement towards the position of District Attorney or elected judge, with power and a cushy job. Finally, judges are politicians, just like lawmakers. They have a public to please by appearing "tough on crime" and not letting rights and laws interfere with their own brand of justice. After all, their next campaign would be pointless without the support of prosecutors and police unions.

In our liberal state, colluders have banned even harmless, victimless crimes. The criminalization of cannabis persists, despite a sea-change around the country. Some forms of consensual adult relationships were, until recently, criminal offenses. Owning the wrong type of gun or selling the wrong type of milk can get you busted—it is even illegal to keep a ferret as a pet in California!

In this book, we will look at the many ways the system colludes against you, spanning infractions through capital felonies, throughout California's history and across the political spectrum.

They say, "you can't fight City Hall." It is true; a citation for a local ordinance infraction is often tougher to fight than a felony criminal charge. Cities and lawmakers have realized that banning something in the name of the public good can short-circuit traditional legal defenses. Prostitution and selling drugs are crimes, but standing around on a street corner violates a city ordinance because you look like you might be thinking of committing a crime.

The Second Amendment protects your right to keep and bear arms, but a city ordinance can prevent you from buying or selling a firearm in your town, in the name of public safety. These laws are tough to fight head on, but easy to change by voting out the people who sustain them.

Many people consider misdemeanors to be trivial, harmless mini-crimes. In fact, many serious crimes in California are classified as misdemeanors and can get you locked up for a year. In California, DUI is classified a misdemeanor for the first three offenses, as long as no one was injured by your driving.

In 2011, the State reclassified many felonies as misdemeanors to reduce overcrowding in State Prison. This resulted in local DA's pressing charges on fewer arrestees, to reduce the burden on their local jails. The spectrum of crime classifications has broad impacts on the entire system. History is another through-line, where we see ripples and echoes of issues from the past. From the rum-runners and gin-joints of the '30s to today's pot farms and dispensaries, prohibition has been an opportunity for both sides of the law.

Of course, this is California, so federal prohibition was often at odds with local interpretations. We grow more wine grapes and marijuana plants than any other state, so, commerce has always been a factor in compliance. Just as loopholes allowed wine grapes and medical marijuana to continue to grow, local law enforcement bullies still find loopholes to bust those who stay within the law.

These themes of abuse by law enforcement and vigorous defense by civil libertarians like myself will recur throughout the book. The laws and police powers in California are stacked against you before you are even arrested. The presumption of guilt by law enforcement and the entire legal system enables the psychopaths in power to channel defendants into jail, prison, or worse.

Before you are arrested, you have likely committed several varieties of crime, giving the cops and DA a smorgasbord of choices to convict you with. The more laxly a law is written, the more intently it seems to be enforced upon unsuspecting citizens. The more vague a law, the more intricately a prosecutor will explore ways to nail you with it.

Suspects are warped through a black hole to a bizarro universe where misdemeanors carry a million-dollar bail, coercion during detention is routine, and judges consistently steer proceedings to their predetermined outcome: a victory for the prosecutor. Being "tough on crime" is seen as a virtue greater than being a strong enforcer of our Bill of Rights.

Fighting this fight against California's corruption and collusion can be exhausting and draining, but also very personally rewarding. Defending the innocent against the awesome power of the State is spiritually satisfying.

Medical cannabis is absolutely legal in California. It has been since Prop. 215 passed in 1996. Despite a public referendum, subsequent law, Senate Bill 420, and now Prop. 64, the colluders continue to attack cannabis patients and providers as if they were dangerous outlaws, outright stealing whatever money they may have on them.

The people who come to me for criminal defense in marijuana cases *thought* they were well within the guidelines of the laws for cultivating and dispensing medical cannabis in California. As it turns out, most of the time, they were. Their proactive compliance and adherence to the law does not keep overzealous law enforcement and DA's from raiding and robbing their grows and dispensaries.

These 'criminals' are some of the nicest, warmest people I've ever met: old hippies, young hipsters, and old-fashioned central valley farmers. They are nice people who are victimized for peacefully growing and sharing a plant, within the laws of the state. These cases are particularly satisfying because the law is on our side, and the overreaching colluders are so far on the wrong side. I get to protect rights, defend justice, and help medical activists, who grow alternative medicine to help others in need.

Self-defense cases are another category I find satisfying to defend. Defending someone who is on trial for defending themselves is a piling on of righteousness. When cops are called to an altercation or a shooting, they are quick to assign blame one way, usually to the person who was injured the least, regardless of the facts. Law enforcement will let a court sort out the details of who did what. At the scene, they usually just want to go through the motions and make sure they don't get sued for failing to remove a dangerous person. The easiest way for them to accomplish this is to arrest one or more parties.

There are two sides to every story. Punching someone is not necessarily a crime. Shooting someone is not necessarily a crime. Your right to defend yourself is sacrosanct. I enjoy helping people defend that right. You are right to defend yourself, others, and your property. I have defended many a "Stand Your Ground" case here in California, where the shooter was demonized, both in the press and in court, for protecting himself from an attacker. The fact that he had used a gun added to the public scorn. But this type of case where life, liberty, and the Constitution are all on trial, was right in my wheelhouse.

There is a righteousness that comes with defending the innocent and protecting our civil liberties, but not every case is a triumph for the accused. As a defense attorney, it would not be just for me to cherry-pick cases and avoid tough clients who face terrible odds. The worst of the worst deserve a fair trial too. A serial killer caught in the act must still be represented before the law. While real criminals do exist in this world, the colluders must still be held at bay, so the perpetrator can get due process.

If the killer is convicted and given a severe sentence, it will be in accordance with his rights, and our rights, to a fair trial. Quelling public outrage should not shortcut justice. Due process, proper procedure, and legal scrutiny, all serve to protect individuals, and ultimately society. It does no one any good to put the wrong person in jail and leave a killer at large. When all the evidence has been legally presented, an aggressive defense has been mounted, and due process has run its course, only then can one be found guilty. That is my job as a defense attorney. Justice cuts both ways, blindly. Remember, what we do to the lesser among us, even the monsters, we do to ourselves.

What does the evidence show? That is the only question a good defense attorney asks. It is also the only question a juror should ask. If the evidence can prove guilt, then the prosecutor will present and argue for guilt. A surgeon operating on a patient after a bank robbery doesn't ask if the person was the robber, security guard, customer, teller, or manager. Likewise, a defense attorney must only ask, "What does the evidence show?" You don't need to lie, cheat, or steal to successfully defend the accused. I focus on the case, the evidence, and due process.

Like a surgeon stepping up to the operating table, I look at the available data. The race, background, or personality of the patient have no bearing on addressing the facts and saving a life. Again, like a surgeon, I can be passionate about my job, while maintaining a clinical regard for the specifics of the case. I get this question from people all the time when they find out I am a defense attorney, "What do you do when you are representing someone and you think they are guilty?" Like a surgeon, it doesn't matter. My job is to review the evidence and best defend their right to a fair trial. My job is to say, "What does the evidence show?"

At the end of the day, I fight for the Constitution, not necessarily for the piece of paper written over two hundred years ago, but for the ideals and human rights it upholds.

The Constitution was written well before California became a state, but it still applies here today. Over the years, we have seen its limits pushed, and its coverage abrogated. Sometimes citizens have pushed back; we had prohibition bootlegging, the Watts riots, the Free Speech Movement, the Summer of Love, draft card burning, the LA riots, the protests that overturned Prop. 8, amnesty cities, the Occupy movement. But these flare-ups merely punctuate the persistent collusion against our rights.

Everyday, criminal defense attorneys fight for your constitutional rights in courts from Crescent City to San Diego. We might be representing a drunk, a stoner, a panhandler, or a kidnapper, but in the end, we are representing *you*:

- Your right to assemble and not be called a gang.
- Your right to sacraments without being called a substance abuser.
- Your right to free speech without being accused of a hate crime.
- Your right to speak out against grievances by the state and not be called a 'terrorist.'
- Your right to remain silent, and not have the state twist your words against you.
- Your right to own, and use, a gun to defend yourself.
- Your right to be secure in your person, homes, papers, and effects.
- Your right to probable cause against unwarranted search and seizure.
- Your right to due process, to fairness within the legal system.
- Your right to not be tried more than once for the same crime.
- Your right to an impartial trial by a jury of your peers.
- Your right to representation by an attorney.
- Your right to a speedy trial.
- Your right to face your accusers.

- Your right to see the nature of the charges and evidence brought against you.
- Your right to not be subject to excessive bail, fines, or cruel and unusual punishment.

Facing you are:

Local police, sheriff, FBI, marshals, troopers, SWAT, task forces, rangers, and other state and federal agencies trying to arrest you, *and*

Prosecutors, elected District Attorneys, Assistant DA's, special prosecutors, secret tribunals, California Attorneys General, and Assistant U.S. Attorneys, all trying to convict you, *and*

Judges and lawmakers invested in suppressing your rights in order to maintain the police-enforcement power structure that benefits their "tough on crime" and "doing something" self-propagating political agendas, *and*

The media, both news and entertainment, that overwhelmingly take and support the side of all the forces listed above.

The last line of defense for accused individuals, and our society in general, is the thin, wool-blend line of defense attorneys who stand between you and the thousands colluding against you.

Balance is important in life. A lifestyle balance between work and play is healthy. A political balance of liberal and conservative is energizing. A balance in the scales of justice is desirable.

Our fight for balance in California occurs in a dark side of the State that few people get to see, a shadow California that is neither liberal nor conservative, but rather, statist and police-supremist, and trods equally over everyone's rights. It is a place that puts "State-Reich" over individual rights.

I fight this imbalance in a justice system run by psychopaths in government, in law enforcement, and presiding over our courts. It is a system that ensures you are screwed from before you get arrested through your life as an ex-con.

This state is California: State of Collusion.

CHAPTER TWO

INTRODUCTION TO PSYCHOPATHS: MEGA-LAW-MANIA

Traits Of A Psychopath:

Boldness = Low fear including stress-tolerance, tolerance of unfamiliarity and danger, high self-confidence and social assertiveness.

Disinhibition = Poor impulse control including problems with planning and foresight, lacking affect and urge control, demand for immediate gratification, poor behavioral restraints.

Meanness = Lacking empathy and close attachments with others, disdain of close attachments, use of cruelty to gain empowerment, exploitative tendencies, defiance of authority, destructive excitement seeking[4].

If you are arrested in California, the deck is stacked against you. For decades, the cops, prosecutors, judges, and politicians in power have eviscerated your constitutional rights to make their jobs easier to perform. Their livelihoods rely on law enforcement winning, and those in their path losing. You are collateral damage along their career path.

Collusion at the highest levels tilts the tables against you, and towards the "police powerists" who use convictions as stepping stones and power

4 Patrick, C.; Fowles, D.; Krueger, R. (August 2009). Triarchic conceptualization of psychopathy: Developmental origins of disinhibition, boldness, and meanness. Development and Psychopathology. Cambridge University Press. 21 (3): 913–938. doi:10.1017/S0954579409000492. PMID 19583890.

chits. These powerful jobs attract people who desire power: psychopaths. Government jobs with uniforms, authority, guns, and badges are an attractive lure.

Studies have shown a number of careers that appeal to those with psychopathic tendencies. Jobs with overt power and authority are overly-represented on those lists. Law enforcement jobs are available to a broad spectrum of characters: From school yard bullies to Ivy League "Mean Girls." There is a position of authority over others for every socio-economic level of abuser.

By controlling the entire legal process: investigation, arrest, evidence, prosecution, sentencing, and even writing new laws, the psychopaths in power are sure to win. But, winning is not enough for a psychopath. Their opponent must also lose. They must be made an example of. A psychopath does not think the way you and I do.

Players in California's judicial system, from law enforcement to politicians, have colluded against our liberty, rights, and way of life for their gain. Their megalomania is our loss.

'Psychopath' is not a medical term. It is used as a catch-all for a number of conditions and diagnoses that involve anti-social behavior. The Diagnostic and Statistical Manual of Mental Disorders, (DSM) does have descriptions for antisocial, narcissistic, and other personality disorders. However, it is common for these and some of their variations to be lumped under the term 'psychopath.'

A psychopath does not need to be a raving mad lunatic—far from it. They are usually functioning members of society in positions of responsibility. Some examples of a stereotypical psychopath as depicted in modern books and movies are Norman Bates, from the aptly named, *Psycho*; Dr. Hannibal Lecter, the cannibalistic psychiatrist from the

"Silence of the Lambs" movie and book series; Dexter Morgan from the *Dexter* books and Showtime series, who worked in law enforcement; and Francis Underwood, US Representative who rose in power to President of the United States in Netflix' House of Cards.

These cool-headed, highly functioning, guileful criminals charm you whilst plotting your demise. These cold-blooded killers, who are defined by their inability for and complete lack of human compassion, are good representations of an archetypal psychopath, rather than the drooling, wild-eyed crazy person that the term 'psychopath' may initially conjure.

Psychopathic personality is a disorder that can be generally described as characterized by detached emotions, reduced inhibition, high stress tolerance, Machiavellianism, lacking empathy, lacking guilt, egocentricity, charm, manipulation, impulsivity, and a reckless disregard for others. However, it is these very same traits that define the psychopath, that can propel a person (in certain careers) to a position of authority.

Dr. Kevin Dutton is a research fellow at the Department of Experimental Psychology at Oxford University. In his book, *The Wisdom of Psychopaths*[5], Dr. Dutton lists the top careers that attract psychopaths. Many of these jobs require coolness, charm, and risk-taking, in order to be effective. Some of these career choices also give perfect cover to those with antisocial aspects to their personality.

The Top 10 Careers With The Most Psychopaths

1. CEO
2. Lawyer

5 Dutton, K. (2012). The wisdom of psychopaths: Lessons in life from Saints, spies and serial killers. London: William Heinemann

3. Media (Television/Radio)
4. Salesperson
5. Surgeon
6. Journalist
7. Police Officer
8. Clergy
9. Chef
10. Politician

These careers attract and require big egos, confidence, charm, stress endurance, and a strong will. Chillingly, because these jobs put people in the limelight, they thereby also put one in a position requiring interaction with and, at least on the surface, accountability to many people.

The functioning psychopath CEO, chef, clergy, journalist, media personality, or salesperson must win our trust in order to succeed at their job. They often have to do so while seemingly in the public eye under public scrutiny. They can be polarizing figures, but they have fans and followers that will willfully follow them, as faithful to these psychopaths as they are to their favorite professional sports team, actress, or poison-laden 'diet' product.

However, a person can choose which athlete to cheer for or which chef to dine with. We have no say in which cop arrests us, which prosecutor tries to jail us and charge us with penalties that will stick with us for life, nor the judge who presides over this system infiltrated by bad apples with very little accountability. In fact, the bad apples in the system are often given peer-support by the other bad apples within the same system.

The careers that attract psychopaths do so because they are roles that have authority and power over the public. Remember, power corrupts but it also intoxicates. Indeed, power has been likened many times across the ages as an aphrodisiac and was most notably in modern times described as the "ultimate aphrodisiac" by Henry Kissinger as quoted by the New York Times in 1973.

Psychopaths can flourish as police officers, prosecutors, judges, and politicians. They used to call these roles "civil servants," but the tables have certainly turned. We, the public, empower these roles under the color of authority to wield their power complete with badges, gavels, and other totems of authority. This also includes the shield of law that has been built up by this psychopathic class to protect themselves. They are shielded from repercussions if they actually get caught doing something wrong.

It is not a coincidence that psychopaths end up in these jobs. As children, nascent criminal psychopaths often expressed a desire to work in law enforcement. A pair of researchers, Stanton E. Samenow Ph.D. and Dr. Yochelson, studied the criminal mind. They found a large percentage of career criminals they interviewed had aspired to become police when they were younger[6].

It is important to remember here that law enforcement not only includes police and sheriffs, but also prosecutors. It is also no secret that most judges are former prosecutors. Here is a lawyer joke that illustrates that point perfectly: "Question: Why does the judge sit at the bench? Answer: Because there's not enough room at the prosecutor's table."

According to the researchers studying criminals, "They reported being attracted by the uniform, the badge, the gun, the fast police cruiser and, most of all, the thrill of pursuing and catching the 'bad guys.' It was the excitement and the ability to wield absolute power over other human

6 Samenow, S. (2013). Criminals Who Become Cops. Psychology Today. Retrieved 26 December 2017, from https://www.psychologytoday.com/blog/inside-the-criminal-mind/201302/criminals-who-become-cops

beings that attracted them as well as the prospect of being cited as heroes for doing so."

One has to wonder if these criminals were the more physical type of kids rather than the intellectual children. I wonder if this same study was conducted specifically on white collar criminals, criminals who use their intellect to commit crimes rather than physically commit them, if their aspirations would have been to become prosecutors, judges, or politicians.

It is not fair to say that every cop, prosecutor, judge, or politician is a born psychopath. In fact, the moral cops, prosecutors, and judges who are good and just are some of the greatest people that I have met in my life. I don't doubt that many cops, prosecutors, judges, and even politicians may have gone into their careers with glowing hearts full of good intentions.

While some members of law enforcement and the legal system are inherently good, some were sick people beforehand and were attracted to the role, whilst others were corrupted by an environment that enables psychopathic behavior. Indeed, prisons are full of criminal minds—on both sides of the bars.

It is widely acknowledged that people who are put into positions of authority often abuse their power. No doubt everyone has heard the expression, "Power corrupts and absolute power corrupts absolutely." This phrase comes to us from Lord Acton, who used it in a famous letter to Bishop Mandell Creighton in 1887. This means that good people will be corrupted into acting badly when given too much power and authority over others. It also means that bad people who are given too much power and authority will act even worse when the veil afforded by their position allows them to act with impunity.

Citizens, us, *We the People*, can often be subject to the whims of bullies and sadists with the power to destroy our lives. Innocent people can be subjected to a 'power trip' police encounter, arrested by a megalomaniacal cop, jailed by a sadist, prosecuted by a manipulative Machiavellian, and judged by an ego-tripping sociopath.

Maniacs with badges, guns, and gavels have undue power over our lives.

The concept that power can be a corrupting influence was the motive behind our American Founding Fathers' construction of a system of checks and balances. It is why James Madison, a grand political architect, sought to divide power rather than concentrate it when crafting the U.S. Constitution. Dividing power, making those who have it 'checked' by competing groups and having the whole system held accountable by the citizens, was Madison's brilliant solution. This division of power—checks and balances and accountability in the U.S. Constitution—is mirrored in the Republic of California's constitution.

Our California system was originally designed with the notion that you cannot trust government; that powerful government positions will be sought out by corrupt people, or in today's terms, psychopaths.

We have lost our way.

In careers with power, there are complex hierarchies of authority. Police and sheriff deputies have ranks and officers; prosecutors have a District Attorney, senior attorneys, and politicians to account to. Judges have politicians and higher appellate courts to please, and government administrators themselves fall into a pecking order of authority. From dog-catcher to council member to Senator, in this system, ordinary people can slowly and unwittingly become destructive agents, especially if their peer group consists of a majority of corrupt individuals.

We've all heard of the 'blue wall of silence' where even a 'good' police officer won't tell on a bad officer when he or she has done something wrong or illegal, and will actively cover it up. Even if the minions serving under psychopaths eventually become aware of destructive ends, relatively few people have the resolve or integrity needed to resist authority.

There are two famous modern studies of the corrupting influence of power; the Milgram Experiment and the Stanford Prison Experiment. You may recognize these from the news, Psych 101 class, or from their depictions in popular culture. The Milgram Experiment was conducted at Yale in 1961. It was a series of experiments dealing with obedience to authority figures conducted by Yale University psychologist Stanley Milgram[7].

The study measured the willingness of participants to obey an authority figure who instructed them to perform acts conflicting with their personal conscience. An ad in the local Connecticut newspaper asked for subjects, inviting "500 New Haven men to help us complete a scientific study of memory and learning" and offering "Four dollars for one hour of your time."

The Milgram Experiments involved random pairs of volunteers—a 'teacher' and a 'learner' who were supervised by an 'experimenter', who, for the purposes of looking like an authority figure, was dressed in a white lab coat. The cover of the experiment was that it was to test memory. Under the supervision of the staff experimenter, the teacher read a list and the learner—behind a blank wall—was expected to repeat it from memory, with the teacher encouraged by the Experimenter to administer painful electric shocks to the learner if the items were not properly repeated.

The electric shocks were ever increasing in nature and the levels were clearly labeled, "SLIGHT SHOCK," "MODERATE SHOCK," "STRONG SHOCK" and "VERY STRONG SHOCK" in black and "INTENSE SHOCK," "EXTREME INTENSITY SHOCK," "DANGER SEVERE SHOCK" and

7 Milgram, S. (1963). Behavioral Study of obedience. The Journal Of Abnormal And Social Psychology, 67(4), 371-378. http://dx.doi.org/10.1037/h0040525

"XXX" in red. The teacher had a dial and a button and heard the painful reactions from the learner beyond the wall. The Experimenter encouraged the teacher to turn up the voltage to more and more painful levels as the test progressed, ostensibly as negative reinforcement to provoke better recall.

But here is the catch: there was no learner and there was no memory experiment. Milgram was testing how far a random person off the street would go in punishing a stranger when encouraged to do so by an authority figure. Again, the experimenter *was* in a lab coat. The learner was in on the experiment, and the reactions to the painful shocks were pre-recorded so that every teacher heard the exact same painful screams and pleadings of having a heart condition as they administered the electric shocks.

When instructed by an authority figure, most of the Milgram participants progressively tortured a stranger up to what they thought was a dangerous voltage. A surprising 65% of experiment participants were prepared to administer the potentially lethal highest level of shock (450 volts!) marked by big red capital letters as "XXX" to subjects who had done nothing wrong other than forget some words on a memory test.

These subjects, the teachers, were not psychopaths or sadists, they were just regular people drawn at random. But, under the instruction of an authority figure who clearly was exhibiting psychopathic behavior, they went along with committing torture. This shows how one bad apple in a position of authority in a police force, prison, or government bureau can poison others into doing bad things willingly. It's also bad news for someone falsely accused of a crime where, most juries follow this rule—they convict. Despite the shocking exception once or twice a decade, exploited by the media, where a seemingly guilty person is acquitted by the jury, most juries convict. Juries convict because they have a predilection, a preprogrammed disposition, to convict.

They do this, in accordance with Milgram, because persons in authority, the prosecutor in a suit along with a parade of officers in shiny uniforms and guns, and usually with the implied approval of the judge, ask them to. In fact, this human tendency is extremely hard to counter in court in a trial situation for a defendant. How do you effectively change human nature in 12 people, whom you've never met, who, whether or not they're willing to admit it, are either already biased against the accused for just being there? Also, they may not even care whether the person is guilty or not but may be sadistically just looking forward to inflicting pain on someone else in order to feel some sense of power.

Add to this the perpetual state of cynicism and outright fear that the 'lamestream' media seem to pulse out nonstop and you've got an uphill battle from start to finish. One of the things that I do in jury trial, which has been very successful, is openly and honestly talking to potential jurors about the Milgram Experiment.

I can't change their behavior or makeup but I can remind them that the courtroom demands them to be at their best, to put aside any feelings of hatred, pettiness, or negativity caused by an influence of power. I remind them that their conclusion on the case is what matters—not the opinion of the prosecutor or the law enforcement witnesses. I remind them that their job is to think critically, not be obedient to voices of those who are in positions of authority.

Milgram summarized the experiment in his 1974 article[8], "The Perils of Obedience," writing:

> "The legal and philosophic aspects of obedience are of enormous importance, but they say very little about how most people

8 Milgram, S. (1973). The perils of obedience | Harper's Magazine. Retrieved 26 December 2017, from https://harpers.org/archive/1973/12/the-perils-of-obedience/

> behave in concrete situations. I set up a simple experiment at Yale University to test how much pain an ordinary citizen would inflict on another person simply because he was ordered to by an experimental scientist. Stark authority was pitted against the subjects' [participants'] strongest moral imperatives against hurting others, and, with the subjects' [participants'] ears ringing with the screams of the victims, authority won more often than not. The extreme willingness of adults to go to almost any lengths on the command of an authority constitutes the chief finding of the study and the fact most urgently demanding explanation."

Experiments like Milgram's have been used to explain "the banality of evil," a phrase coined by Hannah Arendt to describe Nazi soldiers blindly, stupidly following the orders of their leaders towards outright sadistic ends. In modern law enforcement, there are psychopaths holding rank that influence the behavior of peers and subordinates.

However, these authority figures in law enforcement may have climbed to a head position specifically due to their psychopathic behaviors and their talent and ability to impose their will on others. This leads to a culture of corruption, collusion, and cover-ups where their subordinates, just like the Nazi soldiers, will likewise blindly follow the psychopathic orders of their department and unit heads and chiefs.

A decade after the first Milgram Experiment, a similar study used real people and real interactions in a physical setting to test the corrupting influence of authority. It has become known as, "The Stanford Prison Experiment." Stanford psychology professor, Dr. Philip Zimbardo, conducted a study to investigate how readily people would conform to the roles of guard and prisoner in a role-playing exercise that simulated prison life.

Prison guards have a stereotypical reputation still today, as cruel or even sadistic. Zimbardo wanted to assess if it was their character or the environment that made men brutal against others. Participants were randomly divided into Inmates and Guards, and moved into a mock jail in a Stanford building basement. The participants adapted to their roles well beyond Zimbardo's expectations, as the guards enforced authoritarian measures and ultimately subjected some of the prisoners to psychological torture. The results of the experiment have been argued to demonstrate "the impressionability and obedience of people when provided with a legitimizing ideology and social and institutional support[9]."

"How we went about testing these questions and what we found may astound you. Our planned two-week investigation into the psychology of prison life had to be ended after only six days because of what the situation was doing to the college students who participated. In only a few days, our guards became sadistic and our prisoners became depressed and showed signs of extreme stress." (Zimbardo, 2013)[10]

These experiments were done in a lab with random subjects, with no previous bias or racism against the other party. They blindly inflicted pain on others because they were instructed it was the right thing to do.

Imagine how personal bias, stress, adrenaline, fear, ego, racism, and a badge of authority could push the results to a further extreme. Especially in an organization that encouraged members to conform to a culture of power over subjects.

Law enforcement are not working in lab conditions. They do not have

9 How Zimbardo's Prison Experiment Reveals Social Roles' Effect On People's Behavior. (2017). Psychologistworld.com. Retrieved 26 December 2017, from https://www.psychologistworld.com/influence-personality/stanford-prison-experiment

10 Zimbardo, P. (2013) Stanford Prison Experiment. Retrieved 26 December 2017, from http://www.prisonexp.org/

a professor to discuss their real-time actions with. They are given carte blanche to enforce laws as they see fit in the field.

A psychopathic person who craved that power, and sought it, would be ecstatic to find a green light to abuse others once given a badge.

CHAPTER THREE

COPS ACTING BADLY: PSYCHO COPS

Law enforcement careers provide an ideal environment where the criminally-minded individual can find cover for their criminal and psychopathic inklings. This is obvious to children who are not yet aware they have a psychopathic disorder. Kids love playing cops and robbers and exerting power over one another. Some kids cannot tell the difference between the cops and the robbers and grow up to be one or the other, interchangeably. Family, upbringing, opportunity, education, or just plain dumb luck may be the determining factor that puts one child on the path to becoming a criminal, and the other on the path to becoming a police officer.

Of course, most cops are not criminal psychopaths. But the few that are thrive behind the shield of a badge. Not many careers reward evil with healthcare and a pension. As we see from the Milgram and Zimbardo experiments, a few bad apples can make the whole barrel stink. Exposed to powerful peers who push the legal limits, many 'good guy' cops fall in line. After a while, the culture of an entire division or department can change to resemble its worst elements.

One might expect police to be model citizens. But the "Thin Blue Line" of silence does not always include their spouses. In 2014, the Philadelphia Inquirer reported: "National studies show that 40 percent of police families experience domestic violence, compared with about 10 percent of the general public[11]." If a cop would smack his wife, it is not a big leap to smacking a suspect.

Externally, law enforcement agencies do not want a reputation of violating the law and the rights of the citizens. It is bad for business, bad politically, and bad for community relations. Internally, no agency wants the liability of willfully putting mentally ill police on the streets. Law enforcement supposedly has screening in place to help weed out psychopaths during hiring and training. But the reality is that the nature of a psychopath makes it difficult to catch them. By definition, psychopaths are clever, Machiavellian, and charming.

There is a component of the Police Officer Standards and Training ("POST") called the "Peace Officer Psychological Screening," which was initiated in 1955 and last updated in 2017. The purpose of that screening is to ensure that every peace officer is "free from any emotional or mental condition that might adversely affect the exercise of the powers of a peace officer and to otherwise ensure that the candidate is capable of withstanding the psychological demands of the position[12]." It is interesting to note that there are hundreds of online forums, blogs, and study guides on how to beat this test.

If a crooked law enforcement applicant was crafty enough to get an education, stayed under the radar, and out of jail thus far, they are sure to be able to slip through most screening processes. They may even come across as the perfect recruit. When a bad apple is discovered in a police agency, is the screening process reassessed to figure out what went wrong? I've never seen that headline.

---

11 Philadelphia Inquirer (2014). Police officers police families. Philadelphia Inquirer. Retrieved 26 December 2017, from http://articles.philly.com/2014-09-11/news/53775430_1_police-officer-police-families-philadelphia-police-department

12 Weiss Spilberg, S., & Corey, D. (2017). Police Officer Psychological Screening Manual . Lib.post.ca.gov. Retrieved 26 December 2017, from http://lib.post.ca.gov/Publications/Peace_Officer_Psychological_Screening_Manual.pdf

On the other end of the spectrum, Police Departments are known for screening applicants to weed out those that are too intelligent. An exam called the Wonderlic Cognitive Ability Test ranks applicants on a scale from 1 to 50. This weeding out of intelligent applicants came to light in 1996 when Robert Jordan of Connecticut scored a 33 on the test and was overlooked for the next phase of interviews[13].

The average score of police officers nationally is 21-22. Jordan sued, and the response by the city of New London, CT claimed that "People within certain [I.Q.] ranges achieve a degree of job satisfaction and are likely to be happy and therefore stay on the job." The 2nd U.S. Circuit Court of Appeals in New York upheld a lower court's decision that this practice of discriminating against intelligent applicants is okay. In other words, police departments want to hire dumber cops who don't question things, and they have the blessing of the courts.

Crafty psychopaths can slip through the tests, and the more intelligent applicants are filtered out. This sets up an environment where Milgram and Zimbardo's experiments can come to life in the real world.

The mix is volatile. First, take police psychopaths who exert power over compliant peers. With the unspoken police code known as the "Blue Wall of Silence" behind them, they can subjugate a community to their will. The pressures of the job and the stress of split-second decision-making amplify things. Combine this with a lack of training, especially in the proper use of force and the federal militarization of local police. Give them a uniform, a badge, and a gun.

Complete the cocktail with constant media idealization on primetime every night of 'cops breaking the law because they can,' as well as a

13 Rucke, K. (2014). Can Someone Be Too Smart To Be A Cop?. MintPress News. Retrieved 26 December 2017, from http://www.mintpressnews.com/can-someone-be-too-smart-to-be-a-cop/192106/

contemporary America that has come to near-worship the act of compliance with any government demand as well as government authority figures. This makes for a potential American law enforcement becoming an occupying force bent on the submission of all citizens.

There are countless cases of individual police officers acting badly, exerting excessive force, planting evidence, or even murdering innocent civilians in cold blood. These are terrible tragedies and perhaps could have been prevented by an awareness of the fact that powerful positions will attract bad people and can corrupt even the best of people.

More diligence should be taken: we need better screening, training of police, and regular on-the-job counseling. Law enforcement agencies will argue that these bad cops are lone wolves—a bad egg that slipped through the system. But too often the system is corrupted from within and a culture of crime, greed, and evil permeates entire police divisions and departments.

The paucity of police training is absurd. The Free Thought Project did a survey of police training requirements[14] and compared them to the requirements for becoming a hairstylist. In California, the State Board of Barbering and Cosmetology mandates 1,600 hours of training to be licensed. A separate state board overseeing police officer standards requires a minimum of 664 hours to be a cop. Ongoing on-the-job police education and training is limited to an average of only an hour a month.

The law is constantly changing; communities are constantly changing; technology is constantly changing; yet police in California spend less than one percent of their work time improving themselves professionally. This makes it nigh impossible for police organizations to adapt in the face of change. Training on tasers, Black Lives Matter, protesters, legalized

14 Agorist, M. (2014). Hairstylists are Required to Attend Significantly More Training Than Cops. [online] The Free Thought Project. Available at: http://thefreethoughtproject.com/hairstylists-required-attend-significantly-training-cops/ [Accessed 26 Dec. 2017].

cannabis, body cameras, and other opportunities to do their jobs better are passed over. Advancing knowledge and training are not core values of the law enforcement mission. This is a reason why so many problems persist decade to decade.

Fear has silenced many from shining light on endemically corrupt law enforcement organizations, but in the past, some have been exposed.

Oakland PD Riders

The Oakland Police Department has a track record of abusing their power in the community. This is the same organization that, in 1991, paid a $42,000 settlement to rapper Tupac Shakur after allegedly brutally beating him for jaywalking. Moreover, during the 2001-2011 timeframe, Oakland paid $57 million to victims of police abuse—the largest sum of any city in California[15].

Nearly twenty years ago, a group of decorated senior cops established their own 'gang' within the Oakland PD. The group of four officers known as "The Riders" had a reputation to have kidnapped, planted evidence, and beaten citizens. These were veteran officers, respected by their peers, and looked up to by rookies. It was one of these rookies—ten days on the job and fresh out of the Academy, who blew the whistle on the Riders.

The whistleblower rookie testified to seeing the other cops using excessive force, kidnapping, brutally beating suspects in custody, falsifying reports, planting evidence, and more. Racial undertones were obvious: of the 119 plaintiffs, all but one were African-American.

A criminal case was brought against the four cops in 2000. One was acquitted, two had the case dismissed after two mistrials, and the fourth, the alleged ringleader, fled and is still wanted by the FBI.

15 Johnson, S. (2015). How a Dirty Police Force Gets Clean. POLITICO Magazine. Retrieved 26 December 2017, from https://www.politico.com/magazine/story/2015/03/oakland-police-reform-115552

Delphine Allen was the first person to come forward to sue the City and OPD for his treatment at the hands of the Riders. He was represented by legendary attorney John Burris and, eventually, 118 other victims signed on. The lawsuit bore Allen's name: *Allen v. City of Oakland*. During the criminal trials, Allen testified that the officers beat him with their batons and planted drugs on him.

Though the criminal cases were not conclusive, the City of Oakland agreed to a settlement of nearly $11 million for the 119 civil plaintiffs who claimed they were victimized by the Riders. This resolved the civil rights cases claiming the Riders abused authority, committed crimes, planted evidence, and that the Oakland Police Department turned a blind eye to the abuse. In total, the victims had spent more than 25 years behind bars based on false charges and evidence at the hands of the Oakland PD.

In 2013, nine years after the settlement, U.S. District Judge Thelton Henderson found the Oakland Police Department had failed to fully implement reforms as required in the settlement. To guarantee compliance with the settlement, Judge Henderson appointed former Baltimore Police Department Commissioner Thomas Frazier as Compliance Director. The Compliance Director holds unprecedented powers to require corrective action even for conduct not specified in the Settlement Agreement. Oakland has spent another $53 million on reforms and oversight[16].

It is interesting to note that the three officers who stood trial moved on to law enforcement and security consulting careers elsewhere—being an Alpha Dog is a hard lifestyle to break.

Even though the officers who stood trial were not convicted, the Riders case exposed the system and the department as corrupt. Settlements and

16 Oakland Police Department. Wikipedia. Retrieved 26 December 2017, from https://en.wikipedia.org/wiki/Oakland_Police_Department

Federal watchdogs tell the bigger story. Hopefully, the wider reforms will protect Oakland residents going forward.

LAPD Rampart Scandal

In the Los Angeles district known as "Rampart," systematic and widespread police corruption set a high watermark in the 1990s[17]. Being so near to Hollywood, this case blurs into the plots of *LA Confidential*, *Training Day*, *Internal Affairs*, and *The Shield*. More than 70 police officers either assigned to or associated with the Rampart CRASH unit were implicated in some form of misconduct. The range of offenses included unprovoked shootings, unprovoked beatings, planting of false evidence, frame-ups, stealing and dealing narcotics, bank robbery, perjury, and the covering-up of evidence of these activities[18]. Ironically, CRASH is an acronym for Community Resources Against Street Hoodlums.

There were a number of troubling public incidents that exposed the CRASH team and the problems at Rampart over a few years in the late 1990s. Here is a timeline with facts from the PBS investigative program, *Frontline*:

March 18, 1997 – Officer Kevin Gaines Road Rage Shootout

Undercover L.A.P.D. officer, Frank Lyga, shot and killed off-duty Rampart CRASH member Kevin Gaines who was acting erratically and threateningly in a case of apparent road rage. Gaines flashed gang signs, followed Lyga's car, brandishing a .45 ACP handgun as Lyga radioed LAPD for backup. Lyga explained that while driving, Gaines threatened him with a gun. "In

17 Glover, S., & Lait, M. (2003). Ex-Chief Refuses to Discuss Rampart | StreetGangs.Com. Streetgangs.com. Retrieved 26 December 2017, from http://www.streetgangs.com/police/rampart/082303_ex_chief_uncooperative_#sthash.9vBawRrf.dpbs

18 Editorial (2014). D.A.'s blind spot. The Free Library. Retrieved Dec 26 2017 from https://www.thefreelibrary.com/EDITORIAL%3b+D.A.%27S+BLIND+SPOT.-a083421919

my training experience, this guy had 'I'm a gang member' written all over him." Investigators on the case discovered that Gaines had allegedly been involved in similar road rage incidents, threatening drivers and brandishing his gun. Gaines was an associate of known Blood gang members.

November 6, 1997 – Officer David Mack Bank Robbery

An armed robbery of an LA Bank of America near the USC campus made off with $722,000. In the course of the month-long investigation, the assistant bank manager confessed to her role in the crime and implicated her boyfriend, Rampart CRASH officer David Mack as the mastermind. Mack took the fall, never revealing the location of the money. He served only a portion of his 14-year sentence, joining the Mob "Piru Bloods" in jail. Before his arrest, Mack was seen in Las Vegas with his former partner Rafael Perez, where they lost thousands of dollars. Mack never ratted out his accomplices in the robbery.

February 26, 1998 – Rampart Station Beating

A CRASH team officer brought a gang member into the station for questioning. The handcuffed man was allegedly beaten to the point of vomiting blood. Two officers were fired in the incident, and the victim received a large civil settlement.

May 1998 – Missing Cocaine

Officials in the L.A.P.D. property room discovered that six pounds of cocaine evidence were missing. Within a week, detectives focused their investigation on L.A.P.D. Rampart CRASH unit member Rafael Perez.

August 25, 1998 – Perez Arrested

When first stopped and arrested by detectives, Perez asked, "Is this about the bank robbery?" It wasn't. It was about the 6 pounds of missing cocaine, which investigators believed had been checked out by Perez, under another officer's name, and sold on the streets of Rampart through a girlfriend. Some of the stolen cocaine was checked in by LAPD officer Lyga, who had shot Rampart member Gaines in self-defense. After five days of deliberations, the jury announced that it was hopelessly deadlocked, with a final vote of 8-4 favoring conviction.

In preparing to bolster their case for a retrial, investigators discovered an additional eleven instances of suspicious cocaine transfers. They believe that Perez stole evidence from Lyga to try to implicate him, as revenge for shooting Gaines. Detectives were able to identify dope "switches," where Perez had ordered the cocaine evidence out of Property and replaced it with Bisquick.

September 8, 1999—Perez Cuts a Deal

Rafael Perez made a deal with prosecutors under which he pled guilty to cocaine theft and agreed to provide prosecutors with information about other Rampart CRASH officers involved in illegal activity. In exchange, Perez received a five-year prison sentence and immunity from further prosecution of misconduct short of murder.

Thus began a nine-month confessional during which time Perez met with investigators more than 50 times and provided more than 4,000 pages of sworn testimony. Before he was done, Perez had implicated about 70 officers in misconduct, from bad shootings to drinking beer on the job[19].

19 Boyer, P. (2001). Bad Cops. [online] The New Yorker. Available at: https://www.newyorker.com/magazine/2001/05/21/bad-cops [Accessed 26 Dec. 2017].

The CRASH unit indulged themselves like an elite force within the LAPD. They trained their own new members, socialized with their own, and even gave out informal awards for injuring or killing civilians. They operated like any organized criminal gang such as LA's Bloods or Crips. Indeed, several members of the Rampart Division associated with the Piru Bloods, both during their careers and later from prison. Rampart officers were employed by West Coast rap mogul Suge Knight as security. Suge Knight has also been connected to the gang[20].

Gang Laws

The troubling case of the Rampart Division brings up a glaring inequity. Gang laws are probably the most draconian and unconstitutional laws that we have in California. While it certainly is necessary to deal with criminal gangs for the betterment of society, if the public actually knew how the "criminal street gang" statutes as contained in California Penal Code sections 186.22-186.26 functioned, and how they were applied in court, I have no doubt that 90% of the public would vote to change them in some way.

As it is right now, these laws are liberally applied to young minorities and the vast powers that they give prosecutors in a court are wielded to produce conviction results that would make loaded dice jealous. However, even though the gang laws are so easy to apply to young minority men in court to double, triple, or up the sentences to life, I have often wondered why these same laws are not applied to bad cops.

When gang laws are so wide open and so easy to apply to just about anyone, wouldn't corrupt cops count as a gang? They wear the same uniform, meet specifically to break the law, and have each other's backs–

20 Philips, C. (2003). As Associates Fall, Is 'Suge' Knight Next?. LA Times. Retrieved 26 December 2017, from http://www.latimes.com/local/la-fi-suge1aug01-story.html

just like the Crips and Bloods. Maybe if these draconian gang laws were applied more outside the demographics of young minority men, society would reconsider them.

However, while lovers of Justice wait with baited breath for the public to come to arms over the unfairness of gang laws, prosecutors should at least, for the appearance of fairness, apply these same gang laws to law enforcement officers who act like criminal street gangs.

Christopher George Latore Wallace was born in Brooklyn. In the 1990s, he rose to prominence in the East Coast rap scene as the "Notorious B.I.G." At the height of the East Coast-West Coast rap feud, "Biggie," as he was known, was gunned down in a drive-by shooting outside an LA party after the Soul Train Music Awards[21].

The murder of the Notorious B.I.G.[22] aka "Biggie Smalls" remains unsolved. A 2002 book by Randall Sullivan, *Labyrinth*, compiled information about the murder of Biggie. In the book, Sullivan accused Marion "Suge" Knight, co-founder of Death Row Records and a known Bloods affiliate, of conspiring with a Rampart LAPD officer to kill Wallace and make it appear as the result of a bi-coastal rap rivalry. If these allegations are true, it shows that the line between criminal street gangs and law enforcement is much thinner than most people would believe.

What the previously mentioned experiments, as well as case studies of police corruption that have come to light show is that the psychopathic psychology that drives young men to become gang members to terrorize and murder in our streets, is sometimes no different than the drive to become a police officer.

---

21 Philips, C. (2007) Slain Rapper's Family Keeps Pushing Suit.Los Angeles Times. Retrieved on December 26, 2017 from http://www.latimes.com/local/la-me-biggie4feb4-story.html

22 Sullivan, R. (2005). The Unsolved Mystery of the Notorious B.I.G. Rolling Stone. Retrieved on December 2017 from https://www.rollingstone.com/music/news/the-unsolved-mystery-of-the-notorious-b-i-g-20110107.

This doesn't mean that all police are psychopaths, it just means that a psychopath, a person driven to impose his will on others, has options on what uniform they will wear. The same kid could have turned left one day and gone to school and gotten a C+ on a test, or turned right and gone to a market with some friends and shoplifted. The passing C+ grade would have gotten him into the Police Academy to abuse power with a badge, or the juvenile record and the stint at juvenile hall might have nudged him to a gang to assert his aggression under a red or blue bandana.

War On Drugs

Our long since failed "War on Drugs" provides a fertile ground for cop psychopaths. In a war, rights take a backseat. In a war, we look the other way if a soldier commits an atrocity because they are 'keeping us safe.' In a war, we throw away rules in favor of winning that war. Wars are to be won. Our conditioning that we are at war against drugs creates a perfect vacuum for crooked cops with no conscience to operate. This happens so much that, off the top of my head, I can think of several recent cases in Northern California. In jurisdictions that I actively practice in, narcotics officers have ended up playing both sides of the War on Drugs.

In January 2015, thirty-seven-year-old Yuba County Sheriff's Deputy Christopher "Mark" Heath traveled to Waco, Texas, to testify in a federal case against Phillip "Butch" Koss, accused of participating in a family-run marijuana trafficking ring. In January 2016, Deputy Heath was arrested in York County, Pennsylvania, for possession with intent to deliver 247 lbs of marijuana.

Prior to his bust, Heath was an officer, a hero protecting the community. He had been involved in over 60 drug busts as an investigator for the Narcotics Enforcement Team (NET-5). Judges were reverent to him in court. When defense attorneys filed suppression motions against him, asking judges to dismiss cases because he had lied in a warrant or made an unlawful arrest, the defense attorneys lost, and judges handed Heath the victory. Judges towed the modern-day California court party line and guarded Heath's aura of integrity with zealousness and returned scorn to defense attorneys who would dare question it.

In May of 2015, El Dorado County Sheriff's Deputy Mark Andrew Zlendick was arrested. He was a longtime sheriff's deputy who was assigned to the South Lake Narcotics Enforcement Team (SLEDNET), a multi-agency task force designated to take drugs off the streets. That is, until he himself was busted for possession of a controlled substance, trafficking methamphetamine, conspiracy, and possession of paraphernalia. He was caught in Nevada when police were investigating possible domestic violence based on a hastily ended 911 call with his girlfriend.

While investigating, police found Zlendick to be in possession of methamphetamine and cocaine. Though there were only 38 grams of the drugs when Zlendick was arrested, further investigation revealed that he had actually stolen more than a pound of methamphetamine and cocaine from the South Lake Tahoe Police Department's evidence locker from seized drugs that had been slated for destruction. Further, a search of his workstation yielded 3.4 grams of cocaine in his desk.

Yet, Zlendick too, like Heath, was previously a hero in his community, including the courts and district attorney's office. In 2013, he was awarded Crime Scene Investigator of the Year by the El Dorado County Sheriff's Office. After he was arrested and made bail, the county made sure to take care of their 'War on Drugs' hero, Zlendick; they placed him on paid administrative leave pending the outcome of the criminal investigation.

How many of his fellow officers have testified under oath in court as an expert regarding their ability to recognize the signs of drug trafficking or being under the influence of drugs? You would think it would be fair game in court to cross-examine those officers on why they missed these signs with one of their own colleagues and whether or not they voted for Zlendick as Crime Scene Investigator of the Year. Recently, I attempted to cross-examine a fellow El Dorado County Sheriff's deputy who has an assignment as a drug investigator on these same points during a jury trial and was shut down in short order by the judge and deputy district attorney.

I won that jury trial and in the process set a record (at that time) for one of the largest medical marijuana grows ever successfully defended in court at 396 plants. I've since gotten more acquittals with plant counts in the thousands, however, I couldn't help but consider that Zlendick's ability to steal from a police evidence locker room really wasn't just a one-man job.

In 2012, in my own backyard of Contra Costa County, the former head of Contra Costa vice squad was sentenced to fourteen years in federal prison. The cop, Norman Wielsch, pleaded guilty to five felonies after undercover state Department of Justice agents caught him stealing drugs from the evidence locker to sell on the street for cash. His co-defendant also alleged later that the two ran a brothel together and that Wielsch used his position to shut down the competition.

However, the psychopath pattern of a deplorable individual with great charisma is the same, Wielsch was a career police officer, serving for 25 years, and had spent the seven years prior to his arrest 'serving' as the commander of the state-run Central Contra Costa County Narcotics Enforcement Team (CNET).

San Leandro cop Jason Fredriksson was arrested for selling pot in 2011. The Police Detective, who was also known as "Big Dirty" was charged with furnishing marijuana to a confidential informant for sale[23]. He was also having an affair with said informant while his wife worked as a dispatcher for the same San Leandro Police Department. Evidence of illegal marijuana sales was later found at their home. Of course, both were placed on paid administrative leave after all this came to light.

His paid leave allowed "Big Dirty" to keep raking in his almost $200,000 a year salary from the SLPD. Not bad for someone with just a high school diploma. He and his wife used their 'his and hers' taxpayer salary to buy a house in very exclusive Danville for $1.1 Million.

Frederickson was also a SWAT member which brings up the issue of fetishes. Within the criminal law field, cops, sheriff deputies, and prison guards have reputations for being philanderers. It makes one wonder about what really motivates SWAT team members to dress up in black, paramilitary uniforms, complete with bondage-like masks, and brandish weapons at the powerless.

Looking at the on-the-job exploits of psychopath cops, we must also consider their personal lives. Psycho-sexual drives are strong, and can feed off work stress and adrenaline rushes. There are people strongly attracted to the police uniform and the accouterments. The psychopath cop feels powerful and invincible in his militarized state-power costume. Strippers, sexy Halloween costumes, bedroom role-players, and the Village People are examples of police-play along with uniform fetish. Cops equal power, and some take it into the bedroom. Psycho cops project their masculine power both in and out of bed.

When cops use their power to sexually victimize the young and the innocent, things get dark and reprehensible. Recently, in the East Bay of the

23 Lacabe, M. (2011). San Leandro cop Jason Fredriksson arrested for selling pot. San Leandro Talk. Retrieved 26 December 2017, from http://sanleandrotalk.voxpublica.org/2011/05/20/san-leandro-cop-arrested-for-selling-pot/

San Francisco area, dozens of law enforcement officers from several agencies were implicated in the serial sexual exploitation of a minor, that went on for years and years. The young woman known by the pseudonym, 'Celeste Guap,' was a minor at the start of her exploitation by police officers and sheriff deputies. Over a few years, more than two dozen law enforcement officers, from five different agencies, exploited Celeste Guap sexually, trading favors, cash, and police protection in exchange for her sex work.

This tragedy came to light in June 2016 when one of the cops who was victimizing Celeste ended his own life and left a suicide note listing the crimes and the other perpetrators he was aware of. In response, a few shady Richmond PD officers covertly whisked Ms. Guap away to Florida for 'rehab,' outside the reach of Bay Area investigators. This ruse was uncovered quickly.

The number of cops engaged in shady or illegal behavior with Celeste Guap is likely much higher than discovered. Law enforcement agencies circled the wagons to protect their own, and some prosecutors seemingly joined the obfuscation.

The Contra Costa DA Mark Peterson investigated thirteen cops implicated, but only filed charges against one retired cop who paid cash for sex. Peterson claimed that the other cops were cleared since no cash was exchanged, and the sex was "consensual" with a known prostitute. As if her exploitation by cops into sex work made her to blame.

Around a year later, Peterson was found to have improperly used more than $66,000 of funds from his campaign to cover personal expenses. On June 14, 2017, Mark Peterson resigned from office after pleading no contest to a single count of felony perjury. He had been charged by the California attorney general with 12 counts of felony perjury and one count of felony grand theft and was sentenced to perform 250 hours community service.

Police know they wield power over sex workers and can extort favors from them. "Criminalization of sex work creates a situation where the police have a lot of power—information about sting operations, discretion to arrest or not arrest a sex worker, whether or not to call this ad on Back page," said Katherine Koster of the Sex Workers Outreach Project. "It creates situations where a sex worker exchanges favors to shield themselves from charges or arrest."

The DA in Alameda County took a much different view than did Peterson in Contra Costa. DA O'Malley filed charges against three Oakland police officers, a Contra Costa Sheriff's deputy, and a Livermore police officer[24].

Nearly three dozen cops were implicated in the sexual exploitation of a young woman, some while she was a minor. Yet only a few will face trial or discipline. The word "consensual" cannot be used when a law enforcement officer exploits a minor or a sex worker for sexual favors. When the threat of force or fear is a precursor to sex with a young woman, even a sex worker, that is rape.

What's Up, Pitchess?

Background checks and access to public records are standard when reviewing a potential witness at trial. As a defense attorney, I want to know if a witness has a bias, or particular history, that would have bearing on my client's case. This discovery is important and both sides fully review the background of witnesses before talking to them on the stand.

For example, if a career criminal has a history of informing to police in exchange for leniency, I'd want to bring that up during cross-

24 BondGraham, D. (2016). Contra Costa District Attorney Declines to Charge Nineteen Cops in Celeste Guap Sex Exploitation Scandal. East Bay Express. Retrieved 26 December 2017, from https://www.eastbayexpress.com/SevenDays/archives/2016/11/04/contra-costa-district-attorney-declines-to-charge-nineteen-cops-in-celeste-guap-sex-exploitation-scandal

examination so the jury could hear it. Or if the eyewitness was once convicted of a hate crime, the jury should know he might have a grudge. The credibility of witnesses is important to the process. But what if that witness is a cop?

In California, defense attorneys must file what is known as a "Pitchess Motion" in an effort to receive background information on the employment and disciplinary actions of police. The law in California protects the sterling-plated image of cops and tries to put them on the stand as paragons of honesty and virtue. If a cop has a history of violence, racial profiling, substance abuse, coercion, dishonesty in filing police reports, or other misconduct, it likely has bearing on the credibility of his testimony. At least a jury should have the information to help inform their verdict.

Per the theme of this book, the State of Collusion is working against you when it comes to discovering the prior bad acts of a cop testifying at trial. Pitchess motions are hard fought by attorneys on behalf of law enforcement. Since evidence obtained by police and police testimony is usually the linchpin used by prosecutors to seal a case, is it surprising that judges rarely grant Pitchess to defense attorneys, citing the right to privacy and lack of public interest in exposing the cop's background? Nonetheless, filing a Pitchess motion is an important step to a criminal defense in the attempt to keep the system working correctly.

"But wait a minute, what about Brady?" might be what some of you are thinking now. As a refresher, *Brady v. Maryland* was the case that identified evidence which either helped the defense or hurt the prosecution as exculpatory evidence and it became mandatory for the prosecutor to disclose, supposedly. If a cop had a history of excessive force or racial bias, wouldn't that be Brady material and wouldn't the prosecutor have a duty to disclose it? The answer is "No" in California, and you'd most likely be laughed out of court by sneering judges and arrogant prosecutors for attempting to point out this simple, glaring truism.

I've developed a motion to get prosecutors, for safe measure, to run a criminal background check on law enforcement witnesses, just like they do on all citizen witnesses, aka most defense witnesses. The argument goes like this:

Prosecutors have a duty to run criminal histories on all witnesses, there is no exception in the law for law enforcement. This procedure is different than Pitchess because Pitchess only covers time at work whereas criminal background check would cover everything.

Theoretically, now, an officer can be charged with domestic violence on a Monday night and testify with impunity on Tuesday morning without any evidence of his actions being heard by the jury. Nevertheless, prosecutors fight tooth and nail against this motion and most judges refuse to enforce such an order, presumably because it might hurt a cop's feelings to run a simple background check where, if there's nothing there, he or she would have nothing to fear.

Some states see the wisdom of sharing background data on all witnesses, including police. Though police misconduct and personnel records are "confidential" in 23 states, and have limited access in another 15, there are 12 states that classify police disciplinary records as public records, in most cases. The law here in California makes police personnel records explicitly confidential, and it is not easy to get a judge to grant access. This maintains the "Us versus Them" position that lawmakers and Law Enforcement have towards citizens.

Even when a judge does release Pitchess records, you don't get a copy of the complaints made by the citizens or any accompanying Internal Affairs records, just names and contact information of the people that made the complaints. But if you do not ask, you will never know; so filing Pitchess motions are table stakes for defense attorneys in California.

In closing, just as in every other field, there are good cops and there are bad cops. A problem is created because, for the average citizen, the perception of police officers is that of halo-mantled guardian angels. Nightly, television programs exalt police regardless of their means and motives. In the real world, one bad cop can spoil the whole bunch, making the ramifications of police misconduct a serious threat to the safety and liberty of the public.

CHAPTER FOUR

PROSECUTORS ACTING BADLY: PSYCHO PROSECUTORS

Gang membership and police careers are options for blue-collar psychopaths, but evil is not limited to any socio-economic group. White-collar careers like working as a deputy in the district attorney's office or sitting on a bench as a judge, do not have the adrenaline rush of violence, but deliver dopamine power trips as the psychopath twists the law to their will.

Just like there is only one sheriff in a county, and all the officers that work for the sheriff are deputies, the district attorney's office functions the same way. There is one district attorney, and all of the lawyers who work under the district attorney are known as deputy district attorneys or assistant district attorneys.

Those who gain employment as a deputy district attorney are frequently on a good path to become a judge or a politician. A deputy district attorney can no doubt benefit from the public's stereotype of them as wearing the 'white hat' and keeping the public safe by 'fighting against criminal scum.'

Besides being on a fast track for public office, deputy district attorneys also enjoy complete immunity from ever being sued by a defendant for any reason. If a deputy district attorney knowingly charges someone who is innocent with a crime and pursues prosecution despite knowing full well that the person is innocent, they're immune from being sued!

How's that for accountability? How do you think this quality of 'untouchability' affects a prosecutor's mindset? Do you think that being absolutely immune from being sued for any type of crime that they commit as a prosecutor, such as false imprisonment, kidnapping, conspiracy, attempted murder, and even murder itself, can affect prosecutors so that they feel superior to the rest of us? After all, they are generally untouchable and unaccountable for their deeds while acting as prosecutors.

Naturally, there may well be a minority of prosecutors who are fundamentally good and who bring a sense of Justice and Fairness to their job. These voices in the district attorney's office, if they survive the environment long enough to establish a career, are often relegated to more menial positions. They may be tolerated by their office as long as they don't try to voice their opinions too frequently.

Many people who have bad experiences with police officers often describe them as having an eighth-grade mentality. We can all relate to this image of a middle-school bully, someone who's not known for being the smartest kid in class, maybe a jock-like personality who is rougher, physical and more likely to shoulder check you in the hallway than say a nice word to anyone.

This same bully mentality keeps and grows the boy's power by making sure that their social circle tows the line on their opinions as well. They thrive off making others feel bad and, as such, they are prone to putting others down. We can imagine "Biff" from Back to the Future in this role.

The prosecutor version still displays a type of eighth-grade mentality, but instead of the jock bully putting you down, it is the 'mean girl' or the James Spader character from an '80s John Hughes film, the guy with the perfect hair and sweater who is intelligent, privileged and *knows* he's better than everyone else.

District Attorney's offices tend to be highly political as well as fractured. The dynamics are closer to a college sorority or fraternity than to what you see on Law and Order.

While many law enforcement jobs have some nominal screening for the criminally minded, prosecutors' offices have no such screening. Law School is a barrier to entry, and I can attest that those are a hectic three years that will strain all who endure it.

You might think that, like young college students, liberal before they have to get a job and start paying bills and taxes, most law students are seeking to become attorneys to help people, fight for justice, and protect the rights of their clients.

However, there are those who enter law school knowing that on the other side is a platform for them to subjugate the weak to their will. I remember my first few weeks of law school. Class is conducted using the "Socratic" method, meaning a professor conducts class by asking questions, not directly teaching you about the law. It also means that a professor can call on anyone at any time, or someone could raise their hand and answer the question.

I remember being jolted in those first few weeks of law school, listening to everyone around me prattling on and on, sometimes making very little or no sense at all, and at the same time being utterly unconcerned with whether or not anyone else was listening. There were lots of people who just liked to hear themselves talk.

There were lots of people who clearly thrived on being intellectually 'superior' to others. There were lots of airs put on and lots of name brand dropping and status items displayed. Just like CEO, politician and law enforcement officer, "lawyer" is on the list of occupations that attract psychopaths.

However, think about this: is a psychopath, someone who is attracted to power, going to apply to be a public defender? A job where you start off with relatively low pay and permanently carry low social status in the eyes of the public, or are they going to apply at the district attorney's office where the pay is higher, they receive a halo from the public and media, and where the future is fast-tracked for judgeship or political office?

Whether public defender, prosecutor, or private attorney, all attorneys are officers of the court, and we all swear the same oath to the Constitution in order to become attorneys. However, the duties between a defense attorney and a prosecutor differ. A defense attorney has a duty to their client. A prosecutor, having no client, has a duty to represent "the people" and justice in general. That means that a prosecutor's job should be to push for justice, not a conviction. After all, we are supposed to be innocent until proven guilty.

These differing duties are at the root of a lot of the public misperception about the justice system; having a duty to a client does not enable a defense attorney to lie, cheat, or steal so they can 'get their guilty client off.' Neither does having a duty to justice hone a prosecutor into becoming a finer human being every day. If anything, the public's halo and day to day, minute by minute perk that deputy district attorneys have is more conducive to creating a dangerous personality than it is to creating a Christ-like public savior of Justice.

Being in law enforcement, a prosecutor gets a badge. One time, I was in the middle of a very serious jury trial, and the prosecutor asked the judge to hold up court for a day, including all the witnesses and all the jurors, so that he could go get interviewed for a free mass transit pass.

The BART subway/mass transit trains for the Bay Area has a policy of letting law enforcement officers ride free so the system gets extra security for their riders. However, I don't think the policy was intended to give deputy district attorneys free rides, and I'm sure the jury wouldn't have liked the fact that trial was delayed for such a trivial reason. Of course, the judge granted his request.

In fact, prosecutors rarely lose in front of judges. They are rarely ever reprimanded by judges, even in extreme situations where it is clear by all standards that they deserve a hand slap. Having to argue a legal issue against a prosecutor in front of a judge is like being in a rigged game. A judge is more likely to either be an unconditional cheerleader for the prosecutor, or a kept pet, owned by and devoted to the prosecutor.

According to the *LA Times*, "A 2010 report by the Northern California Innocence Project cited 707 cases in which state courts found prosecutorial misconduct over 11 years. Only six of the prosecutors were disciplined, and the courts upheld 80 percent of the convictions in spite of the improprieties, [a] study found[25]."

In 2011, the Yale Law Journal looked into the matter of prosecutorial misconduct[26]. They found that the scope and scale of the problem is difficult to fully investigate. They give several reasons why this issue is hard to prove.

First, prosecutors who engage in willful misconduct presumably do not want to be discovered and therefore take steps to conceal their misdeeds. Even a scrupulous prosecutor who witnesses a colleague engage in misconduct may nevertheless fail to report it for fear of professional repercussions.

---

25 Dolan, M. (2015). U.S. judges see 'epidemic' of prosecutorial misconduct in state. LA Times. Retrieved 10 February 2018, from http://www.latimes.com/local/politics/la-me-lying-prosecutors-20150201-story.html

26 Lebowitz, D., Lerer, T., Keenan, D., & Cooper, D. (2011). The Myth of Prosecutorial Accountability After *Connick v. Thompson*. The Yale Law Journal. Retrieved 10 February 2018, from https://www.yalelawjournal.org/forum/the-myth-of-prosecutorial-accountability-after-connick-v-thompson-why-existing-professional-responsibility-measures-cannot-protect-against-prosecutorial-misconduct

Second, prosecutors' offices enjoy considerable autonomy in shaping their internal policies. Likewise, individual prosecutors exercise almost unlimited discretion over whom to prosecute and which offenses to charge.

Third, the vast majority of known instances of prosecutorial misconduct come to light only during the course of a drawn-out trial or appellate proceeding. But most criminal cases in the United States result in plea bargains, which are rarely the subject of extensive investigation or judicial review, creating a heightened risk of undetected prosecutorial misconduct in cases which are resolved through plea bargaining.

Finally, those in the best position to report misconduct, namely, judges, other prosecutors, and defense attorneys and their clients, are often disincentivized from doing so for both strategic and political reasons.

At the federal level, Federal Rule of Criminal Procedure 16 (Rule 16) governs discovery and inspection of evidence in federal criminal cases. Rule 16 entitles the defendant to receive documents, records and other evidence or materials subject to discovery.

A report released in 2011 by the Federal Judicial Center found that 12 percent of federal judges acknowledged that federal prosecutors do not usually follow a consistent approach to disclosure. Even though a 12 percent rate of inconsistent disclosure by prosecutors shouldn't be tolerated, this figure was from survey responses by judges, who are usually former prosecutors and notoriously favorable to them.

The inconsistency of prosecutor disclosure was higher when defense attorneys were asked about their experiences with prosecutors, ranging between 30 percent on the low end and 75 percent on the high end[27].

When a prosecutor cheats and wins, it is a win for the office, the

27 Hooper, L., Rauma, D., Leary, M., & Thorpe, S. (2011). National Survey of Rule 16 of the Federal Rules of Criminal Procedure and Disclosure Practices in Criminal Cases. Federal Judicial Center. Retrieved 10 February 2018, from

County, and for the DA running for re-election. Jurors proudly march out of the courtroom feeling that they 'did the right thing' after participating in a process that clearly skews for the prosecution. Meanwhile, for the person wrongfully convicted, their life is ruined.

The National Registry of Exonerations reported in 2014 that for the previous fifteen years, nearly 1,500 people had been convicted of crimes and later exonerated. It is estimated that nearly half of all wrongful convictions are due to official misconduct[28].

That is a lot of lives ruined by bad actions from bad prosecutors. Even when prosecutorial misconduct is discovered, those prosecutors are rarely punished, in only about 2 percent of such cases. When there is an official sanction against the prosecutor, it often amounts to the proverbial slap on the wrist[29].

In my private practice, I have encountered many examples of prosecutors acting like entitled psychopaths. I don't have to work too hard to come up with examples of prosecutors doing the wrong thing and not caring about it. Below are a few from the top of my head.

I once had a client who had previously pled guilty to charges related to consensual homosexual advances in public. Stings by law enforcement against homosexuals were more common at the time. The judge, the prosecutor, and his attorney all promised him he would only have to register as a sex offender on Megan's List for the three years of his misdemeanor probation. Yeah, for making a date with a dude in an otherwise empty public bathroom.

This was in California, not the Bible Belt. The client came to me over a decade later because he was obligated to register as a sex offender for life,

28 Shepeard, C. (2014). Rampant Prosecutor Misconduct Rarely Punished. Truthout. Retrieved 10 February 2018, from http://www.truth-out.org/news/item/27644-rampant-prosecutor-misconduct-rarely-punished

29 An Epidemic of Prosecutor Misconduct. (2013). Center for Prosecutor Integrity. Retrieved 10 February 2018, from http://www.prosecutorintegrity.org/wp-content/uploads/EpidemicofProsecutorMisconduct.pdf

not just for the three years as he had been promised. Despite the assurances of the judge and attorneys, the law at that time required sex offenders to register for life with no end period[30].

I was able to reverse the entire conviction because he had been misinformed about the lifetime consequences of the law. With his conviction vacated, the client was no longer required to register. Nevertheless, despite a letter to the police department along with proof of the dismissal from court, when my client didn't register on his birthday, the police showed up at his house with their guns to arrest him. Moreover, district attorney's office filed a new case against him for failure to register.

The prosecutor knew full well she had just lost and my client had been released of the burden. Out of malice, she went after an innocent man for not registering as a sex criminal, even though his conviction had been reversed. Ruining lives for sport is par for an evil prosecutor's course.

I had another client who was a victim of identity theft by a criminal cousin. The criminal committed a crime, was found guilty, and served his time under the name and identity of his innocent cousin. Upon release, the shady cousin vanished in the wind and his innocent cousin was tracked down for probation violations.

This is not a lighthearted hijinks from The Patty Duke Show; my client faced serious repercussions and prison for what his criminal cousin did. It was easy to prove my client's innocence, as the booking photo showed the criminal cousin had a large scar across his forehead, and my client, though similar in appearance, had no scar.

Open and shut, right? Not in this case; the DA persisted in holding

30 The law regarding registration under Penal Code section 290 did not change until senate bill 384 passed the California legislature and was signed by Governor Jerry Brown in October 2017. Sex registration is now three-tiered requiring registration for 10 years, 20 years, or life.

my client accountable for the acts of his cousin, even though the judge and prosecutor knew he was factually innocent.

It took four to five appearances over months to get the case against my client cleared, in the face of resistance from the malingering prosecutor who would not let go. When I pointed out that I would set the matter for a formal hearing, the prosecutor's response was apoplectic, "Are you trying to threaten me?" Yes, I was threatening her with doing her job. Since when is pointing out a non-case a problem? Only entitled prosecutors on the losing side would think so.

For many years, it has been illegal to sell or distribute high-capacity firearm magazines. Possessing high capacity ammo clips only became illegal recently, in July 2017. Even a third-grader knows that the Constitution protects us from ex post facto prosecution for activity done before the law was passed.

Nonetheless, I have had several prosecutors in different counties attempt to press forward with trial knowing that the magazines had been obtained and 'grandfathered' before the law was passed. This is a common dirty trick by prosecutors to paint a defendant into a corner, crank up their bail, and color perception against them, all in an attempt to run up charges. They get away with this more often than you think.

In all of the instances mentioned above, I was able to get the charges dropped and secure justice for my clients. Had they settled on a plea, or chosen a less experienced attorney, their lives would have been dramatically different due to the willful evil of bad prosecutors.

Top Cops In The Land

Local prosecutors are not the end of the line of malice. As the District Attorney is a politician, DA's often matriculate up to higher offices with even more power.

The top prosecutor in the land is the Attorney General of the United States. We saw former Alameda Deputy District Attorney Ed Meese ascend to the role of AG under President Reagan, and assert himself as the moral arbiter of what was 'decent' for the entire country. There are more and more recent examples that hit home here in California.

Janet Napolitano is not from California. She grew up and served most of her career in New Mexico. She did her undergraduate studies at Santa Clara University in the Bay Area, but had little to do with our State or our education system beyond that. She was elected as the Attorney General and later Governor of New Mexico, and appointed by President Obama to head the Department of Homeland Security. In 2013, she left her $200,000 a year job at the DHS to become the President of the University of California system for over $700,000 a year.

The most interesting part of Governor Napolitano's career is not how an attorney who never tried a criminal trial rose through the ranks to become a top law enforcement official. That can be explained by her own internal psychopathic pragmatism to twist laws via her office to increase her power.

What really astounds is how a person from out of state, with no higher education executive experience, and a long record of violating people's rights, can comfortably sit at the head of the Nation's most prestigious, liberal-minded, free-thinking, public education institution.

Berkeley was the seat of the Free Speech Movement (which Ed Meese battled as a local district attorney just down the road). UC students have gone on strike to protest all manner of constitutional and human rights transgressions. Protests for women's rights, against wars, against compulsory ROTC, demonstrations against the death penalty, protests against the California House Un-American Activities Committee (HUAC), and protests against racial discrimination, are a few of the headlines.

In her career as a U.S. attorney, Attorney General, Governor, and ultimately Secretary of Homeland Security, Janet Napolitano embodied everything protesters have railed against throughout the history of UC. Napolitano militarized the border with the National Guard, increased deportations of immigrants, violated our physical privacy with invasive TSA searches, targeted veterans groups as right-wing terrorist cells, and wasted billions of dollars in failed contracts on the 'theater of security.'

Any one of these actions would have been enough to motivate a student protest at a UC campus forty years ago. But when Janet Napolitano was appointed as UC President[31], there were only a handful of student protests across the system. This is what is most frightening; we are getting less and less wary of pragmatic, opportunistic, psychopath attorney politicians in our midst.

It seems that we are not getting the lawmakers and law enforcers we want, but the psychopaths we deserve.

United States Senator Jefferson Beauregard Sessions the Third could not have less in common with the average Californian. The Alabama native served as a U.S. attorney, and as the Alabama Attorney General prior to his time in DC. He was appointed to the role of Attorney General for the United States by President Trump in 2016. His job is similar to your local District Attorney's, but at a federal level, plus an army of federal lawyers and police (ATF, TSA, DEA, etc.) ready to do his bidding.

Throughout his career, Sessions has used his office to attack individual rights, especially those of blacks, LGBTQ, cannabis users, and immigrants. As power begets power, he has risen from a minor Southern crank to the rank of America's top law enforcer.

31 Costello, S. (2013). Napolitano's expected appointment stirs controversy at UC. The Daily Californian. Retrieved 10 February 2018, from http://www.dailycal.org/2013/07/17/napolitanos-expected-appointment-stirs-controversy-at-uc/

Speaking of "Jefferson," another famous (albeit fictional) Southern boss named Jefferson comes to mind. Jefferson Davis "Boss" Hogg, the crooked commissioner of TV's Hazzard County. The venal and greedy Boss Hogg wielded the cops like a private goon squad to suppress the independent-minded Duke boys, whilst furthering his dastardly schemes.

If you still harbor strong negative feelings towards Boss Hogg, it is a credit to the late character actor Sorrell Booke, who brought J.D. Hogg to life over the entire series run. He was actually an Ivy-league Yankee! Booke was born in upstate New York, and earned degrees from both Columbia and Yale, where he studied acting. Fluent in five languages, Booke served in Army Intelligence during the Korean War. He lived most of his life in California, and passed away near Los Angeles in 1994.

As grand a man as Sorrell Booke was, his Hogg character was grandly vile. But through all his capers and cons, Boss Hogg kept a moral code. He refused to allow any of his schemes to cause physical harm to anyone. He would foil his own plans to protect the Dukes, or anyone, from death or injury. If only the other Confederate President namesake had such scruples...

We are not sure that "Boss" Sessions has ever set foot in California, but he sure has it out for our citizens and our values. As Sessions rolled back federal protections for transgender people, he claimed it should be left up to each state to choose for itself.

Then, a few weeks later, the Attorney General announced that his office and federal authorities would start going after cannabis users in states that have voted to legalize its use. This later move shows a complete disregard for state rights, and a complete lack of an internally consistent moral compass.

Sessions is an example of a prosecutor turned up to ELEVEN, and using his office to enforce his biases and whims. It seems Californians and perhaps all of America will suffer from a small-town Alabama prosecutor's personal grudges.

What a wacky world where Jefferson "Boss" Hogg is morally superior to AG Jefferson Sessions. And woe that Sorrell Booke isn't around to recast him.

It takes a cruel indifference to others, to the Constitution, and to Justice to pick and choose vulnerable people to target. Using power for personal and political gain is expected from a comedic villain, but it is pure psychopathy when wielded by a prosecutor like Sessions

The Prosecutor's Deck Is Stacked

Compounding the imbalance of justice are the relative workloads of prosecutors in the district attorney's office and those of the public defenders representing indigent clients. The State throws waves of resources into prosecuting a case: police, detectives, investigators from the district attorney's office, and a team of prosecutors. The number of work hours concentrated on putting someone in jail is astounding. Compare that with the overwork of public defenders and the short time each gets with his or her client or case before trial.

The situation puts the defendant and the defender behind the eight ball, facing the full weight and aggression of the State. The situation is often sarcastically called 'meet 'em and plead 'em,' because a client may have just seen his public defense attorney for the first time before standing to declare their arraignment plea or even plea bargain before the judge.

In some jurisdictions around the country (Detroit, New Orleans, Fresno), the public defender has statistically less than an hour to prepare for each case[32].

Further, prosecutors begin their case with it bundled as a tidy package,

32 Lee, J., Levintova, H., & Brownell, B. (2013). Charts: Why You're in Deep Trouble If You Can't Afford a Lawyer. Mother Jones. Retrieved 17 April 2018, from https://www.motherjones.com/politics/2013/05/public-defenders-gideon-supreme-court-charts/

with prepared evidence and professional witnesses (cops). Defense attorneys must craft their cases from square one.

The DA is an elected politician. Judges are elected politicians. Politicians of all stripes know the power of speaking to the public of lower crime rates and lower budgets. This means they want a greater amount of prosecutions and convictions and, at the same time, to cut back on government programs, except for, of course, law enforcement.

This means that those who have to rely on public defenders are in a situation where they have prosecution on steroids and a defense attorney who does not have all the resources he or she would want. Because politicians control county budgets, this puts the defense of our most vulnerable in the hands of people intent on having more convictions and more 'criminals' in jail. Power and psychopaths are a deadly combination.

Power Begets More Power

A prosecutor for the District Attorney's office can let the job go to his or her head and begin acting more and more like a power-hungry psychopath. Or, if the prosecutor is already a psychopath, he or she can let his or her head affect the job. Through various forms of prosecutorial misconduct, a greedy and ambitious deputy district attorney can tip the scales of justice towards convictions, and use those faulty convictions to climb higher in the District Attorney's office, into public office, or onto the judge's bench.

Being a prosecutor is a very powerful position that should require adhering to strict ethics and undergoing frequent scrutiny. In spite of giants in the legal field, like Alan Dershowitz, decrying for years that "prosecutorial misconduct is rampant," no such scrutiny exists[33].

33 Gershman, B (2008). Prosecutorial Misconduct, Preface by Dershowitz, A. (2nd ed.). New York: Clark Boardman Callaghan/West Group.

In fact, prosecutorial misconduct is not a new problem. In 1935, the U.S. Supreme Court in *Berger v. United States*, 295 U.S. 78, defined "prosecutorial misconduct" as "overstep[ping] the bounds of that propriety and fairness which should characterize the conduct of such an officer in the prosecution of a criminal offense." In their zeal to win, a prosecutor can falsify evidence, suborn perjury, intimidate witnesses, or encourage the police to do these things under the guise of 'Justice.'

Because they are the 'good guys,' they feel the end justifies the means. Passive misconduct is just as malicious, when a prosecutor aids, abets, encourages, turns a blind eye to, or laughingly cheers on police misconduct, wrongly-obtained evidence, and failure to disclose exculpatory evidence. There is also the act of a prosecutor vigorously defending in court a bad search, bad police conduct, or arguing that lawful conduct should be prosecuted as a crime, knowing that prosecutors almost always win in front of judges.

For the malevolent prosecutor who willingly alters or distorts facts in order to jail an innocent, repercussions are unlikely. These clever psychopathic attorneys can point to their hectic workload, or plead ignorance, or have one of the many sympathetic judges write off their deeds as harmless error. The odds of a prosecutor getting away with murder are much higher than a crafty serial killer's.

Of course, just as with corrupt police or sheriff deputies, non-accountability plays a big role in fostering the dynamic of corrupt prosecutors. Permissive or corrupt judges who are supposed to be a link in the system of checks and balances to prevent corrupt prosecutors, share some responsibility for creating non-accountability in prosecutors. However, in a rare instance of a judge calling corrupt prosecutors out, the Chief Judge of the United States Court of Appeals for the Ninth Circuit,

Alex Kozinski, wrote in a 2013 case, U.S. v. Olsen, that "There is an epidemic of Brady violations abroad in the land."

The term "Brady violations" comes to us from a 1963 case, *Brady v. Maryland*, where the United States Supreme Court ruled that prosecutors had to disclose to defense attorneys information which may help the defense. Although the problem of cheating prosecutors is such an epidemic that the Ninth Circuit was forced to acknowledge it in the Olsen case, the problem with the Olsen ruling is that the court still left it up to prosecutors to decide whether or not information is Brady material.

Thus, defense attorneys, and their clients facing serious prison terms, are still at the mercy of prosecutors as to whether or not the prosecutors will actually disclose Brady material. Interestingly, Judge Kozinski's next sentence in the Olsen opinion after noting the "epidemic of Brady violations abroad in the land," was, "Only judges can put a stop to it." We are still waiting on that one.

CHAPTER FIVE

JUDGES ACTING BADLY: PSYCHO JUDGES

Question: Why does the judge sit at the bench?

Answer: Because there's not enough room at the prosecutor's table!

Ba-Dump-Bump!

It is important to remember that law enforcement not only includes police and sheriffs, but also prosecutors. It is also no secret that most judges are former prosecutors.

There's a common expression around courthouses up and down the state that a recently-appointed judge has let "the robe" go to his or her head and now the former colleague, friend, or law partner has got "black robe disease." According to a *Los Angeles Times* report by Maura Dolan, 43 California judges were reprimanded for misconduct in a recent year. Two of those judges were reprimanded for having sex in chambers. One judge, who moonlighted as a law professor teaching evidence at night school, used his chambers to have liaisons with his former law students. He also tried to get his law students jobs at the district attorney's office.

Think about the already cozy relationship between prosecutors and judges. The law students who were sleeping with a married judge in his chambers wanted to work where? The District Attorney's office! The judge cheating on his wife in his chambers with his former students had pull to get people jobs where? The District Attorney's office! Psychopaths love exploiting relationships and power imbalances.

The judge disciplined for sex in chambers was having amorous trysts with none other than his court clerk. Dolan writes, "The vast majority of complaints against judges result in no discipline, and most misconduct is resolved by sending judges private letters[34]." She later quotes UC Berkeley law professor Christopher Kutz as stating that a judge's conduct must be extreme before the system even takes the step of disciplining them.

Keep in mind, these are judges that got caught behaving badly. The vast majority are probably never caught.

The goal of many prosecutors is to eventually become a judge and wield even more unquestionable power over people. From the bench, a judge can allow or discard evidence, testimony, and even entire defenses. If a case is pre-judged based on bias, the judge can steer the entire proceeding to the conclusion they desire. In addition to willful interference in a case, bad judgment by a judge can make them partial. Judges having sex with jurors, witnesses, or prosecutors; judges abusing substances both on and off the bench; and inattention or apathy to a case can all stack the odds against the innocent.

Judicial misconduct is even harder to prove than prosecutorial misconduct. Even when the judge's colleagues sitting on appellate courts can't find a way around a trial judge's misconduct in a case which resulted in a criminal conviction, the appellate courts will most often just call the trial judge's misdeeds "harmless error" and the conviction will be maintained. When you and I go outside the law, we are arrested by police with guns. If a judge goes outside the law, it's merely called "error" on paper.

34 Dolan, M. (2015). 43 California judges were reprimanded for misconduct last year. latimes.com. Retrieved 26 December 2017, from http://www.latimes.com/local/california/la-me-judges-discipline-20150404-story.html

Thus, megalomaniac judges are not hard to find. Take Judge Robert Bowers from Solano County. Bowers, married, began having an affair with an alternate juror sitting on one of his cases. The affair supposedly began after the jury verdict was returned on the case but before the defendant was sentenced. The affair came to light when Bowers was arrested for felony domestic violence against his estranged wife six weeks after the jury verdict.

Not surprisingly, Bowers has a history of making erroneous rulings that have resulted in criminal cases being overturned. I am not alone in witnessing his disparaging treatment of defense attorneys. Incidentally, I observed Bowers in court as the trial judge for a shaken baby case that my friend and colleague, Jaye Ryan, tried in his courtroom in Fairfield, California (Solano County). Ms. Ryan was convinced that her client was innocent, and she had the science to back it up. Unfortunately, Ms. Ryan and her innocent client had the deck stacked against them; a dishonest prosecutor's office and megalomaniac, corrupt judge Bowers.

The Solano County prosecutors had been caught red-handed suppressing hundreds of pages of documents about several homicide autopsies, including documents related to a secret investigation into the competency of their expert doctor who performed the autopsies. Basically, the Solano County District Attorney's office, when confronted by autopsy evidence that wasn't helpful for their case, would hire another doctor to do a 'second autopsy' to help seek convictions. The science of performing a second autopsy is dubious, as the evidence has already been man-handled and possibly contaminated.

The same thing happened in this case, the doctor who did the autopsy was told by the lead detective that the defendant confessed to shaking the baby which led to its death. The doctor then wrote an autopsy consistent with this 'evidence.' The problem is, the defendant never said it. It was a lie. When Ms. Ryan informed the autopsy doctor of the truth, the doctor changed his opinion to match the physical evidence; that shaking the baby was not the cause of death, that the death was consistent with an accidental fall.

The prosecutor's office then hired another expert, Dr. Michelle Jorden, to conduct a 'second autopsy' with a small amount of remains that were left over. You would think that justice would have a chance here. You would think that, even if Ms. Ryan couldn't vindicate her client, she could still at least get the jurors to see reasonable doubt regarding the autopsy evidence. But judge Bowers was there, compensating for the corrupt prosecutors, and secured the conviction for them, acting as if he were on their team.

Throughout the entirety of the trial, the judge acted completely one-sided and unfair towards the defense. In fact, during closing argument, the place where an attorney is supposed to be able to argue, Bowers would not allow Ms. Ryan to do so. For instance, she was not permitted to argue that the officer who falsely told the first doctor that the defendant confessed was a "liar." This is not only standard closing argument, but was well-justified by the facts of that case.

Bowers belittled Ms. Ryan in front of the jury, seemingly stopping her at every opportunity. Ms. Ryan was devastated when her client, whom she considered factually innocent, was convicted by the jury. This is just one example of a wrongful conviction accomplished by a biased judge looking to get a conviction—either out of siding with the prosecution, an evil nature, or both.

Things are so bad in the Criminal 'Justice' System, in terms of cops who thwart the fair administration of law, evil prosecutors who just like to inflict punishment on whomever is in their way, and out of control judges at the top of the food chain who will never attempt to correct things.

Take, for example, the next big trial that Ms. Ryan did and the very Aryan-looking Contra Costa County judge, that was presiding over it. This was a four-co-defendant murder case where all the accused were black. The judge, for whatever reason, had well beyond the normal number of bailiffs in the courtroom. It looked like such a racially hostile environment that one of the prospective jurors, a black man who had been excused from the case, approached Ms. Ryan and told her that the courtroom resembled a "slave ship up in there." A posse of armed, uniformed bailiffs towering over black defendants in chains.

During jury selection, the judge sat there and validated the prosecutor's removal of every black member of the prospective juror pool. There were not many black people called to jury duty for this trial, and the few who were called were sent away by judge and prosecutor. There is no excuse for willfully denying defendants a jury of their peers.

Ms. Ryan repeatedly battled the judge over her client's numerous and serious medical conditions. The judge would then receive information about jailhouse medical requests, presumably from the bailiffs, who are actually sheriff deputies assigned to the courtroom. She would summarily block Ms. Ryan's attempts at seeking medical attention for her client.

For instance, Ms. Ryan noted in court that her client had made dozens of requests for medical assistance in jail that had been ignored. He had an embarrassing yet serious bladder disorder that caused an urgent need to urinate. The judge countered that the defendant had actually only made two previous medical requests and that the judge's sources confided that the defendant has not shown signs of urine stains on his underwear or on his courtroom chair. Again, how would a judge know this? Who was she getting her information from, or was she making it up? This is why we have the 6th Amendment's guarantee to confront our accusers.

A few weeks later, Ms. Ryan was able to find forty-four medical requests and bring them to court. When Ms. Ryan made a record stating that the judge was obviously conducting a secret inquiry and demanded to know the source of the Court's information, especially since a lot of it was completely false, the Judge flatly stated that there was no secret inquiry and denied Ms. Ryan's requests. This is straight-up psychopath behavior.

When Ms. Ryan tragically died in the middle of trial, the judge's true evil nature uncloaked itself; she called the attorneys into chambers and did everything she could to avoid declaring a mistrial. Again, even a random person would be intelligent enough to figure out that if someone's attorney dies in the middle of trial, particularly a murder trial where the client is facing life, the judge has to declare a mistrial. You can't just substitute someone else in and keep going.

Attorneys are not players on a high school sports team. Cases are not a game of musical chairs. Her decision was either completely moronic or completely evil. Here's the Catch-22: if the judge's actions were completely stupid and idiotic, she shouldn't be on the bench. On the other hand, if she's not completely moronic, then she's a zealously evil demon, hellbent on conviction no matter what, and certainly shouldn't be on the bench. Either way, I feel extremely worried about any person of color who has the misfortune of having a case in her courtroom.

According to the U.S. Courts, which keeps statistics on judicial misconduct, it is very rare for a judge to face action for misconduct. In 2012, of the 1,364 complaints filed, only eight were concluded against the judge[35]. The rest were dismissed or found in favor of the judge. Those are fantastic odds.

35 Complaints Against Judges - Judicial Business 2012. (2013). United States Courts. Retrieved 26 December 2017, from http://www.uscourts.gov/statistics-reports/complaints-against-judges-judicial-business-2012

Judges are public figures and most decisions they make are publicly recorded. What is frightening to consider is that prosecutors and law enforcement act, and make their decisions, outside of the public eye. There is also not the same type of systematic review that judges have with higher courts above them.

Given that the general public claims to distrust lawyers as a profession, and also distrusts politicians, consider that judges are both. Which brings us to…

CHAPTER SIX

POLITICIANS ACTING BADLY: PSYCHO POLITICIANS

For a psychopath seeking optimal power, the close reach of a gun or a gavel is not enough. For these psychologically twisted megalomaniacs, their lust for power and will to subject others can drive them to larger political stages. Sometimes their plotting leads to crimes and misdemeanors at the highest level.

We established that Judges and District Attorneys are elected officials, and that makes them politicians. They are in powerful positions to offer favors quid pro quo, tit for tat, and mutual back scratching. But the pure politics of legislative and executive offices give cover and opportunity for psychopaths to collaborate on a grander scale, in all aspects of our lives. In fact, a start in the law is too often a first step up the political career path for a psychopath seeking to climb elected ranks.

Showing a long view of our political process to a moral person, they would logically be disgusted into avoiding it or motivated to shine a light on any shenanigans. Showing a psychopath the operations of politics, pull, and power is like showing raw meat to a hyena. Every opportunity, exploit, and advantage they detect is ripe for their using. Politics can be a career of evil for the truly villainous.

In the history of the United States, more than half of the presidents were lawyers before entering office. The law is a field which brings the mind, working with people, and civic service together. A lawyer certainly knows the fundamentals of public speaking and influential rhetoric. These are good traits for any public figure. But, since both the law and politics attract potential bad actors, law school and legal practice can serve as the 'farm team" for future corrupt professional politicians.

Here are the presidents from the past 100 years who have attended law school:

- Barack Obama

  Law School: Harvard | President: 2008 – 2016
- Bill Clinton

  Law School: Yale | President: 1993 – 2001
- Gerald Ford

  Law School: Yale | President: 1974 – 1977
- Richard Nixon

  Law School: Duke University | President: 1969 – 1974
- Franklin D. Roosevelt

  Law School: Columbia | President: 1933 – 1945
- Calvin Coolidge

  Legal Training: Post College Apprenticeship | President: 1923 – 1929
- Woodrow Wilson

  Law School: University of Virginia | President: 1913 – 1921
- William Howard Taft

  Legal Training: Post College Apprenticeship | President: 1909 – 1913

Some of the men above pushed and bent the Constitution to suit their needs. Their legal training provided them with the confidence and chutzpah to change reality to their will. How many of the above began wars on flimsy pretenses? Which ones took executive privilege to new heights and destroyed lives?

On the flip side, consider some of the names that are not on the list above, the non-lawyers. People often have fond feelings about Teddy Roosevelt, Harry Truman, John F. Kennedy, Jimmy Carter, and Ronald Reagan. But Teddy used his own cult of personality to get elected. Truman fell into the job. We all know what happened to JFK. Carter was a one-termer, and Reagan may have been the puppet of lawyers and spies with darker aspirations. The system is rigged by psychopaths against the good and the great (and the rest of us).

Perhaps Hillary Rodham Clinton is the poster child for psychopathic drive for power. She went to law school at Yale, married another political aspirant, and climbed to the brink of the presidency. She was dubbed "The Lady MacBeth of Little Rock" by journalist Daniel Wattenburg in 1992. As an attorney, First Lady, Senator, and Secretary of State, Mrs. Clinton would change her ideology and values to suit the political outlook. Despite the decades of Al Capone-like politicking, she had enough political clout to still be nominated as the Democratic presidential candidate in 2016, losing to Donald Trump.

Rodham-Clinton's career story is perfect for a book about collusion, psychopaths, corruption, venal power grabs, and disregard for the average citizen's rights. But, as she has little to do with our State of Collusion, we will explore the original poster-boy for abuse of power by psychopaths in high places. California's own President Richard Millhouse Nixon.

Tricky Dick

The "California Lincoln" was how Richard M. Nixon was once described. He came from humble roots in Southern California, became a lawyer in California, then Vice President under Eisenhower. He unsuccessfully ran for California governor and lost the presidential race to JFK before finally winning the Presidency in 1968.

Raised as an evangelical Quaker in Yorba Linda, California, his faith could have exempted Nixon from military draft. Likewise, his work in a government office in 1941 should have exempted him. Nevertheless, Nixon sought an officer commission in the US Navy and urged his superiors to send him from his station in Iowa to operations in the Pacific. He was elected to Congress in 1946 and the US Senate in 1950. It was around this time his political opponents dubbed him "Tricky Dick" for his shady campaign tricks[36]. A lifetime of moral Quaker upbringing done away by a desire to climb political rungs.

While in Congress, Nixon was a member of HUAC, the House Un-American Activities Commission, which led witch hunts for Communists in all stations of society. From the Hill, to Senate, to Eisenhower's Vice President, and eventually President of the United States. Guile and ambition lifted Richard Nixon from the obscurity of a commoner to the most powerful political position in the nation and world.

Nixon's presidency was undone by the "dirty tricks" performed by members of his staff and administration as well as his attempts to cover up their deeds which included breaking into and bugging opponent's offices. Nixon and his close aides also ordered investigations of activist groups and political figures using the Federal Bureau of Investigation (FBI), the Central Intelligence Agency (CIA), and the Internal Revenue Service (IRS)—the domestic armies of the psychopath lawyer turned federal politician. One might wonder if this particular aspect of the Nixon administration was used as the template for the Obama administration, which engaged in the same activities to a factor of ten, but suffered next to zero of the political consequences imposed onto Nixon.

36 Gellman, I. (1999). The contender, Richard Nixon. New York: Free Press.

On November 17, 1973, during a televised question and answer session with the press, Nixon said, "People have got to know whether or not their President is a crook. Well, I'm not a crook. I've earned everything I've got."

Nixon's appeal and statement were made despite his conspiring to burgle and wire-tap offices, deliberately withholding evidence, lying about his involvement, lying about not recalling his involvement when cornered, obstruction of justice, abuse of power, improper use of government agencies, accepting gifts while in office, and owing nearly half a million dollars in back taxes. The ability to lie in the face of all reason is the most distinguishing trait of a psychopathic politician compared to the rest of us who naively place our trust in them.

The national stage gives a psychopath the most powerful pulpit from which to spread their influence. Early in his Presidential career, Nixon began using drugs as a boogeyman to rally behind. He formally declared a "War on Drugs" that would be directed toward eradication, interdiction, and incarceration. The term caught on two years later when Nixon declared drug abuse "public enemy number one," the day after publication of a special message from President Nixon to the Congress on Drug Abuse Prevention and Control. This was the first shot fired in the War on Drugs.

"The Nixon campaign in 1968, and the Nixon White House after that, had two enemies: the antiwar left and black people. You understand what I'm saying? We knew we couldn't make it illegal to be either against the war or black, but by getting the public to associate the hippies with marijuana and blacks with heroin, and then criminalizing both heavily, we could disrupt those communities. We could arrest their leaders, raid their homes, break up their meetings, and vilify them night after night on the evening news. Did we know we were lying about the drugs? Of course we did."

- John Ehrlichman, to Dan Baum for Harper's Magazine in 1994, about President Richard Nixon's war on drugs, declared in 1971.

Famously, Nixon's presidential stay did not end well. The term "Watergate" named after one of the office buildings wiretapped by Nixon conspirators is now used as a catch-all for high level malfeasance, with the suffix "gate" applied to nearly any scandal. In the end, Nixon resigned under threat of impeachment and forty-eight other officials were convicted of wrongdoing related to the break-ins and subsequent cover-up. A thirty-year career of political aspirations at any cost undone by the massive weight of psychopath hubris.

Ronald Reagan

Affable actor Ronald Reagan was not an evil psychopath at heart. Though he was born and raised in small-town Illinois, Reagan came to California in 1937 on a road-trip as a radio announcer for the Chicago Cubs. On that trip he auditioned for Warner Brothers and earned a contract acting job and played many small but memorable supporting roles in films. During WW2, he was stationed in California to help make instructional and public relations films with the First Motion Picture Unit of the U.S. Army.

Reagan ran for Governor of California on a foundation of anti-communism, smaller government, and free markets. Though, it seems that civil liberties were not a priority for Governor Reagan. In reference to burgeoning anti-war and anti-establishment student protests at the University of California at Berkeley, he vowed "to clean up the mess at Berkeley." This assault on free speech started with sending in the lawyers, as we saw with Ed Meese when he was the DA for Alameda County. Later, sending in the California Highway patrol to break up Berkeley protests, and ultimately deploying the National Guard to occupy Berkeley and suppress dissent.

Though not an attorney, Reagan found attorneys to help him accomplish his goals, or so he thought. More likely, crafty, political minded psychopaths were attracted to the affable Reagan and were keen to use his brand and office to further their goals.

Another off-brand move had the NRA member Reagan support a ban on carrying loaded firearms in California. In 1967, Reagan signed the Mulford Act, which repealed a law allowing public carrying of loaded firearms, becoming California Penal Code 12031 and 171(c). This law came in response to arms-bearing Black Panthers marching on the State Capitol in Sacramento. In a trade-off between Constitutional ideals, and hatred of upwardly-minded minorities, Reagan chose to limit everyone's rights to make it easier to weaken and imprison his opposition.

It is important to note that Ed Meese served as the Governor's legal affairs secretary from 1967 to 1968 and as executive assistant and chief of staff to Governor Reagan from 1969 through 1974. The role of whispering in Reagan's ear continued in the White House where Ed Meese began his Washington stint as "Counselor to the President." This was effectively a cabinet and National Security Council level position but without Congressional approval or oversight.

Former Reagan advisor and journalist David Gergen said of Meese in the White House, "He's a tremendously influential and highly-valued adviser to the President who advises on issues all across the board. He's one of the men who has known [the President] so long and so well he's become almost an alter ego of Ronald Reagan[37]."

Meese faced a tough confirmation for his role as Attorney General. He did not last a full term, resigning in the face of an ethics scandal three years into the job.

37 Edwards, L. (2005). To preserve and protect. Washington, D.C.: The Heritage Foundation.

Other controversies during the Reagan years that featured attorney Ed Meese as his counselor and Chief of Staff, Texan attorney James Baker:

- The attack on the First Amendment via the "Meese Report," formally known as The Attorney General's Commission on Pornography. The two-volume, nearly 2,000 page report claimed a "causal relationship between pornography and sexual violence." This was a green light for the government to go after any content they found objectionable. Critical response to the report came from Penthouse International "United States of America v. Sex: How the Meese Commission Lied About Pornography," to the more staid ACLU's "Polluting the Censorship Debate," by Barry W. Lynn, a 188-page summary and critique of the commission report.
- Secretary of the Interior, James Watt (an attorney from Wyoming), was indicted on 25 counts of felony perjury and obstruction of justice by a federal grand jury, accused of making false statements before the grand jury, investigating influence peddling, and grant rigging at the Department of Housing and Urban Development, which Watt had lobbied in the 1980s.
- Inslaw was a legal management software solution provider that created the PROMIS information and document platform for prosecutors. The original 16-bit version of PROMIS was created by the Federal Government, and therefore in the public domain. Changes in the Copyright Act of 1976 resulted in intellectual property rights reverting to Inslaw for five years, in which time Inslaw had made many updates to the software, upgraded it to 32-bit use, and other improvements. Enter Ed Meese and his $800

million plan to upgrade Federal law enforcement technology. As part of the upgrade, Inslaw was contracted to provide an improved version to the government for $9.6 million. Long story short: the Feds refused to pay Inslaw, claiming the original 16-bit license for the old version gave them rights to use and distribute the new and improved version. Two different federal bankruptcy courts ruled that the Justice Department "took, converted, and stole" the PROMIS installed in U.S. Attorneys' Offices "through trickery, fraud, and deceit," and then attempted "unlawfully and without justification to force Inslaw out of business so that it would be unable to seek restitution through the courts." Trials and lawsuits wore on for nearly twenty years. After several appeals, Inslaw has still not been paid.

- The Savings and Loan Crisis in the 1980s was precipitated by Reagan's retroactive elimination of loopholes in the tax code, which wiped out many real estate developments planned with the tax breaks in mind. Nearly a thousand Savings and Loan institutions failed. Several congressmen, senators, and even George. H.W. Bush's son, Neil, were dragged into the mess. Ultimately, the government shelled out $160 billion in taxpayer dollars to bail out the failed institutions. Economist John Kenneth Galbraith called it "the largest and costliest venture in public misfeasance, malfeasance and larceny of all time."
- The $250 million Wedtech scandal involved "no-bid" government contracts going to people and companies that should not have received them. It started with the Bronx based company applying for contracts as a minority-owned business, while fraudulently concealing the fact that they were not a minority-

owned company. In all, more than 20 state, local, and federal government officials were convicted of crimes in connection to the scandal. An independent counsel appointed by Congress charged Ed Meese with complicity, as his close friend lobbied Meese on behalf of the company. Meese was never charged, but he did resign as Attorney General in 1988 due to the scandal.

- The grand-daddy of scandals in the 1980s was the Iran-Contra Affair. This was a complex scheme involving illegally trading weapons with Iran to fund CIA-backed Nicaraguan rebels in Central America as well as money from cocaine smuggling. It began as an arms-for-hostages deal and expanded into a world-wide drug and arms pipeline. Reagan was kept in the dark about the details of the operation by the main conspirators. High-level investigations dug into the conspiracy and indictments were filed against: Secretary of Defense Caspar Weinberger (J.D., Harvard), Assistant Secretary of State Elliot Abrams (J.D., Harvard), Clair George (enrolled at Columbia Law School), plus other members of the National Security Council and the military. While one psychopath lawyer can do a lot of damage, multiple psychopath lawyers working together to break the law can do exponential amounts of damage. Also, the more these criminally-minded psychos work together, the more valid an illegal operation may at first glance appear.

There were so many scandals for such a well-loved, nice guy, from a small town like Ronald Reagan. He certainly needed the collusion of psychopath attorneys and politicians to foment so much corruption. Would the scandals have even happened if Ed Meese was not whispering in President Reagan's ear? In all, the presidency of Ronald Reagan was marked by multiple scandals, resulting in the investigation, indictment, or conviction of over 138 administration officials, the largest number for any U.S. president.

The Torture Memos

Reagan wasn't the only President to employ attorneys with psychopathic tendencies to find cover and absolution for official wrongdoing. George W. Bush never went to law school (though he has a Harvard MBA, and is the only president with an MBA). The Texan president tapped a Korean-American who grew up in Philly, went to Yale for law school, and taught at Berkeley to justify violating International Law.

The University of California at Berkeley has such a reputation of progressiveness and liberal views, it is ironic that it has produced so many villains of the Constitution. For a psychopath lawyer that wanted to aim high, and leave an indelible mark on the planet, rationalizing away Geneva Convention protections with the guile of a sociopath is the pinnacle.

John Yoo is an attorney that has been on the faculty at UC Berkeley since 1993. Starting in 2001, Mr. Yoo worked closely with Vice President Cheney's office to justify the "War on Terror." The use of Guantanamo Bay for the "enhanced interrogation" of "enemy combatants" flowed from Mr. Yoo's legal papers on the subject[38].

His inhumane and defective legal reasoning continued into the warrantless wiretapping of Americans by the NSA in a memo where Yoo said, "Our office recently concluded that the Fourth Amendment had no

38 Yoo, J. (2005). John Yoo commentary on the 'torture memos'. Berkeley.edu. Retrieved 26 December 2017, from http://www.berkeley.edu/news/media/releases/2005/01/05_johnyoo.shtml

application to domestic military operations[39]."

In fact, in Spain and in Germany, charges have been filed against John Yoo for "alleged complicity in torture and other crimes against humanity at Abu Ghraib in Iraq and Guantánamo Bay." Russia has banned him from travel there citing Yoo among those responsible for "the legalization of torture" and "unlimited detention." *Russia* citing an American lawyer for justifying torture and the denial of Due Process? Thanks, Mr. Yoo. You too, Mr. Bush, Jr.

In 2009, two days after taking office, President Barack Obama in Executive Order 13491 repudiated and revoked all legal guidance on interrogation authored by Yoo and his successors in the Office of Legal Counsel between September 11, 2001, and January 20, 2009. He then proceeded to order ten times the amount of airstrikes than his predecessor "W" and became the first ever two-term President to keep the nation in war[40] for each day of his eight-years in office[41].

Psychopaths are relentless in their pursuit of power and influence. Sometimes they are the most powerful person in their neighborhood, county, state, or nation. When a psychopath cannot attain a rank for him- or herself, they will employ minions or puppets to do their bidding. As we have seen in many administrations, including the current Trump administration, the people empowering the head honcho need to be vetted and watched as well, sometimes even more so.

---

39 Memo On Illegal Searches Comes To Light. (2008). Cbsnews.com. Retrieved 27 December 2017, from https://www.cbsnews.com/news/memo-on-illegal-searches-comes-to-light/

40 Parsons, C., & Hennigan, W. (2017). President Obama, who hoped to sow peace, instead led the nation in war. www.latimes.com. Retrieved 17 April 2018, from http://www.latimes.com/projects/la-na-pol-obama-at-war/

41 Purkiss, J., & Serle, J. (2017). Obama's covert drone war in numbers: ten times more strikes than Bush. The Bureau of Investigative Journalism. Retrieved 17 April 2018, from https://www.thebureauinvestigates.com/stories/2017-01-17/obamas-covert-drone-war-in-numbers-ten-times-more-strikes-than-bush

CHAPTER SEVEN

ORANGE COUNTY SNITCH SCANDAL

If anyone needs proof that the California criminal justice system is absolutely corrupt, the Orange County Snitch Scandal is Exhibit A. It's a miscarriage of justice on an epic scale, a particularly egregious example of citizens' rights trampled by career-focused prosecutors breaking the rules and conspiring with cops to score big conviction numbers. Here's a synopsis of the whole sorry, disgraceful saga.

In 2011, Scott Dekraai killed eight people in a Seal Beach hair salon—the deadliest mass killing in Orange County history[42]. Victims included his hairdresser ex-wife, and seven co-workers or customers. Although the case against Dekraai seemed like a slam dunk—he was carrying the murder weapons in his car and admitted guilt at arrest—the Orange County District Attorney's Office (OCDA) and Orange County Sheriff's Department (OCSD) felt it necessary to pad their case with jailhouse informants in a way that just so happens to be unconstitutional. District Attorney Tony Rackauckas wanted the death penalty for Dekraai, and he was determined to get it.

The use of such "snitches" also appears to have been business as usual among the OCDA and OCSD. When Dekraai's lawyer, public defender Scott Sanders, discovered these agencies were engaging in this reprehensible

42 Fields, E., Carpenter, E. et al. (2011). Seal Beach shootings: 8 slain in O.C.'s deadliest mass killing – Orange County Register. Retrieved 26 December 2017, from http://www.ocregister.com/articles/business-321651-medical-beach.html

conduct, what began as a mass murder case evolved into an investigation of the OCDA and the OCSD use of snitches.

Before Dekraai – a Timeline

It wasn't like the public was unaware of the widespread use of snitches by the OCDA and OCSD before the Dekraai case[43]. In 1985, the *Los Angeles Times* reported on the use of jailhouse informants in over 100 major Orange County cases, specifically naming Deputy District Attorney Tony Rackauckas, who by the time of the Dekraai case had worked his way up to the head honcho position as *the* district attorney. But back then, Rackauckas allegedly used a discredited informant named James Dean Cochrum on a regular basis to obtain confessions unconstitutionally and get convictions on otherwise questionable cases.

By 1999, Rackauckas is the head District Attorney. California's chief assistant attorney general tells Rackauckas that the OCDA's office has been defying court orders along with failing to provide informant evidence in a capital case. Rackauckas just ignores the issue.

- 2002 – An Orange County Grand Jury (OCGJ) accuses Rackauckas of protecting cronies from prosecution and demanding personal loyalty from deputies, not the pursuit of justice.
- 2007 – The OCSD boasts its deputies have "excellent expertise in the cultivation and management of informants." The OCDA recognizes the OCSD's "expertise" in this area.

43 Moxley, R. (2017). Snitch Myth? Only To Orange County's Reality-Denying Grand Jury. OC Weekly. Retrieved 27 December 2017, from http://www.ocweekly.com/news/reality-timeline-in-orange-countys-jailhouse-snitch-scandal-contradicts-grand-jurys-report-8201616

- 2008 – An internal OCSD memo recognizes its jail deputies' "cultivation of hundreds of confidential informants."
- 2009 – With the aid of the OCSD, two Santa Ana cops meet with Oscar Moriel, a serial killer. He tells them he can work as a snitch as long as his pending life imprisonment sentence is reduced. He later testifies for the OCDA in three cases.
- 2011 – Just prior to the Dekraai murders, jail deputy Arthur Tunstall testifies he "routinely" cultivates informants during a case involving a jailhouse murder.

That's just a sampling of the collusion between the OCDA and OCSD prior to Orange County's largest mass murder.

The Death Penalty and Snitches

The Northwestern University School of Law's Center for Wrongful Convictions issued a report[44] in 2005 finding that "snitch-dependent prosecutions" are the primary cause of wrongful death penalty convictions. From 1975 to 2004, there were 111 death row exonerations. Snitches were involved in nearly half of these convictions. Inaccurate eyewitness testimony accounts for the next largest number of wrongful convictions, at just 25 percent. When it comes to DNA exoneration of death row convicts, the report states that snitches are involved in about 15 percent of those cases.

There was overwhelming evidence that Dekraai committed those eight killings. Why did the OCDA and OCSD bother to set up a snitch? We can't know the answer to that, but their decision to do so made national headlines.

44 Center on Wrongful Convictions: The Snitch System. (2005). American Civil Liberties Union. Retrieved 27 December 2017, from https://www.aclu.org/other/center-wrongful-convictions-snitch-system

How the Snitch Operation Worked

In popular culture, snitches—or "jailhouse informants" to use the politically correct term—are inmates who happen to overhear another prisoner confess and then go to the authorities. In reality, snitches don't end up "accidentally" in a cell with someone who just has to get his crime off his chest and discuss it with someone whom he just met.

Snitches apply for these gigs with the hope of gaining sentence reductions or jail perks, such as phone calls, special commissary food, or better visitation. If they manufacture a confession by an inmate, there's little for the snitch to worry about. The downside is discovery by other inmates. Nobody likes a snitch (outside of the OCDA or OCSD) and if fellow inmates find out about their activities, snitches risk severe consequences including the loss of their lives.

Some snitches received a great deal of money[45]. Mexican Mafia members Jose Paredes and Raymond Cuevas received more than $150,000 over an 18-month period from local law enforcement agencies. That's your California tax dollars at work. Their way of extracting 'confessions'? Paredes and Cuevas would tell inmates that they (the inmates) had broken the code of the Mexican Mafia, and should start putting their affairs in order, so to speak. The only way an inmate could avoid a grisly death was by cooperating with them.

During the discovery process, Sanders found out his client, Dekraai, was taped by a snitch in their jail cell. The day after Dekraai's arrest, the OCSD moved him to cell 3 of Sector 17, in the county jail system's "intake release center." A more appropriate name is the 'Snitch Tank.' In the cell, a jailhouse informant and Mexican Mafia member named Fernando Perez

45 Saavedra, T. (2014). Money, cable TV, food delivery: How Mexican Mafia snitches lived like kings behind bars. Orange County Register. Retrieved 27 December 2017, from http://www.ocregister.com/articles/cuevas-643108-paredes-informants.html

started a conversation with Dekraai about the murders. During their talks in the Snitch Tank, authorities secretly taped the men for a total of 130 hours.

Sanders was also defending double murderer Daniel Wozniak[46], another high profile case at the time. He later found out that Perez was also talking to Wozniak about his alleged crime, and felt it more than a coincidence. Wozniak was later convicted of killing two people in order to pay for his wedding and sentenced to death.

While preparing Dekraai's defense, Sanders wanted access to Perez's informant records from the prosecutor's office. The prosecutor resisted releasing these records, but Judge Thomas Goethals ordered the prosecutor's office to comply. Sanders received a file containing 5,000 pages and linking Perez to nine cases in which he served as a snitch. Several of these were gang-related.

Perez was facing life behind bars on a third-strike charge of illegal firearms possession when Dekraai was arrested. Because prosecutors varied so much in the amount of discovery material regarding informants turned over to defense attorneys, Sanders believed certain prosecutors were withholding this crucial information.

Legal Informants

It's not illegal to use informants under California law. What is illegal is when law enforcement deliberately uses snitches to obtain incriminating information from defendants when the defendants have attorneys. Remember these defendants have the constitutional right to an attorney as

46 Puente, K. (2016). Daniel Wozniak sentenced to death for killing 2 friends to fund his wedding. Orange County Register. Retrieved 27 December 2017, from http://www.ocregister.com/2016/09/24/daniel-wozniak-sentenced-to-death-for-killing-2-friends-to-fund-his-wedding/

well as to remain silent. If an informant genuinely overhears information, they can report it. However, if the government purposefully uses a snitch to get information from another inmate, then the inmate is acting on behalf of the government as an "agent."

Again, once someone is arrested and has an attorney, the government isn't allowed to talk to them. If the government can't talk to someone, a government agent can't talk to them either. This was the principle of law established in the United States Supreme Court case of *Massiah v. United States* in 1964.

Further, in 2011, Governor Jerry Brown signed legislation adding to the existing law on informant use. Formerly, the law provided that convictions couldn't be established by an accomplice's testimony unless such testimony was corroborated by other evidence connecting the defendant with the offense's commission. This corroboration isn't sufficient if it simply shows the circumstances or commission of the offense. The amendment signed by Brown provides:

> A jury or judge may not convict a defendant, find a special circumstance true, or use a fact in aggravation based on the uncorroborated testimony of an in-custody informant. The testimony of an in-custody informant shall be corroborated by other evidence that connects the defendant with the commission of the offense, the special circumstance, or the evidence offered in aggravation to which the in-custody informant testifies. Corroboration is not sufficient if it merely shows the commission of the offense, the special circumstance, or the circumstance in aggravation. Corroboration of an in-custody informant shall not be provided by the testimony of another in-custody informant unless

the party calling the in-custody informant as a witness establishes by a preponderance of the evidence that the in-custody informant has not communicated with another in-custody informant on the subject of the testimony[47].

Sixth Amendment Violation

For Sanders, such informant secrecy aided the prosecution and he felt defendants had the right to more information about these snitches, including any quid pro quo promises made to them in exchange for their testimony. Sanders argued that the government using informants to coerce inmates into making confessions knowing that the inmates had counsel violated the U.S. Supreme Court's Sixth Amendment interpretation of the right to legal counsel per Massiah.

In January 2014, Sanders filed a 500-page motion alleging the OCDA and OCSD disregarded the law. It wasn't just about the Dekraai and Wozniak cases; the snitch problem was systemic. In his motion, Sanders argued against the death penalty for Dekraai. In additional motions, Sanders argued Dekraai's statements were obtained illegally and further, that the OCDA was so internally corrupt, it should not prosecute the Dekraai case.

The Evidentiary Hearings

In March 2014, evidentiary hearings commenced with Goethals presiding. During the hearings, 28 law enforcement officers and prosecutors testified[48] under oath. The defense claimed the OCSD had a long history of secretly coordinating the movement of informants. Snitches were put in place with

47 Senate Bill No. 687 Introduced by Senator Leno. February 18, 2011. Retrieved on December 27, 2017 from http://www.leginfo.ca.gov/pub/11-12/bill/sen/sb_0651-0700/sb_687_bill_20110218_introduced.pdf

48 Request for Federal Investigation in Orange County, California, November 17, 2015. Retrieved on December 27, 2017 from http://www.constitutionproject.org/wp-content/uploads/2015/11/Request-for-Federal-Investigation-in-Orange-County.pdf

the aim of receiving incriminating information from defendants. They would even threaten defendants physically to get the confessions they wanted.

According to the defense, the prosecutors were well aware of these tactics and allowed them to remain secret. Prosecutors often portrayed these snitches to defense lawyers and judges as people who 'just happened' to overhear these crime details. Was the snitch's credibility in question? The prosecutors went out of their way to conceal any such evidence even when their own notes indicated that a witness had believability issues—serious Constitutional and ethical violations!

The OCSD deputies claimed—under oath—that putting an informant beside Dekraai was unintentional. No snitch program existed on their watch, they said. Unfortunately for them, computerized TRED[49] records (kept secret by sheriff's deputies) were then introduced.

These records, dating back a quarter century, traced inmate movement as well as snitch coordination. Such information should have been made available to defense lawyers but hadn't. Further, the secret logs[50] went well beyond TREDs. From 2008 to 2013, deputies kept logs outlining different ways to get a confession out of an inmate, a sort of 'how to' for snitches. Forging documents, spreading rumors, and coaching the snitch on keeping his credibility are among the insights. Deputies concocted projects with operational names such as "Dead Cockroach," "Smoke and Mirrors," and "Okey-Dokie."

If it weren't such a travesty of justice, this operation and the ridiculous lying about it would be a comedy. Sheriff's deputy William Grover testified

---

49 Moxley, R. (2015). The TRED Deception: Tainted Government Informant Program Blows Another Murder Case. OC Weekly. Retrieved 27 December 2017, from http://www.ocweekly.com/news/the-tred-deception-tainted-government-informant-program-blows-another-murder-case-6479606

50 Puente, K., & Saavedra, T. (2017). O.C. deputies' logs reveal details of informant use, recordings in county jail. Orange County Register. Retrieved 27 December 2017, from http://www.ocregister.com/articles/logs-737439-deputies-sheriff.html

he didn't spend any time, "less than zero," with informants. The logs proved otherwise. In one log, he writes of encouraging the Perez-Wozniak relationship. Deputy Ben Garcia testified under oath that the OCSD didn't have informants—again contrary to provable facts. Deputies also violated the law in other ways, including bringing drugs[51] into the facility to protect their snitches. This didn't occur once or twice, but in several dozen cases.

Shredding Time

Just five days after the snitch investigation reopened in 2014, the OCSD received the go-ahead to shred[52] related—and potentially incriminating—records by the Board of Supervisors. Was this a deliberate decision by the Board? This destruction request was stuck in an 80+ page document addressing the disposition of various OCSD records. One clue: This was exactly when Sanders sought release of these very documents.

Goethals' Ruling

In August 2014, Judge Goethals issued his ruling, using strong language including this statement:

> This court finds that working informants and targeted inmates were at times intentionally moved inside the Orange County jail by jail staff, often at the request of outside law enforcement agencies, in the hope that inmates would make incriminating statements to those informants. Such intentional movements were seldom, if ever, documented by any member of law enforcement. Therefore,

51 Frank, B. (2016). Feds launch investigation of OC DA, sheriff's offices. Southern California Public Radio. Retrieved 27 December 2017, from http://www.scpr.org/news/2016/12/15/67240/feds-launch-investigation-of-oc-district-attorney/

52 Puente, K., & Saavedra, T. (2017). O.C. Sheriff's Department sought permission to destroy jailhouse snitch records. Orange County Register.. Retrieved 27 December 2017, from http://www.ocregister.com/articles/records-741694-department-sheriff.html

> little or no information concerning those intentional movements was ever created or turned over to defense counsel as part of the discovery process[53].

He called many of the witnesses who testified before him "credibility challenged," and noted these were "current and former prosecutors, as well as current and former sworn peace officers. Some perhaps suffered from failure of recollection. Others undoubtedly lied."

NO OCDA in the Second Phase

In March 2015, after Sanders' revelations, Judge Goethals barred the Orange County prosecutor's office from trying phase two of the Dekraai trial – the death penalty phase. The bottom line: Goethals' found the OCDA's office was lying. However, while the judge did enact some accountability by removing the OCDA's office from the Dekraai case, he did nothing about the obvious perjury committed by the individual deputy district attorneys and sheriff's deputies. One has to wonder how long this apparent tradition of two-tiered justice can continue; if you're with the government, you can commit crimes and not be punished and if you're not with the government, you'd better watch out, you'll have the book thrown at you!

When a district attorney's office is recused from a case or can't do it because of a conflict, say one of their own gets charged with a crime, it is the role of the California Attorney General's office to step in and prosecute the case. In this case, rather than simply step in, Kamala Harris' Attorney General's office chose as its first act on the case to appeal Goethals' ruling!

53 Ruling by Judge Goeathals. August 4, 2014. Court Of The State Of California County Of Orange, Central Justice Center. Retrieved 27 December 2017, from http://big.assets.huffingtonpost.com/RulingbyGoethals.pdf

In its appeal, the AG office stated in essence that the OCSD was responsible, that the OCDA had no conflict, and that there was no reason why the OCDA couldn't continue to prosecute the case. Now ask yourself why the AG's initial act was attempting to support a corrupt OCDA and overturn a judge's ruling. That tells you a lot about the depth of this appalling scandal.

Revenge of the OCDA

Retaliation by the OCDA against Judge Goethals was swift and ruthless. After Judge Goethals' began the hearings, an odd development occurred. Orange County prosecutors began blanketly filing "170.6 motions" against him[54], a tactic rarely done by a prosecutor's office. These motions permit any lawyer in California to disqualify a judge from presiding over a case. From January 2014 to May 2015, Goethals was 'point sixed' from more than 100 cases. In the eight years prior to the hearings, he had only 18 such disqualifications. This is corruption sticking up for and supporting corruption.

Appellate Court Ruling

It took until November 23, 2016 for the Appeals Court to decide that Goethal's decision keeping OCDA prosecutors off the case would stand. The Appellate Court's ruling states,

> The OCDA's primary function is to prosecute crimes in Orange County...it must exercise its vast discretion justly and fairly to

54 Foshay, K., & Okwu, M. (2015). Recordings reveal how informant ring operated in Orange County jails. Al Jazeera America. Retrieved 27 December 2017, from http://america.aljazeera.com/watch/shows/america-tonight/articles/2015/5/28/orange-county-snitch-scandal-audiotapes.html

> ensure every defendant is treated fairly, regardless of the severity of the charged offenses. Here, the evidence demonstrated the OCDA had an interest extraneous to its official duties – its loyalty to the OCSD and its desire to protect the OCSD at the expense of Dekraai's constitutional and statutory rights.
>
> This abdication of the OCDA's fiduciary duty violated Dekraai's due process rights. The record before us demonstrates that from the outset, the OCDA failed in its duty as the primary county prosecutor to supervise its prosecution team... and ensure its prosecutors and its law enforcement team complied with its constitutional and statutory obligations. These proceedings were a search for truth[55].

Using scathing language against Rackauckas' corrupt office, the court ruled "Not only did the OCDA intentionally or negligently ignore the [OCSD's] violations of targeted defendants' constitutional rights, but the OCDA on its own violated targeted defendants' constitutional rights through its participation in the [confidential informant] program," and "the magnitude of the systemic problems cannot be overlooked." They added that the prosecutors had a desire to protect the Sheriff's Department at the expense of "Dekraai's constitutional and statutory rights."

That ruling occurred the same day that county supervisors decided to give the Orange County grand jury $400,000, for the purpose of "continuing a previously undisclosed probe into the county's use of informants."

55 Appeal From An Order Of The Superior Court Of Orange County, Thomas M. Goethals, Judge. *The People V. Scott Evans Dekraai.* Court Of Appeal Of The State Of California Fourth Appellate District. Division Three. 11/22/2016. Retrieved on December 27, 2017 from big.assets.huffingtonpost.com/DekraaiCoAopiniorecusalappeal.pdf

Time for Some Compliance

In October 2016, Judge Goethals said it was "time for some compliance" after waiting years for the OCSD to cooperate with discovery requests. It had taken up until then—more than three years after the records were requested—for the deputies' "special handling log" from 2008 to 2013 to appear. Goethals ordered[56] 250 to 300 pages of those logs to be turned over to the defense. Moreover, it appeared from what was turned over that the special handling log had been replaced in 2013 with another document created at that time for "important information," but no one appeared to be able to locate that new log.

Goethals didn't buy the story told by a deputy county counsel that Sheriff Sandra Hutchens' office was diligently searching for that lost "important info" log. "If the Orange County sheriff was sincerely trying to unravel this mystery, I can't see why we haven't gotten to the bottom of it," Goethals said, as reported in the *Orange County Register*. "It seems as if the sheriff believes that she can have documents and she can decide whether or not she can turn them over. That's not the sheriff's place."

Imagine a criminal defendant or a defense attorney willfully and repeatedly disobeying a court order for three years. It wouldn't happen because the defendant or defense attorney would have been jailed and/or fined harshly for such insolence.

Things got so bad that Goethals threatened[57] to hold the sheriff and deputies in contempt of court because they kept failing to turn over evidence. In early December 2016, the OCSD did turn over an additional

---

56 Laird, L. (2016). Judge chides sheriff, turns over more documents in Orange County jailhouse informant case. ABA Journal. Retrieved 27 December 2017, from http://www.abajournal.com/news/article/judge_chides_sheriff_turns_over_more_documents_in_orange_county_jailhouse_i

57 Ferner, M. (2016). Orange County Judge Blasts Sheriff In Jail Informant Scandal: 'What Is Going On Over There?'. HuffPost UK. Retrieved 27 December 2017, from https://www.huffingtonpost.com/entry/orange-county-california-jail-informant-sheriff_us_58545931e4b0b3ddfd8cb972

5,600 pages, but Goethals called this gesture a "document dump," which had relevant and irrelevant material interspersed. "This is a classic strategy. That's what this looks like, folks," he said.

Not surprisingly, some information in the records directly contradicted that of several deputies who had testified under oath. In court, they had stated that they had never dealt with snitches…

The Relatives Weigh In

The relatives of Dekraai's eight victims not only endured unbearable heartache at the violent loss of their loved ones, but had to contend with the OCDA and OCSD's wrecking of what should have been an easy case. At a press conference, they asked that rather than the death penalty, Dekraai receive eight consecutive life imprisonments with no chance for parole terms. Defiantly, the OCDA publicly refused their requests and vengefully swore to pursue the death penalty.

The Upshot

It's been six years since Dekraai killed eight people, and the corruption unearthed by his attorney still resonates. There's still no certainty about how many convictions could be related to these unconstitutional practices, and Sanders is pushing to have every Orange County case for the past 30 years involving a snitch re-examined.

An OCDA internal report[58] points the finger at "a failure of leadership" and "lack of oversight" for this unholy mess. The report notes these omissions led to "repeated legal errors that should have been identified and rectified by management long before the problems reached the current scale."

58 Aguilar, E. (2016). 'Lack of oversight' led to informant scandal in Orange County. Southern California Public Radio. Retrieved 27 December 2017, from http://www.scpr.org/news/2016/01/04/56659/lack-of-oversight-led-to-informant-scandal-in-oran/

It is interesting to note that, as per the *Los Angeles Times* article, Tony Rackauckas worked his way up from being a deputy district attorney using this dishonest and unconstitutional snitch system all the way up to the top job of the district attorney ladder. Another example of a psychopath's career journey to the highest point of the hierarchy.

The fallout continues with more than half a dozen defendants having murder or other serious convictions overturned. Over a dozen defendants were granted new trials or received reduced sentences. Sanders says the number of affected cases could range in the hundreds.

Think about it. It took three years[59], from 2013 to 2016, for the OCDA to even admit a snitch program existed. They deny everything and then decide to 'fess up' in June 2016? Do they think Orange County residents are idiots? Who is the OCDA kidding? The questions no one is asking are, since this program was done for decades at first using pen and paper and then using computers; who sought out the computer programmers to create the computerized snitch system? What job description was put on the work order? How much did it cost? Who authorized the payment? Where did the payment come from? This scandal was no isolated incident, accident, or mistake. This manifest denial of justice was the result of collusion at the top levels of Orange County law enforcement, the very people the public puts their faith in for the upkeep of justice.

Where Are They Now

Here's an update on what's new with or related to some of the snitch scandal's characters:

59 Ferner, M. (2016). Orange County DA's Office Finally Acknowledges Jailhouse Informant Program Exists. HuffPost UK. Retrieved 27 December 2017, from http://www.huffingtonpost.com/entry/orange-county-jailhouse-informant-program_us_575b236be4b0ced23ca81b2c

- Assembly bill 359[60], targeting in-custody informants, was inspired by the huge amounts of money paid to snitches Paredes and Cuevas.
- Perez was sentenced[61] to 21 years in state prison, on charges of being a felon possessing a firearm in public. Under the state's three strikes law, he faced 42 years to life.
- Moriel, who admits he's killed at least six people, has an attempted murder case postponed for the *40th* time. That's no misprint, four-zero, "FORTY."
- Rackauckas, now 74, held a June 2017 fundraiser in Costa Mesa for his upcoming fifth run as DA. Orange County Supervisor Todd Spitzer plans to run against him.

60 Minutes Revelations

Over the years, one jailhouse informant, a serial snitch, had helped the OCDA secure scores of convictions, even though the OCDA records indicate they didn't find him to be a credible source. This informant aged, reformed his life, and became a heroic whistleblower against this scandal. He even bravely appeared on *60 Minutes* at great personal risk, to expose it.

What people who watched the *60 Minutes* episode don't know is that before he appeared there, he had called me, out of the blue, having been referred through the internet, needing counsel on how to go about his dangerous mission. I drove down from the Bay Area to Orange County to meet with him personally. I evaluated whether he had any liability: there was none. I counseled him, organized and scanned all of his extensive

60 Act to amend Sections 1127a and 4001.1 of the Penal Code. ASSEMBLY BILL No. 359. CALIFORNIA LEGISLATURE. Introduced by Assembly Member Jones-Sawyer. February 08, 2017. Retrieved on December 27, 2017 from https://leginfo.legislature.ca.gov/faces/billTextClient.xhtml?bill_id=201720180AB359

61 O.C. Gangbanger who snitched on the Mexican Mafia gets a lighter sentence. (2016). New Santa Ana. Retrieved 27 December 2017, from http://newsantaana.com/2016/03/06/o-c-gangbanger-who-snitched-on-the-mexican-mafia-gets-a-lighter-sentence/

notes detailing the OC snitch system to ensure there would always be a copy in safe hands, and got him emotionally prepped for his TV interview.

In that interview, this informant stated he had had a direct line to the OCDA, "I can get on the phone anytime I want, night or day. I was working right there with Tony [Rackauckas], I would call him up, he'd love it." Rackauckas' response to *60 Minutes* was that this serial snitch was a liar, but then he didn't explain why, if he thought so, he used this informant so frequently. Nor did Rackauckas explain why he never mentioned his belief that this serial snitch was a liar to jurors or the defense attorneys for the defendants the snitch helped to put away.

Grand Jury Sham

Incredibly, on June 13, 2017, the OCGJ (Orange County Grand Jury) issued a report[62] entitled "The Myth of the Orange County Jailhouse Informant Program." In the report, the OCGJ dismissed the idea of a conspiracy between the OCDA and the OCSD in the use of snitches. Although the report did concede a few members of both agencies broke the law when it came to the use of informants, it found no "structured" informant program.

"A handful of special handling deputies drifted from their custodial duties over a period of years, into investigating crimes. The lack of proper supervision and appropriate policies allowed this to continue longer than it should have," according to the report. "This drift does not constitute an OCSD jailhouse informant program, but rather the work of a few rogue deputies who got carried away with efforts to be crime-fighters."

The OCGJ's recommendation: development of some new training and procedures. The report concluded that the entire case was a "witch-hunt

62 Orange County Grand Jury. (2017). The Myth Of The Orange County Jailhouse Informant Program. Retrieved 27 December 2017, from http://www.ocgrandjury.org/pdfs/2016_2017_GJreport/2017-06-13_Informant_Report.pdf

for agency corruption," but, of course, it only involved a few overzealous bad apples, not entire departments. Perhaps a more appropriate title is "The Myth of the OCGJ Actually Doing its Job."

The husband of one of Dekraai's victims terms the OCGJ report "shameful[63]." He asks that Goethals continue to pursue the truth.

The Pursuit Continues: Throwing Out the Death Penalty

Goethals is indeed continuing to pursue the truth. In hearings[64] in the summer of 2017, Goethals pressed deputies about the log books and why the OCSD couldn't explain why no entries were placed in the logs between April and October, 2011. At one hearing, Goethals asked an expert on gathering jailhouse documents for his theories on the missing information. It came down to two: either the deputies were too busy and neglected to put in the necessary effort to journal, or the information was deleted. Take your pick of what you think occurred. Goethals was making a decision whether or not to throw out the death penalty in the Dekraai case, based on whether the OCSD withheld or destroyed evidence.

On August 18, 2017, he made his decision. Goethals ruled[65] that the death penalty was off the table. Understandably, some Orange County residents were enraged, but Bethany Webb, who lost her sister in the carnage, said, "I honor this judge and what it took to do an unpopular thing in Orange County, but the right thing for everyone involved," according to the *Orange County Register*.

---

63 Moxley, R. (2017). Snitch Myth? Only To Orange County's Reality-Denying Grand Jury. OC Weekly. Retrieved 27 December 2017, from http://www.ocweekly.com/news/reality-timeline-in-orange-countys-jailhouse-snitch-scandal-contradicts-grand-jurys-report-8201616

64 Vo, T. (2017). Sheriff's Deputy Says, Despite Gap in Jail Log, Deputies Never Stopped Making Entries. Voice of OC. Retrieved 27 December 2017, from http://voiceofoc.org/2017/06/sheriffs-deputy-says-despite-gap-in-jail-log-deputies-never-stopped-making-entries/

65 Goulding, S., Puente, K., & Saavedra, T. (2017). Judge's decision that Scott Dekraai can't get the death penalty draws strong responses – Orange County Register. Retrieved 27 December 2017, from http://www.ocregister.com/2017/08/18/judges-decision-that-scott-dekraai-cant-be-executed-draws-angry-responses/

On Twitter, Rackauckas expressed "disappointment" on behalf of the OCDA that "Judge Goethals denied the California AG the ability to pursue death penalty against Dekraai." He's probably more disappointed that his bullheaded pursuit of the death penalty, in this case, led to a national scandal focused on his misdeeds.

But Her Emails!

An email[66] revealed in an evidentiary closing argument proves Sheriff Hutchens a liar. She had previously testified under oath before Judge Goethals that all of the jailhouse informant evidence had been submitted and her department would obey his further directives. Oops! On a screen set up in the courtroom, Sanders showed the judge a five-year-old email Hutchens had never produced.

It was a December 2009 email from Deputy Seth Tunstall to his colleagues titled, "Mod L Moves." In it, he referred to colored wristbands the snitches wore, each indicating a dangerousness level. These "levels" gave the snitches anti-police street cred to the inmates they targeted. The email names Charles Flynn, a Santa Anna police department investigator, as wanting Moriel, one of the snitches, placed next to a specific inmate.

A Federal Investigation

The OCGJ's report is not the last word. A federal investigation[67] launched in December 2016 is still underway over allegations that the OCDA and OCSD "routinely" obtained illegal confessions by using snitches. It's one

66 Moxley, R. (2017). One More Buried Record Proves Sheriff Sandra Hutchens' Lies in Snitch Scandal. OC Weekly. Retrieved 27 December 2017, from http://www.ocweekly.com/content/printView/8338377

67 Puente, K., & Saavedra, T. (2017). Feds launch investigation into Orange County D.A.'s Office, Sheriff's Department over jailhouse informants – Orange County Register. Ocregister.com. Retrieved 27 December 2017, from http://www.ocregister.com/articles/-738533--.html

for the record books, as it is just the second time[68] in U.S. history that federal investigators are looking into both sides of one county's justice system. The U.S. Department of Justice is investigating "the possibility of systemic constitutional abuses," according to the *Orange County Register*.

The Justice Department doesn't usually take on a case unless plenty of evidence exists. Should the feds confirm that the civil rights of inmates were violated, that could lead to either a federal lawsuit against the county, or an early settlement by the county. In the latter case, that means huge changes coming to the OCSD and OCDA.

As a last word on this federal investigation, bear in mind that it is a civil investigation only, meaning that, while some people may be sued or fined, there will be no criminal charges and no law enforcement official will go to jail or prison for any of the multitude of crimes committed in carrying out this serious, decades-long scandal.

68 Timeline: Orange County's jailhouse snitch crisis. (2017). Orange County Register, Retrieved 27 December 2017, from http://www.ocregister.com/articles/dekraai-738551-prosecutors-attorney.html

CHAPTER EIGHT

COUNTY JAILS

The quaint notion of a local jail is a misconception. It is not a barred boarding house where drunks sleep it off and inmates play cards with a Barney Fife-like deputy. County and city jails in the State of California have become proxy prisons used to punish convicted felons, while detaining innocent arrestees within the panopticon of prosecutors and law enforcement.

Our criminal justice system is based upon innocence until proven guilty. When someone is arrested, that person has rights. They have the right to receive a fair trial, and they have rights during that trial, but many innocent people are arrested then disappeared away in jail, away from friends, family, social workers, and community.

Jail Versus Prison: A Blurring Definition

Historically, "jails" for the most part are detention centers run by local governments intended to house four types of detainees: those awaiting trial, those convicted of misdemeanor offenses (which by definition carry sentences of less than a year), those convicted of felonies and given probation (which also by definition carry sentences of less than a year), and those convicted of felonies who were given sentences of longer than a year (prison cases) who are awaiting transfer to prison.

Prisons, on the other hand, are state- or federally run facilities, also known as penitentiaries, intended to house people convicted of felony-level offenses with sentences longer than one year. Jails handle a large number of people—ranging from falsely accused innocents to dangerous, convicted felons entering and departing on a day-to-day basis, and offer little in the way of daily routine or long-term support services.

People landing in jails are often intoxicated, injured or mentally ill and have been diverted to jails while law enforcement determines what to do with them. Prisons, however, process a smaller number of inmates in and out each day, follow a strict, predictable daily schedule and offer larger facilities providing broader access to rehabilitation services. Because of the advantages of the prison environment[69], repeat offenders, even those with shorter sentences, will often request time in prison versus a local jail facility[70].

Due to a shell-game scenario perpetrated by the State of California on its county governments, these definitions and the differences between jail and prison have blurred, putting innocent victims of a haphazard justice system in peril.

After arrest, individuals are booked into a local jail facility. Keep in mind that law enforcement doesn't usually charge the arrested individual; the job of charging is reserved for prosecutor, with rare exception. In California, under the law, individuals can be held up to 48 hours—which magically turns into 72 hours in court—before a prosecutor must either file charges or let them go.

After arraignment, which usually includes a bail hearing, if bail is denied or the defendant is unable to post bail, the accused is held in the local jail while awaiting trial. If found guilty, those who are sentenced for one year or less will usually serve their sentence locally in that same county jail.

69 What's the difference between prison and jail?. Cleminfostrategies.com. Retrieved 27 December 2017, from http://cleminfostrategies.com/whats-the-difference-between-prison-and-jail/

70 What is the Difference Between Jail and Prison?. Hg.org. Retrieved 27 December 2017, from https://www.hg.org/article.asp?id=31513

As noted above, county jails were never intended to act as prisons to punish serious offenders. A large function of the local county jail was to house people awaiting their day in court. Approximately 60-75 percent of a California county jail's detainees are awaiting trial, depending on which study you read and in what year. These are people who could not make bail and are in the jail simply waiting for their case to be heard in court. The accused who are awaiting trial are being housed among the remaining 25 percent—an increasingly volatile and dangerous contingent—due to the state's need to divert prisoners from prison facilities to jails.

The Evolution of Jail as Power

The temporary denial of liberty is a relatively recent concept as a form of bond or punishment. In ancient times, punishment was swift and often very brutal. Hammurabi's Code, one of the earliest examples of a codified system of laws, dates back to 1754 B.C. and offers a scaled level of punishments based upon "An eye for an eye, a tooth for a tooth," as well as the presumption of innocence for the accused.

In the centuries before our current system of law, a fine was a simple and humane punishment for those with the financial means to pay, whereas the poor endured corporal punishment, such as a public lashing—quick and to the point. Humiliation and shame were powerful punishments in some societies as well, with the guilty tied up on the pillory or locked in the stocks in town square. Of course, exile and death were punishment for the crimes considered extreme and heinous in that era.

Over time, the dungeon or jail became a status symbol for rulers and despots. From the Middle Ages, the authority to detain a body stemmed from the centralization of power, and a ruler or despot could demonstrate his power over individuals and society with monuments to punishment and physical embodiments of incarceration[71].

Thus the dungeon, the jail, the cage—all symbols of domination and subjugation of the mighty against the weak, the mighty against the few, the rules against the ruled, the State versus its enemies. To whip, shame, or torture another human was common and mundane, but the ruler alone could take and give freedom. Jails were seen as a signifier of power and authority over others.

AB 109: The Downhill Roll Starts

On May 23, 2011, the U.S. Supreme Court upheld a federal court order regarding *Brown v. Plata*. The case proved that prison overcrowding in California constituted cruel and unusual punishment and was the cause of inmates' inadequate medical and mental health care. The state was forced to reduce California's prison population to less than 137.5 percent of design capacity (at the time they were at roughly 180 percent of capacity).

The state's solution was to pass AB 109, known as "Realignment," which pushed a portion of the prison population back down to local county facilities that were not subject to the order and had more room, relatively speaking. Certain felonies became punishable by serving 'prison time' in the county jail. Parole violations for these same offenses would also be served in local jails.

This placed an increasing number of serious criminals alongside a population of people serving lightweight sentencing for lightweight crimes as well as those awaiting trial. It also put strain on the guards who now had to watch a more volatile and dangerous population, often lacking

71 Turning, P. (2012). Competition for the Prisoner's Body: Wardens and Jailers in Fourteenth-Century Southern France. In Classen, A., & Scarborough, C. (2012). Crime and punishment in the Middle Ages and early modern age. Berlin: Walter de Gruyter.

the experience and training to do so, and taxed facilities not built to accommodate or separate the influx of prisoners.

The logical solution to prison overcrowding would have been to put fewer people in prison. Enter Californians United for a Responsible Budget (CURB). CURB is a coalition of 70 grassroots organizations working together to not only reduce the number of people in prisons and jails, but also to reduce the number of prisons and jails in the state and divert spending from corrections to human services, education, healthcare, housing, and jobs.

CURB has quite sanely pointed out the obvious, stating, "The only sustainable way to end overcrowding is to reduce the number of people imprisoned in California." Along these lines, CURB has suggested decriminalizing drug possession, reducing sentences for youth and preventing excessive sentences.

Rather than imprison fewer people, however, the State of California began implementing the Public Safety Realignment initiative, which pushed roughly 25,000 inmates out of the state's prison system in its first two years, according to the Public Policy Institute of California. By giving county jails a monetary incentive to absorb the prison overflow, realignment made California's prison overcrowding look substantially reduced on paper (even though it fell short of *Brown v. Plata*'s initial goals and timeline).

But this reduction in prison population was a shell game at best. In the past five years, California's jail population has predictably grown while the prison population has fallen. The average daily population in local jails has increased by at least 12 percent. Larger counties have seen jail population surge more than 18 percent, with hardest-hit Fresno's jumping by an astonishing 29.6 percent.

Not only are jail populations booming, those new occupants are there for the long haul. The California State Sheriffs' Association found that, in 2013, more than 1,100 prisoners in the state's county jails were serving 5 to

10-year sentences, with 44 of them serving sentences of 10 years or more[72]. This is really bad for a reason that may not be obvious; jails are meant to hold people for sentences of one year or less, prisons for one year or more. Prisons have yards and a bit more accommodation knowing that the stay is for the long haul. For instance, someone in prison may be able to have a guitar whereas, in county jail, you are pretty much locked in a tiny box twenty-two to twenty-three hours a day.

While crime has to have its consequences, society must still be humane. After all, what we do to the least among us, we truly do to ourselves. We might be okay with bringing a dog to a groomer for a day knowing that it will be locked in a small cage after the haircut before we pick it up after work but we wouldn't think about leaving it in those small confines whilst we go on a two-week vacation. For that, we would get a kennel, knowing that the dog can get out, run around and interact with others during the day. God help us if we sink to the point where we systematically do to humans what we would not dare do to dogs.

Prop. 47: The Rolling Gains Momentum

Compounding the *Brown v. Plata* decision was the passage of California's Proposition 47 in 2014. Known by its ballot title, "Criminal Sentences. Misdemeanor Penalties. Initiative Statute," or by the moniker supporters bestowed, "Safe Neighborhoods and Schools Act," this initiative looked great on paper—it turned many non-violent crimes into misdemeanors punishable at the city or county level; meaning that non-violent criminals, such as drug offenders, thieves, shoplifters, and forgers, were kept out of the state prison.

Proposition 47 was supported by diverse advocates from the American

72 Petrella, C. (2014). Consequences of California's Realignment Initiative. Prison Legal News. Prison Legal News. Retrieved 27 December 2017, from https://www.prisonlegalnews.org/news/2014/jun/12/consequences-californias-realignment-initiative/

Civil Liberties Union to conservative Newt Gingrich. While Los Angeles' Mayor Garcetti implied the law was related to increased crime rates in his city and San Diego Police Chief Shelley Zimmerman called it "a virtual get-out-of-jail-free card," Stanford University law scholars called the legislation effective, reporting that in 2014 alone the state prison system was spared over 13,000 inmates, saving the state $150 million. The downside to the state prison system saving $150 million by reclassifying crimes as misdemeanors is that the criminals committing those crimes become the problem of local district attorneys and jails, once again shuffling a state problem to the local level[73].

More often than not, those accused of these less severe crimes are not tried, meaning they take a plea bargain and are released within days or weeks, as opposed to months or years. In counties that were already having problems with overcrowding prior to the passage of AB 109 Realignment and Prop. 47, such as many rural counties for instance, repeat offenders see the local jail as a revolving door and as little impediment to committing more petty crimes to sustain an unhealthy lifestyle such as personal drug habits due to addiction.

Had those local county jails not been overburdened with crimes pushed down on them by the state, something which district attorneys must take into account, these troubled people could break the cycle of crime and, facing a rather lengthy time incarcerated in jail or prison, they could opt to do the equal amount of time in a drug program. To get an addict into treatment, you need both a carrot and a stick. A substantive jail or prison sentence versus serving the same time in a drug treatment or dual diagnosis program usually does the trick.

Judges and attorneys who not only truly care but are also fiscally-minded about the cost to taxpayers, could help 'steer' offenders into

73 Parker, C. (2015). California's early release of prisoners proving effective so far, Stanford experts say. Stanford News. Retrieved 27 December 2017, from http://news.stanford.edu/news/2015/november/prison-early-release-110215.html

treatment, job training, social services, health and mental care. Instead, these low level offenders, usually addicts or mentally ill, encounter the same law enforcement officers over and over as they get caught in a cycle of petty crimes with little support or punishment. It can't be a good experience for the officers either; they must get frustrated doing the same thing over and over again, living a life out of a nightmarish Groundhog Day.

When I take a case, an aspect that I believe to be a very important part of my job is to make sure my client won't have to hire me again. When I have made pitches for programs for addicts or those suffering from mental health issues, judges and prosecutors are more often than not very supportive as long as the crime isn't too violent and I can prove that the root of the crime was addiction or mental illness, and that my client wants the help, hasn't had this opportunity before, and wants to change his or her life.

A Culture of Intimidation and Rights Violations Grows at the Local Level

"The degree of civilization in a society is revealed by entering its prisons." —Fyodor Dostoyevsky

"It is said that no one truly knows a nation until one has been inside its jails. A nation should not be judged by how it treats its highest citizens, but its lowest ones." —Nelson Mandela

"Speak up for those who cannot speak for themselves,
for the rights of all who are destitute. Speak up and judge fairly;
defend the rights of the poor and needy."
—Proverbs 31:8-9

Placing a growing number of convicts at the local level puts a massive population of citizens in the direct line of sight of bullying, abuse, and manipulation by law enforcement; a problem that is far less common when inmates are held at a distance in state-run prisons. In theory, the local jail is run by the local sheriff or police, who are on the same side of the law as the district attorney or prosecutor. But proximity creates an opportunity for the jailer to coerce, bully, eavesdrop, or abuse inmates to help the prosecution gain evidence towards a coerced confession or wrongful conviction.

Jailers rarely see their inmates as innocents being held until trial, especially jailers who are now expected to oversee an ever-growing population of more seasoned criminals. Given the fragility of human psychology and the two-tiered dichotomy of jail, eventually all orange jumpsuits will be seen as less than human serial numbers, dangerous threats to civilization that must be caged. That perception makes it easier for those officers working at the jail who are predisposed to sadism to abuse the rights of the detainees.

County jails in California are ripe with the history of abuse and rights violations. This history arguably permeates the entire system. May we never forget the important lessons of the Stanford Prison Experiment as well as the tests run by Milgram.

I've covered in Chapter Seven of this book the Orange County Snitch Scandal. However, that is not an isolated incident of criminals in jail *on the other side of the bars*. In early 2016, retired Los Angeles County Sheriff Lee Baca pled guilty to a felony related to corruption and civil rights violations carried out by his department.

The story begins in 2011, when the Federal Bureau of Investigation concerned about charges of widespread violence, abuse, and corruption in the Los Angeles County jail system began an undercover investigation. The

FBI enlisted an inmate named Anthony Brown, 44, to report misconduct and wrongdoing by jail guards. Brown had previously been an informant for the FBI, so his background and presence in the jail were perfect for an insider perspective on conditions[74].

Brown was provided a cell phone—a serious piece of contraband inside a jail facility—to communicate with FBI handlers and share evidence of wrongdoing gathered from observation and jailhouse gossip. The plan was working, until a random shakedown of Brown's cell turned up the phone. When the sheriff's department staff reviewed the phone's logs, perhaps expecting to see communications with a girlfriend or evidence of ongoing criminal activity, they found something altogether different—the most frequently called numbers on Brown's contraband phone reached the FBI's Los Angeles field office.

In order to begin damage control, the sheriff's department first needed to know how deep in it they were. After a middle-of-the-night session spent bullying and harassing one of Brown's handlers, interaction with the female FBI agent proved fruitless, and sheriffs determined that they needed time alone with Anthony Brown to discover what he had revealed to the FBI. So, they made him disappear.

During "Pandora's Box," a secret operation executed by an LASD investigative unit ironically named "Operation Safe Jails," Anthony Brown was released from jail, immediately rebooked as a new inmate and sent to a new location. Every 48 hours, to stay ahead of the jail booking and inmate tracking computer, "Anthony Brown" was released and rebooked with new data: a new name, new booking number, new physical description.

74 Fremon, C. (2013). OPERATION PANDORA'S BOX: Will Hiding a Federal Informant Result in Criminal Indictments for Members of the Los Angeles Sheriff's Department? |. Witness LA. Retrieved 27 December 2017, from http://witnessla.com/operation-pandoras-box-will-hiding-a-federal-informant-result-in-criminal-indictments-for-members-of-the-los-angeles-sheriffs-department/

Even data on his required medication had to be intricately maneuvered to make sure he received his prescription without alerting the FBI to his whereabouts. Meanwhile, the cadre of Pandora's Box officers would interrogate, entice, reward, and interview Brown on what he had shared with the Feds.

For over two weeks, the FBI lost contact with their informant, and U.S. Marshals could not find the inmate they were due to transfer to state prison. After secreting Brown away for 18 days, he was re-entered into the database with his real biodata and numbers and was flagged for transfer to prison. In fact, four of the Operation Pandora's Box team members personally drove Mr. Brown to the California State Prison at Lancaster.

Eventually, the Feds filed charges against the conspirators in the Pandora's Box case, citing "Conspiracy Against Rights" (when two or more persons conspire to injure, oppress, threaten, or intimidate any person in any State, Territory, Commonwealth, Possession, or District in the free exercise or enjoyment of any right or privilege secured to him by the Constitution or laws of the United States) and "Deprivation of Rights Under Color of Law" (essentially the same charge levied against those in law enforcement).

The indictments and prosecutions culminated with the Los Angeles County Sheriff at the time, Lee Baca, being taken down. However, Baca didn't plead guilty to the cruel plot to hide a prisoner and violate his rights; he merely admitted in a plea agreement that he'd lied to federal authorities. Others involved in the scandal are still awaiting trial. Eileen Decker, U.S. attorney for the Central District of California, noted that Baca's guilty plea "demonstrates that the illegal behavior in the Sheriff's Department went to the very top of this organization. More importantly, it illustrates that those who foster and then try to hide a corrupt culture will be held accountable."

As much as jailed inmates are abused and mistreated, they must also deal with feeling as though they have no recourse to report abuses when they do occur. In 2015, in Santa Clara County, located just north of San Jose, a Blue Ribbon Commission was formed by the county Board of Supervisors to investigate reports of rampant wrongdoing at the county's three jails.

One commissioner, Wes Mukoyama, a jail chaplain, said that one inmate told him a "guard recommended he tear up a grievance or he would retaliate." Alison Brunner, another commission member and Executive Director of the nonprofit Law Foundation of Silicon Valley reported that some inmates say, "they have been actively retaliated against." Systemic abuses in the Santa Clara jail system came to light early in 2015 after mentally ill inmate Michael Tyree was beaten to death while in custody[75]. Three guards were later charged with Tyree's murder.

Inmates' fears of retaliation are exacerbated when grievances must be submitted directly to guards for filing, rather than to a prison counselor or social worker, putting the abuser in a position to destroy the report and retaliate for its submission.

Santa Clara's Blue Ribbon Commission issued a report in 2016 culled from interviews with nearly 1,000 inmates, 33 staff members, and eight inmate family members. The report found numerous instances of correctional officers using excessive force "in routine jail movements and lockdowns. Interviewees emphasized that officers' use of force does not always stop when an emergency ends; physical violence and pepper spray often continue even after an inmate is fully restrained and no longer a threat to anyone's safety."

75 Prodis Sulek, J. (2015). Jail abuse: Santa Clara County commission hears complaints that guards retaliate about inmates who file grievances. The Mercury News. Retrieved 27 December 2017, from http://www.mercurynews.com/bay-area-news/ci_29208064/jail-abuse-santa-clara-county-commission-hears-complaints

Inmates also reported, "Some officers use physical force against inmates who 'talk back'...and that a few officers use force disproportionately with vulnerable inmates, such as those who are mentally ill, elderly, or without family, because these inmates are less able to speak up for themselves."

The revelations in Orange County, the undoing of the Los Angeles Sheriff's Department, and the exposure of intimidation and bullying in Santa Clara are indicators of a culture of abuse in California jails. Many of these abuses have gone on for years, across the state, at an operational and organizational level bordering on bureaucratic.

It is not just in big city jails in California that these abuses happen. They are happening on a smaller scale as well, today, in a county jail near you. Let's just hope it doesn't take the death of an inmate for an independent commission to be empaneled to raise a little awareness to let the situation cool down until the scenario repeats and gradually escalates until there are even bigger tragedies.

The dirty tricks and abuses in jail are not always grand conspiracies perpetuated from the highest levels. Sometimes they are mundane, banal, matter-of-fact bullying that happens when you put a wannabe-boss-man-psychopath-brute in a position of power over a vulnerable population. I've heard lots of stories and seen a lot with my own two eyes while visiting with my in-custody clients. I know this to be true.

Some of the inmate abuses commonly reported in county jails include:

- Purposefully "losing" or destroying inmate grievances
- Arbitrary enforcement of policies and overt favoritism
- Mixing up or withholding medications
- Forced cold-turkey withdrawal of psychiatric medications
- Deliberately providing an inmate ill-fitting clothing
- Withholding menstrual pads from female inmates

- Beatings or sexual abuse by jail staff
- Denying meal and hygiene opportunities
- Jail staff looking the other way when violence occurs against an inmate
- Intentionally housing a disturbed or violent inmate with a targeted detainee

There is a move called the "Morning Bus" that is as routine as it is cruel and defeating. A jail guard wakes an inmate very early in the morning and moves them to a holding cell for transfer to court. The inmate misses the morning meal, loses sleep and sits in anticipation of a trip to see the compassionate face of their lawyer or a glimpse of sunshine. But cruelly, the targeted inmate is not loaded on the bus because there was never a court transfer in the works to begin with. The inmate is returned to their cell, hungry and confused, the supposed victim of a clerical error.

This same trick was commonplace in my home county of Contra Costa except that the inmates would be transported to a court within the county only to 'find out' that the inmate didn't have court that day so the inmate would not only suffer the negatives of the "Morning Bus" routine, but also be housed in a cramped, stressful courtroom pod all day only to be bussed back to his cell late in the day. This move was referred to as a "Dry Run."

Inmate Phone Systems: A Rich Source of Income and Intel

When an innocent person is held in a cage before trial, they are scared, alone, and susceptible to coercion by jail officers and their co-conspirators. District attorneys are happy to have any bit of evidence that can help them increase their conviction rate and look "tough on crime" for the polls.

It is unfortunate that detainees held pre-trial are lumped in with convicts that have truly and deservedly lost their liberty. This not only puts innocents in harm's way, it also pits jail staff against all inmates in a good-versus-evil standoff. But even convicted felons have rights. The county phone systems are often abused to deny an inmate's rights.

I've had clients who were denied jail calls for days after their arrest. Further, when an inmate gets to a phone and is able to call, all such calls in county jails are recorded. This is a 'safety feature' supposedly imposed by the jail to ensure plots and crimes are not discussed between inmates and the outside world. This can lead to prosecutors and law enforcement hearing things that should not be shared with a jury, for example, privileged attorney-client conversations.

In Contra Costa County, east of San Francisco, unless an attorney has provided a written request on letterhead to Custody Services Bureau, Main Detention Facility, 1000 Ward Street, Martinez, CA 94553, the attorney-client call will be recorded and available for live monitoring. Detainees have no expectation of privacy, and the district attorney can listen to all calls except the few that are on the pre-approved attorney list.

Global Tel Link is a leading provider of inmate telephone communication and payment systems. Through GTL and other services like it, family members can put money on an inmate's account for use in making calls. These calls then make money for the jail while also providing a rich source of evidence that can be eavesdropped on or replayed in violation of attorney-client privilege. You can see why the county loves this vendor relationship and is constantly seeking to expand it.

How many inmates have been coerced into taking a bad plea bargain based on innocent information shared on GTL phones that, in light of the circumstances, would have looked really bad to a jury? I've seen it more than once where prosecutors in a big case are desperate because there's not enough evidence to convict—and they know it. They proceed to carefully go through all of a defendant's phone calls and mine gold to force a plea bargain.

Imagine an inmate and his significant other processing the stressful and difficult time of one of the pair being incarcerated by arguing. The prosecutor can then take that conversation, normal under the circumstances, and spin it in front of a jury, "He's a violent, vicious man, no doubt an abuser of women too—did you hear what he said to his girlfriend in anger over the phone while in jail?" Imagine someone watering down or changing the facts behind their arrest to a family member or significant other over the phone while incarcerated for the obvious reason that they want to lessen the impact of their arrest to their loved one. 'Why, your client is a liar! The story that he told his girlfriend on the phone is different than the story that he told his mother which is different than the story that he told the detective on the night of the arrest. Which story is the jury going to believe now? Your client better take the offer.'

Conclusion

Every prisoner—from a petty thief to a serial rapist—must be afforded basic rights if we are going to be a civilized society. Equally important, those *accused* of crimes have rights and deserve fair treatment along with a fair trial. When jails are looking at revenue rather than justice, when the state is more concerned with falsely deflating prison populations than the proper handling of citizens, when local jails and jailers are overwhelmed by a number and type of prisoner they're not equipped to handle, that is when the system cracks open with conflicts and unfathomable problems.

What is incomprehensible is why the California Legislature thought that putting people from overcrowded prisons into a county jail—where some counties had room but others were already bursting themselves—was a solution. Everyone knows what runs downhill. If you don't address the source of a problem, and only treat its symptoms, then you haven't done anything at all except put off the inevitable.

Heaven forbid that we should study just how much of our local law enforcement, prosecutor, and county jail resources are spent dealing with mentally ill people. While it's heresy to suggest cutting the budget of police and sheriff, what if we found that 30 percent of their resources were being utilized dealing with the mentally ill? What if we then cut the budget of law enforcement by 15 percent and used it to fund programs assisting the mentally ill?

One Law of Nature that we should all be keenly attuned to is that good begets good and bad begets bad. However, society is perpetually screaming all day, every day until red-faced, 'Get the bad guy, get the bad guy!' We should further analyze where we really want to put our resources and whether or not we really want the net of criminality to be so wide where lawbreaking isn't determined by deeds so much as happenstance.

CHAPTER NINE

THE HISTORY OF CANNABIS PROHIBITION

The "Left Coast" has had a long, uneven relationship with bowing to federal powers. California has led the nation in passing many groundbreaking laws, while only half-heartedly enforcing many national edicts. Its size, fame, robust economic power, and progressive ideology have given California a perceived mandate for its, at times, rogue behavior.

Consider that Sacramento is 2,375 miles away from Washington, D.C.—about as far apart as two cities can be while remaining within the continental U.S.—and it's no wonder California acts like a teenager whose parents are away. At the same time, California wields substantial size, both in terms of land mass (third in the nation) and, more importantly, population. With an estimated 39 million residents in 2015, California is by far the most populous state in the union. In fact, the state holds an astonishing 12 percent of the total U.S. population, with larger numbers than those of the 20 smallest states combined. And let's not forget this size translates to control over 55 (10 percent) U.S. Congressional seats, meaning that California wields immense power within the very federal system it frequently chooses to sidestep.

Historically, California's economy has been the epitome of boom and bust. It has weathered a number of financial storms over the centuries and has repeatedly pulled back from the precipice in the nick of time. Currently, the state is riding a tide of economic rebound and expansion, thanks, in part, to absurdly diversified economic drivers including technology, agriculture, aerospace, tourism, and entertainment.

With this type of power behind it, it's no surprise that when California becomes one of the pioneers, with a broad-minded law such as same-sex marriage, the nation eventually follows suit. And that when the federal government imposes a new regulation, California does not always comply with the spirit, or letter, of that law.

In the earliest decades of the 20th century, the United States endured an age known as the Progressive Era. Far from what we might now consider progressive, this period was known for the wave of stringent reforms and social constraints that swept the nation. Between 1920 and 1933, the 18th Amendment to the U.S. Constitution, combined with the Volstead Act, banned the production, sale, and distribution of alcohol in the United States.

But well before the federal prohibition on alcohol, the state of California prohibited cannabis in 1913. In fact, the ban on cannabis in California predated the federal ban—known as the Marihuana Tax Act of 1937—by a full 24 years. California's Poison Act made the possession of "extracts, tinctures, or other narcotic preparations of hemp, or loco-weed, their preparations and compounds" illegal. It was amended two years later and forbade the sale or possession of "flowering tops and leaves, extracts, tinctures and other narcotic preparations of hemp or loco weed (Cannabis sativa), Indian hemp, except with a prescription[76]."

Marijuana was not commonly known or used as an intoxicant by Californians at the turn of the century. Note that within the Poison Act, the plant wasn't even referred to as marijuana, but by its scientific name, *cannabis*. So why was this unknown plant lumped in with "narcotics

76 Gieringer, D. (1999). The Forgotten Origins of Cannabis Prohibition in California. Contemporary Drug Problems, 26(2), 237-288. http://dx.doi.org/10.1177/009145099902600204

and poisons" as part of a relatively obscure pharmacy code? What was happening in California at the time that would cause a ban on a plant no one had really heard of? In a word: Racism.

The terms used to describe cannabis in the 1913 law are telling. "Indian Hemp." "Loco Weed." "Narcotic." These terms allude to East Asians and Hispanics and hint at the close ties between drug bans and the vast prejudice against immigrants at the time.

In fact, Henry J. Finger, a powerful member of California's State Board of Pharmacy and the entity responsible for passing the Poison Act, pointedly tied his disdain for "Hindoos" to drug use in a 1911 letter: "Within the last year we in California have been getting a large influx of Hindoos and they have in turn started quite a demand for Cannabis Indica. They are a very undesirable lot and the habit is growing in California very fast; the fear is now that it is not being confined to the Hindoos alone but that they are initiating our whites into this habit[77]."

The majority of the "Hindoos" Finger refers to were actually Punjabi Sikhs who had arrived in California in relatively small numbers, but faced even harsher discrimination and anti-immigrant derision than Chinese immigrants of the time. Contrary to Finger's accusations, these Sikh emigres largely abstained from drug use, but that didn't stop him from making the claims[78].

The history of Chinese immigration in the U.S. is irrevocably tied to three things: the California Gold Rush, the Transcontinental Railroad, and opium. Between the beginning of the Gold Rush in 1848 and the Chinese Exclusion Act of 1882 (which halted the entry of Chinese laborers into the U.S.), it is estimated that 300,000 Chinese entered the country, with roughly three-quarters of them settling in California.

77 Ídem, page 18
78 Ídem, page 20

This massive influx of Chinese workers alienated Americans and led to rampant racism, discrimination, and persecution. Opium was the intoxicant of choice for some Chinese, and when use of the drug spread, it was perceived as one of the myriad of evils, along with gambling and prostitution[79], the Chinese were accused of inflicting on innocent Americans. So little was known about cannabis, that it was lumped in with narcotics, like opium, by lawmakers looking to spread further discrimination.

After the Mexican Revolution ravaged Mexico between 1910 and 1920, tens of thousands of Mexicans came north into the United States looking for jobs and a new start. By some estimates, the number of Mexicans entering the country more than quadrupled to as much as 100,000 per year in the 1920s. These new Americans competed for land and jobs in California and faced crushing discrimination, just like their Chinese immigrant brethren.

The "loco-weed" attributed to the wildness of Mexicans was not truly the ditch weed or loco-weed of cattle ranches but, rather, cannabis. White lawmakers were not sure what cannabis was, but they knew that "Loco Mexicans" smoked it, and wanted to ban it in order to, once again, leverage marijuana to further racist agendas[80].

How Hemp Made Enemies and Fueled Racism

At the time of cannabis prohibition in California, the state had many significant crops. After the Gold Rush years, grains—wheat and barley in particular—flourished in the state. By 1910, California was a noted producer of grapes, citrus, deciduous fruits, and nuts. Cannabis was not among these bumper crops, but something called "hemp"—the fibrous

79 Ahmad, D. (2007). Opium Debate and Chinese Exclusion Laws in the Nineteenth-century American West. Reno: University of Nevada.

80 Steinhauer, J. (2015). The History of Mexican Immigration to the U.S. in the Early 20th Century | Insights: Scholarly Work at the John W. Kluge Center. Blogs.loc.gov. Retrieved 27 December 2017, from https://blogs.loc.gov/kluge/2015/03/the-history-of-mexican-immigration-to-the-u-s-in-the-early-20th-century/

stem of the cannabis plant—was making news and stirring marijuana detractors[81].

By the time cannabis was banned federally in 1937, many states had imposed their own prohibitions against it, often for racist reasons, as was the case in California. While there are many 'conspiracy theories' about why cannabis was banned federally, most point to some type of collusion between publisher William Randolph Hearst, Secretary of the Treasury Andrew Mellon, DuPont Chemical, and Harry Anslinger, the commissioner of the Federal Bureau of Narcotics.

It's hypothesized that DuPont, Hearst, and Mellon (the richest man in the world at the time and a heavy investor in DuPont) attempted to suppress the growth of natural hemp to promote the profitable development of synthetic fibers, namely DuPont's new nylon polymers.

Others speculate that Hearst battled hemp to prevent its possible use in paper production, given that he was heavily invested in timber for producing newsprint for his own publications. Theorists accused Hearst of using his vast newspaper network to run a smear campaign tying hemp to negative publicity around rampant marijuana use and drug-fueled crime sprees.

In truth, old-fashioned racism played a far larger hand in cannabis prohibition than backroom bargaining by anti-hemp fat cats. But even with a motive of racism, Hearst can't escape the specter of guilt. In his book, "The Emperor Wears No Clothes," the late pro-marijuana advocate Jack Herer claims that Hearst's involvement in anti-marijuana yellow journalism was fueled by the loss of some 800,000 acres of Hearst-owned Mexican timberland to Pancho Villa's army. According to Herer, no race was safe from Hearst's vitriol:

81 Olmstead, A., & Rhode, P. (2004). The Evolution of California Agriculture, 1850-2000 in Jerome B. Siebert (ed.), California Agriculture: Dimensions and Issues, pp.1-28., Oakland: University of California Press.

> Non-stop for the next three decades, Hearst painted a picture of the lazy, pot-smoking Mexican, still one of our most insidious prejudices. Simultaneously, he waged a similar racist smear campaign against the Chinese, referring to them as the 'Yellow Peril.'
>
> From 1910 to 1920, Hearst's newspapers would claim that the majority of incidents in which blacks were said to have raped white women, could be traced directly to cocaine. This continued for 10 years until Hearst decided it was not 'cocaine-crazed negroes' raping white women—it was now "marijuana-crazed negroes" raping white women[82].

It's not surprising then, that we find many parallels between the prohibition of marijuana in 1937 and the prohibition of alcohol in 1920 when it comes to the wielding of undue political influence to racist ends.

Prohibition and the Rise of Wheelerism

The Prohibition movement of the early 20th century was led by white, protestant Americans, ultimately by the Anti-Saloon League (ASL) whose pressure politics overran the more moderate temperance movement of the late 19th century. These cutthroat pressure politics, often called "Wheelerism," were the specialty of ASL head Wayne B. Wheeler.

Unlike the temperance groups that addressed other societal concerns and tended to vote along party lines, the ASL focused doggedly on defeating "wet" politicians in favor of pro-prohibition "dry" politicians and were not above using coercion and intimidation to reach their goals. Powerful

82 Herer, J. (1985). The emperor wears no clothes. Van Nuys: Ah Ha Pub.

Wheeler was central to these tactics. According to Justin Steuart, Wheeler's former Publicity Secretary:

> Wayne B. Wheeler controlled six congresses, dictated to two presidents of the United States, directed legislation in most of the States of the Union, picked the candidates for the more important elective state and federal offices, held the balance of power in both Republican and Democratic parties, distributed more patronage than any dozen other men, supervised a federal bureau from outside without official authority, and was recognized by friend and foe alike as the most masterful and powerful single individual in the United States[83].

So singular was the ASL's focus, that any group aligned with dry causes was considered their ally, regardless of political affiliation or platform. This included suffragettes since the majority of women supported prohibition on moral grounds, as well as racists. Though health and salvation were often the public battle cry of prohibitionists, prejudice was always an underlying motivation.

The roots of the prohibition of cannabis as well as the prohibition of alcohol are directly attributable to a prejudiced majority persecuting minorities. In fact, every region had their favorite minority to persecute, making a national movement possible. In the Northeast, immigrants from Ireland and Italy had deep cultural and religious roots in the consumption of alcohol. Pushing temperance was a way to subjugate the new Catholic Americans and make their arrival and stay less welcome.

83 Okrent, D. (2010). Last call, the rise and fall of prohibition. New York: Scribner.

In the South, landed gentry promoted the notion of prohibition as a way to promote 'Southern Values' of racial segregation, subordinating women, and 'honor.' It was a way to prevent blacks from enjoying the same privileges as white gentlemen, who could drink in their homes and private clubs. In the Southwest, alcohol abuse was painted as a problem for Indians and Mexicans, and temperance as a way to keep those peoples subdued.

In the Midwest, the very heart of the temperance movement and home to the Anti-Saloon League, it was religious fervor and political hunger that motivated activists. On a global scale, World War I and the fight against the Germans turned the nation against the beer drinkers from Europe, not to mention whiskey-drinking Irish and wine-loving Catholics[84].

The 18th Amendment to the United States Constitution was ratified by the required 36 of the then 48 states. California was the 22nd to ratify. Only two states rejected the amendment: Connecticut and Rhode Island. Ultimately, however, the amendment proved unenforceable. The 48 states proved too large, with too much coastline and land mass to patrol for illegal imports and nefarious home brewing. The government lacked an efficient central body to effectively enforce the law, and American thirst for alcohol proved too unquenchable to stop.

While many Americans rather openly disregarded the Prohibition Amendment entirely, it was the stock market crash of 1929 and subsequent Great Depression that ultimately led to the relatively quick end to Prohibition. Federal tax revenues from individuals and corporations plummeted by half between 1930 and 1932, and the government scrambled to find new revenue streams.

84 Coker, Joe L. (2007). Liquor in the Land of the Lost Cause: Southern White Evangelicals and the Prohibition Movement. Lexington: University of Kentucky Press.

While the end of Prohibition didn't entirely make up for this lost tax revenue, it certainly infused the government with much-needed cash—and quickly. Ratified at the end of 1933, the 21st Constitutional Amendment—which repealed the 18th Amendment—drove the total percentage of federal tax revenue generated by alcohol from a paltry 2 percent in 1933, to a sizeable 13 percent just three years later[85].

The Grapes of Wrath

The agricultural wealth of California is renowned. In the 1920s, California was the nation's leading agricultural state, as it continues to be to this day. Grapes were a very important part of the state's economy during this period. In fact, by 1919, California produced 80 percent of the country's grapes. Fifty years later, cannabis would begin its path toward becoming a $14-billion-dollar industry in the state. Prohibition would prove impossible to effectively implement for both alcohol and cannabis when California's economy depended on the production of both[86].

The Napa wine industry was just beginning to take off at the start of Prohibition, and though it nearly wiped out the wine industry, it had a reverse effect on the grape growers in the state. Prohibition prevented the commercial production and distribution of alcohol, but it did allow for the growing of grapes as well as home, medicinal, and sacramental wine production.

Wine sales plummeted, while grape sales skyrocketed. One reason for this was the wide-scale distribution of wine bricks, condensed grapes that could be dissolved in a gallon of water and fermented. Estimates calculate

85 Boudreaux, D. (2008). Alcohol, Prohibition, and the Revenuers. Foundation for Economic Education. Retrieved 27 December 2017, from https://fee.org/articles/alcohol-prohibition-and-the-revenuers/

86 Brady, E. (2013). How Humboldt became America's marijuana capital. Salon. Retrieved 27 December 2017, from http://www.salon.com/2013/06/30/how_humboldt_became_americas_marijuana_capital/

that home winemaking grew nine times over during Prohibition, largely due to the distribution of wine bricks from coast to coast.

Many well-known wineries of today, including Beaulieu Vineyards and Beringer Winery, were allowed to stay open during Prohibition under the guise of producing sacramental wine. Still, other wineries hid illegal wine production behind new fields of prunes, peaches and other fruits planted where acres of grape vineyards had once stood[87].

The success of grape production in California during Prohibition mirrors the prohibition of cannabis in the 1970s, when California marijuana began its rise to popularity, and up to today. In fact, our own federal government can take an immense amount of credit for driving the popularity of California-grown marijuana past the previously more popular Latin American varietals like Acapulco Gold and Panama Red. At the time, the U.S. government sponsored a controversial program to spray Mexico's booming marijuana crops with the herbicide paraquat.

Instead of deterring Americans from smoking marijuana for fear of illness from the toxic paraquat, it simply drove them to homegrown alternative sources. False claims of death and disease caused by smoking paraquat-contaminated Mexican weed spread like wildfire, and by the time the paraquat program was halted in 1979, roughly 35 percent of marijuana smoked in California was grown in the state. By 2010, it's estimated that 79 percent of pot smoked in the entire U.S. was grown in the Golden State[88].

Commercial sale of cannabis was illegal, but agricultural production boomed. People grew it on their secret farms, in closets, hidden forests, and backyard gardens. Medicinal marijuana is a part of the consumption,

87 Stunning Prohibition Facts. Wine Folly. (2014) Retrieved 27 December 2017, from http://winefolly.com/update/prohibition-facts/
88 Ídem 72

but the majority is consumed illicitly, purely for recreational use—just as grapes were during prohibition.

There's no doubt that agriculture is an important part of the California economy, and a reason it continues to act like an unsupervised teenager, eschewing federal governance at will. According to the USDA, California agriculture is a $46.5-billion-dollar industry, and it's estimated to generate at least $100 billion in additional, related economic activity[89]. While almonds ($5.8 billion) edged out grapes ($5.6 billion) as California's largest legal cash crop, many estimates place the state's marijuana production at far more than almonds and grapes combined.

According to a 2006 report[90] published in The Bulletin of Cannabis Reform and prepared by Jon Gettman, Ph.D.; the former head of the National Organization for the Reform of Marijuana Laws (NORML), the country's annual marijuana production was valued at nearly $36 billion, with California responsible for more than one-third of that value, or $14 billion.

A 2012 book, *Marijuana Legalization: What Everyone Needs to Know*[91], written by experts from Pepperdine and UCLA, among others, disputed these figures. The 2012 book estimates the total value of the crop at $2.1 to $4.3 billion, still a significant value, but they also admit that any estimate is unreliable as much of the production and distribution occurs out of sight. With so much of the economy invested in weed and grapes, you can imagine that local California authorities would have a different view of enforcement than federal authorities.

---

89 California Agricultural Statistics 2013 Annual Bulletinite This For Me. (2015). USDA. Retrieved 27 December 2017, from http://www.nass.usda.gov/Statistics_by_State/California/Publications/California_Ag_Statistics/2013/2013cas-all.pdf

90 Gettman, J. (2006). Marijuana production in the United States. The Bulletin of Cannabis Reform. Retrieved 27 December 2017, from https://www.documentcloud.org/documents/408191-mjcropreport-2006.html

91 Caulkins, J., Hawken, A., & Kilmer, B. (2012). Marijuana Legalization: What Everyone Needs to Know. Oxford: Oxford University Press.

Law of Supply and Demand

When a product is prohibited, the demand for it does not cease. The risk of producing and delivering a contraband finished product increases, as do the costs of production. The prohibition of alcohol was not a problem for rich white people who could afford to continue consumption. The laws were meant to control drinking by poor ethnic immigrants and other minorities including poor blacks, both urban and rural. Racists could have a champagne toast to the success of prohibition.

This gave rise to bootleggers and speakeasies providing alcohol. Ships brought liquor barrels down from Canada and unloaded them on the hundreds of miles of beaches along the California coast. Beer and booze ran up from Mexico. While prohibition was a Federal law, the local authorities saw it as an opportunity to control, regulate, and profit from this black-market industry. According to the *LA Times*, the prohibition era head of the LAPD vice detail ("The Purity Squad"), ran gambling joints on the side and then quit to become a bootlegger[92]. Mob boss Charles Crawford, boasted of a private telephone line into LA's City Hall.

Daniel Okrent, the author of *Last Call*, a book on the rise and fall of Prohibition, sums up the situation in the Bay Area concisely: "In San Francisco, Prohibition was only a rumor[93]." In 1920, the Democratic Party held its national convention in San Francisco, and Mayor Sunny Jim Rolph furnished every delegate with a bottle of whiskey delivered to their hotel rooms[94].

In 1922, there were approximately 1,492 speakeasies in San Francisco, which spoke volumes about the 83 percent of San Franciscans who did not

92 Holland, G. (2012). A bit of digging unearths tales of L.A. bootlegging, crooked cops. LA Times. Retrieved 27 December 2017, from http://articles.latimes.com/2012/oct/11/local/la-me-holland-tunnels-20121012

93 Ídem 69

94 Nolte, C. (2011). Prohibition was only a rumor in S.F.. San Francisco Gate. Retrieved 27 December 2017, from http://www.sfgate.com/bayarea/nativeson/article/Prohibition-was-only-a-rumor-in-S-F-2352835.php

vote for Prohibition, reports Ellen Gorchoff-Fey on San Francisco City Guides[95].

While the rich and elites drank imported whiskey in swank underground clubs, the poor went dry, paid too much for inferior liquor, or worse, went blind drinking home-made alcohol contaminated with methyl alcohol.

The prohibition of marijuana made its street price increase, and the reward for growing it very lucrative. But the illicit retail business for cannabis was much sketchier than the speakeasies. The rich could afford quality marijuana from a trusted source. Hollywood and hippies seemed to have an abundance of pot in the '70s. It was almost part of the California culture. But at the street level, tainted or fake marijuana was a risk.

Even today, with marijuana laws loosening, we see people poisoning themselves with chemicals marketed as "air freshener" or "spice," which are toxic cooked up artificial cannabinoids. Prohibition is an artificial skewing of the marketplace that leads to crime, fraud, and racism. Legalization brings equality to the marketplace and allows everyone safe, affordable access.

Conclusion

During Prohibition, planted acres of grapes grew from 1920 to the end of the alcohol ban. Of course, wine sales tanked, except for those who had exclusions and loopholes for medicinal and religious purposes, or took to wine brick production. In a similar fashion, when marijuana was legalized in California for medicinal use via the Compassionate Use Act of 1996 (Proposition 215), planted acreage grew, and the state government's

95 Sfcityguides.org. A Note On Speakeasies. [online] Available at: http://www.sfcityguides.org/public_guidelines.html?article=1331&submitted=TRUE&srch_text=prohibition&submitted2=TRUE&topic [Accessed 6 Feb. 2018].

vague language gave producers wide berth to interpret the "growth" of the medical marijuana sector. Passing with just 55 percent of the vote didn't exactly spell "mandate," either.

The 21st Amendment ended Prohibition in the U.S. in December, 1933. Later in the Century, California citizens and legislators took steps to loosen the federal grip on marijuana prohibition in the 1990s with Prop. 215, thus creating an open clash between the rights of Californians versus the power of the federal government. California's Senate Bill 420 (S.B. 420) in 2003 and the Adult Use Act (Proposition 64) in 2016 further estranged the State and Federal authorities. As Washington, Colorado, and more than 27 other states pass wider reaching marijuana legalization laws, it will be interesting to see how California and other states fare—and how the feds respond.

CHAPTER TEN

CANNABIS LAWS

The Will of the People regarding medical cannabis was elegantly and eloquently expressed in the Compassionate Use Act by way of Prop. 215. It clearly established the right for a patient and their caregiver in California to obtain and use cannabis to treat illness. It is a perfect gem of a law. BUT, it only applied to the rights of an individual patient.

An apple a day may keep the doctor away, but we are not all able to grow our own trees. We have community gardens, apple farmers, and grocery stores for that purpose. It gets a bit more complicated with marijuana.

The larger cannabis community of cultivators, dispensaries, and collectives were still in a nebulous area in California even after Prop. 215. The proposition protected your right to grow and use, and even to obtain, but the grower or supplier who gave the patient the medical cannabis could still be considered outside the law by law enforcement. There were holes in the medical law that needed to be patched; very sick patients cannot be expected to nurture and grow their own medicine, and medicine providers should not have to work in fear of arrest for helping heal the sick.

The Compassionate Use Act went into effect on January 1, 1997. However, it took until 2003 for the State Legislature to write and pass laws to address the larger medical cannabis economy. The time in between was no safer for cannabis providers than the time before 215. The will of the people was certainly not the will of law enforcement and many lawmakers.

The Legislature in Sacramento needed to pass new laws to codify the larger cannabis picture and further protect patients and providers.

State Senator John Vasconcellos was a lifelong politician that looked least likely to be a career politician. He was born and educated in the South Bay, first at Bellarmine Prep, and later at Santa Clara University. He served as an Assemblyman in Silicon Valley before there was even Silicon there. He was a gregarious man of the people who marched with Cesar Chavez from Delano to Sacramento and met with every constituent who asked for a meeting.

Vasconcellos had a political foundation that spanned decades and both sides of the aisle in the Capitol. His seniority and respect were second only to Speaker Willie Brown's. He personally was an advocate of the legalization of marijuana. This made Vasconcellos the perfect person to help craft the future of marijuana in California[96].

California Attorney General Bill Lockyer named Senator Vasconcellos co-chair of the Medical Marijuana Task Force to sort out a system for safe and affordable distribution to qualified patients. His co-chair was Republican District Attorney from Santa Clara County, George Kennedy. The creation of the Task Force was a result of "Item C" in the text of Prop. 215 which encouraged the "federal and state governments to implement a plan to provide for the safe and affordable distribution of marijuana to all patients in medical need of marijuana."

Vasconcellos and the Task Force brought together the various stakeholders, from narcotics officers to patients. His work integrating viewpoints and stakeholders was essential to the bill passing. Eventually, the Task Force had converted foes of Prop. 215 like the California District

---

96 Plotkin, H. (1992). Politics on the cutting edge. The New Politics, San Jose Metro. Retrieved 27 December 2017, from http://plotkin.com/AdobeAcrobat/10.29.92page19.pdf

Attorneys' Association, the California Sheriffs Association, the California Medical Association, and the California Nurses Association, into supporters of the legislation that would become known as Senate Bill 420.

> "Because there was such a clear public statement in the voters' passage of Prop. 215, and yet such utterly contrary viewpoints regarding how it ought best be implemented, we were faithful to our commitment to assure that each of the words used in the statute was carefully fashioned, extensively vetted, and the result of intensive and laborious compromise and consensus[97]."

The consensus building continued up until the last minutes before the vote. The almost-final draft that Vasconcellos was prepared to send to the Senate for vote put the responsibility of setting cultivation guidelines on the State Dept. of Health Services, after public hearings on the matter. Governor Gray Davis opposed this language on grounds that it would put a burden on the Health Services Department[98]. Sen. Vasconcellos negotiated a last-minute compromise with Attorney General Bill Lockyer, setting guidelines of a 1/2 pound of marijuana and up to 6 mature or 12 immature plants.

These guidelines are not legal limits, but rather advice to law enforcement on what may or may not constitute "too much" for the typical cannabis patient's needs. Prop. 215 carefully omitted any stated limits, leaving the number to whatever was "medically necessary." Police, in general, may not have understood the notion of a "right" to medical

97 Vasconcellos, J. (2012). An open letter from retired CA senator John Vasconcellos. Bay Area News Group blog. Retrieved 27 December 2017, from http://www.ibabuzz.com/politics/files/2012/02/Vasconcellos-SB-420-ltr.pdf

98 Gov. Davis Signs Medical Marijuana Task Force Bill - SB 420. (2003). CA NORML Legislative News. Retrieved 27 December 2017, from http://www.canorml.org/leg/xleg/vascoSB 420.html

cannabis in 2003, but they would certainly latch on to the magic numbers of "1/2 pound of marijuana and up to 6 mature or 12 immature plants" when looking to make a bust.

The Medical Marijuana Program Act, otherwise known as "SB 420," passed in October 2003 with the Assembly 42-32 in favor and the State Senate supporting 24-14. It put into effect a number of provisions that extended protections and programs for the nascent legal medical cannabis industry in California.

The new law was a formal recognition by legislators of the patient rights declared in Prop. 215. This was a win in and of itself, to have politicians vote to recognize and support legal medical use of cannabis. Further, it is the State of California asserting its supremacy on the issue. Section 420(1)(e) reads:

> The Legislature further finds and declares that it enacts this act pursuant to the powers reserved to the State of California and its people under the Tenth Amendment to the United States Constitution.

Sacramento had thrown its weight behind the will of the people, declaring that the mighty state of California would stand up for patient rights against the command of the Federal Government.

Provisions signed into law in the CA Health and Safety Code starting at Section 11362.7:

- Set definitions and rules for caregivers
- Set rules for Voluntary ID card system
- Addressed medical cannabis access for probationers, parolees, and prisoners

- Limited cannabis smoking in certain areas, along the lines of no-smoking provisions
- Set possession and cultivation guidelines
- Respected local community guidelines when higher than the State's
- Covered patients for "transportation" of medical cannabis
- Established patient collectives and co-ops

Some of these provisions were needed clarifications to protect patient rights, others did not clarify things at all, and some were used by law enforcement as a green light to go after marijuana cases with the backing of the Legislature.

Caregivers

The new law set out many definitions and rules for caregivers, ostensibly to help protect them from undue arrest, and to allow them to be secure in their role of providing cannabis as medicine to patients.

It specifically lists healthcare, residential care, clinic, home health, and hospice workers as covered by the definition of caregiver. It retains the 215 definition of anyone designated to provide care, but the further definitions are helpful. Caregivers need the backing of the law to give the medical care needed by their patients. Many state workers, social workers, and nurses might have had apprehensions about administering cannabis. This law protects them, and anyone assisting them in the administration of the medicine.

The law wisely made it clear that a caregiver could have any number of patients under their care, but only if they were all in the same county. If a caregiver had a patient in their care in one county, the law specified that the caregiver could not provide care to any patient in any other county.

This may have been a nod to simplifying the ID system bureaucracy administered by the Counties. In practice, this can prevent a caregiver from having patients in both the adjacent cities of West Sacramento (Yolo County) and Sacramento (Sacramento County).

Voluntary ID Card

To help law enforcement identify patients versus abusers when looking to hassle cannabis users, the State set up a program for a voluntary ID card system. This was a State ID card program that was administered by local county health departments. Remember that the Compassionate Use Act did not require any written proof or documentation of medical need. It allowed a verbal recommendation from the patient's physician. This should work for a jurisdiction that respects a patient's access to medicine, but, across the state, law enforcement would bust cannabis users and let the courts sort out medicine from recreation.

The logic behind an ID card system is that when approached by law enforcement for growing, obtaining, or using cannabis, the patient could show a card with a unique ID number that the officer could verify via a phone call or online lookup. This should have settled the matter of an individual growing, possessing, or using cannabis as medicine. Maybe this system helped some people, but in virtually every one of the cases that I have encountered where my clients possessed a state ID card, the cards were either ignored or mocked by law enforcement.

It is still easy for an officer to claim the cannabis was not within the medical guidelines in the officer's "training and experience" or that the cultivation was, in the officer's opinion, not exclusively for medical use. Patients and caregivers with cards and medical recommendations still get arrested by crooked cops and prosecuted by shady prosecutors.

The upside is that Prop. 215 and SB 420 laid out a framework for an affirmative defense. If the cop or DA don't respect the law, at least a jury or a higher court on appeal might.

Many counties resisted the notion of legal medical marijuana for years. San Diego and San Bernardino Counties claimed that since cannabis was illegal on the federal level, they could not be compelled to recognize the provisions of SB 420. They took their case all the way to the United States Supreme Court. On May 18, 2009, their appeal was denied. They now offer ID cards.

Three counties refused to implement ID cards altogether. Sutter, Mariposa, and Colusa Counties are still not participating as of 2017, well over a decade from the law passing. An excuse used is that since instituting the program will cost the county money, they cannot be compelled to spend funds to support it. Other counties nominally comply with state law for issuing ID cards and compliance, while still arresting and prosecuting patients who have them.

In fact, the California Attorney General published additional guidance to law enforcement on how to work within—and around—medical cannabis laws. "If the officer has probable cause to doubt the validity of a person's medical marijuana claim based upon the facts and circumstances, the person may be arrested and the marijuana may be seized. It will then be up to the person to establish his or her medical marijuana defense in court[99]."

To provide a double layer of privacy, police cannot identify whether persons are medical marijuana patients by their name or address, but only by a unique identification number. Santa Cruz County and San Francisco

99 Guidelines for the Security and Non-diversion of Marijuana Grown for Medical Use. (2008). Department of Justice. Retrieved 27 December 2017, from http://ag.ca.gov/cms_attachments/press/pdfs/n1601_medicalmarijuanaguidelines.pdf

County take privacy a layer deeper. They do not share patient information with the state and submit anonymously to the state database.

The ID card program code is the wordiest of the provisions. To be fair, it is creating a new bureaucracy designed by committee to appease a hundred different points of view. The bulk of the remainder involves identifying processes and crimes related to the ID card program, such as fees, policies, County responsibilities, penalties for fraud, faking an illness, and misuse of program data.

A standout provision that shows forethought and concern is the item related to cannabis for those often forgotten by society; prisoners, parolees, and probationers are specifically directed to apply for and obtain cannabis ID cards. It does not let them smoke in jail, but it will protect them from a shakedown by the Parole Office or the local fuzz looking to jam up the town's usual suspect.

Smoking Rules

California has been a non-smoking state since our ban on indoor smoking went into full effect in 1998. SB 420 made it clear that smoking cannabis is still smoking and went on to list other places and activities that were not okay for toking. It proscribed the smoking of medical marijuana within 1,000 feet of a school, youth center, or recreation center unless done within a residence. It goes out of its way to specifically ban cannabis smoking on a school bus—you know, just in case that needed to be clarified.

The law further explains that employers and facilities do not need to accommodate the use of medical marijuana on their premises.

Moreover, cannabis smoking while driving a car or boat is prohibited. Note that this part of the law only addresses the smoking of cannabis, not the intoxication or other uses of the medicine. Per SB 420, eating pot brownies while driving was not prohibited. The topic of impairment from medical marijuana and the relation to driving was to be later addressed by another voter initiative, Prop. 64, discussed below.

Guidelines

Medical necessity is best determined by a doctor upon diagnosis with a patient. Cops and DA's should not pick and choose how much medicine is too much. Prop. 215 wisely left the amount to cultivation and possession of cannabis up to the medical needs of the patient.

A patient might need to grow 40 plants to make sure she has enough bud to last her the rest of the year. To the uniformed, perhaps 40 plants would seem like too large a crop for one person. But if she could only grow during the season, and was not able to nurture her crop optimally, and some of the crop would mold or be unusable, and she used cannabis in the form of edibles as the best way to combat the effects of cancer and thus needed more cannabis than someone who smokes it, perhaps 40 plants is the right number.

If a patient lives in a town where there are no dispensaries, perhaps he would stock up on enough medicine to last a few months between visits to the city where dispensing was allowed. If he had two pounds of medicine in his home, or in his car returning from a dispensary visit, it would be the right amount of medicine for his needs over a period of time.

Or maybe a patient juices cannabis and makes a smoothie each morning to address the symptoms of her illness. Juicing requires lots of cannabis bud and/or leaves. For this patient, having hundreds of live indoor plants is in line with her medical condition and needs.

Cops don't always see things that way. Where they see more than a few plants, or more than a few ounces, they see a crime. They also see an easy mark for seizure, taking any money and property that they find along with a grow or cannabis product. After all, the thrill of pointing an assault weapon in an elderly woman's face during the arrest may only be surpassed by the reward for pulling in assets which are added to law enforcement's own budget.

The law sets guidelines for cops to follow when determining if an amount of medicine is within the amounts determined by the Senate in 2003. It gave the Attorney General the right to suggest a different set of guidelines based on medical and scientific review. But as you can guess, the AG never bothered to change the guidelines.

The guidelines laid down in Health and Safety 11362.77. (a) state a qualified patient or primary caregiver may possess no more than **eight ounces of dried marijuana** per qualified patient. In addition, a qualified patient or primary caregiver may also maintain no more than **six mature** or **12 immature marijuana plants** per qualified patient. It is easy to see how a legitimately ill person could easily need much more than these guidelines and be vulnerable to arrest as a pot dealer.

Thus, there was a contradiction between Prop. 215 and SB 420. Prop. 215 allows for your doctor to recommend what you need and was passed by the voters. On the other hand, SB 420 put the eight ounces and 6/12 plant limits on medical users and was passed by the state legislature. Who won in the inevitable legal battle on this issue? In 2008, in *People v. Kelly*, the California Supreme Court struck down the SB 420 limits as an unconstitutional amendment to the voter initiative, Prop 215. It is amazing that to this day, I still have cops and prosecutors cite to the unconstitutional SB 420 guidelines as justification for an arrest and prosecution. In fact, most lawyers that practice in this area out of necessity will seek a court ruling before a trial to prevent law enforcement from attempting to testify in front of a jury that the "law" only allows for 8 oz., or 6 mature or 12 immature plants, per patient.

At the time of the passing of SB 420, some municipalities had their own standards for patient cultivation and possession. Sonoma County, for example, set their guidelines for possession of up to 3 pounds of dried cannabis per year, and cultivation of up to 30 plants within 100 square feet of garden. These local rules are allowed to persist, and cities and counties are allowed to set higher numbers than the state law. However, in court, in a jury trial, anything other than, "Was the amount that the patient possessed reasonably related to his or her medical needs?" is completely irrelevant and, in fact, unlawful. Educating judges and prosecutors on medical cannabis law has been frustrating, to say the least.

Indeed, rather than set higher numbers, in the absence of the right to lower or eliminate them, we have seen local municipalities use whatever means they can to restrict patient rights. Cities and counties now effectively ban cannabis by using local "zoning" ordinances to severely restrict or ban altogether cultivation and dispensing within their lines.

Zoning ordinances are effective at "mitigating a public nuisance in the name of public health and safety." A zoning violator, aka a patient growing their own medicine, will get an abatement ticket and often have only a few days to abate the problem. A city zoning bureaucrat becomes the cop, judge, and executioner of your medical garden. Zoning laws have become the go-to means for municipalities to effectively ban medical cannabis thanks to the California Supreme Court's ruling in 2013 in *City of Riverside v. Inland Empire Patients Health and Wellness Center*[100] which held that

100 California Supreme Court. (2013). *City of Riverside v. Inland Empire Patients Health & Wellness Center, Inc.*. Harvard Law Review. Retrieved 27 December 2017, from https://harvardlawreview.org/2014/02/california-supreme-court-upholds-local-zoning-ban-on-medical-marijuana-dispensaries-ae-city-of-riverside-v-inland-empire-patients-health-wellness-center-inc-300-p-3d-494-cal-2013/

cities and counties can outright ban both brick and mortar as well as mobile dispensaries under their zoning authority.

Fighting zoning action on constitutional or procedural grounds are two of the few immediate defenses available for this backdoor attack on otherwise legally allowed behavior. The best way to beat zoning laws is to vote out the politicians who passed them and vote in politicians who support safe access to legal medicine. Do you want home invasions or do you want a regulated dispensary with an open door to law enforcement and its own security where grandma can go every few weeks and safely buy her brownies which have been quality checked?

Recognizing Co-ops and Collectives

One of the biggest accomplishments of SB 420 is the legal recognition of collectives and cooperatives. Though 215 gave you the right to grow and use medicine, it did not address how you could obtain it if you did not have a green thumb or if you didn't have a backyard but your friend did.

Bruce Margolin is a veteran attorney in the defense of Californians' right to safe access. He served as director of Los Angeles NORML and helped write Prop. 215. Bruce is a champion of the cause and one of my heroes as a criminal defense attorney. He has been in this fight since the beginning and saw firsthand the years between 215 and SB 420:

> The day after California voters approved Proposition 215 in November 1996, the phones at NORML chapters around the state rang nonstop. Californians with health conditions wanted to know where they could find safe, legal medical marijuana. Back then, they were told that, according to the law, they could grow themselves or appoint a caregiver to grow it for them. They couldn't legally buy

or transport their medicine. In a non-agrarian, far-flung city like Los Angeles, this was not a workable solution for most people[101].

The ambiguities and mandate of Prop. 215 led to the legislature passing and the governor signing SB 420. Though there was not much detail about the association of patients and caregivers to collectively cultivate, the few words that were there opened up today's legal cannabis economy. The actual wording is:

> 11362.775. Qualified patients, persons with valid identification cards, and the designated primary caregivers of qualified patients and persons with identification cards, who associate within the State of California in order collectively or cooperatively to cultivate marijuana for medical purposes, shall not solely on the basis of that fact be subject to state criminal sanctions.

On these words alone a billion-dollar industry legally flourishes in California. Did I say business? The sale of cannabis is not addressed in SB 420. This created a Twilight Zone where patients have legal rights to medicine, caregivers can give it to them, and caregivers can be paid for their work, ***yet*** the direct sale of medicine is not covered.

Almost as an afterthought, the following line is tagged onto the end of 11362.765(a) "nor shall anything in this section authorize any individual or group to cultivate or distribute marijuana for profit."

This has led to a type of Cargo Cult around the formation of 501(c)(3) or, more appropriately, 501(c)(4) non-profit organizations for the

101 Medical Marijuana Ordinance Must Protect Patients Rights, Privacy. (2010). Culture Magazine. Retrieved 27 December 2017, from http://ireadculture.com/medical-marijuana-ordinance-must-protect-patients-rights-privacy/

cooperative cultivation and dispensing of cannabis. This has become an *ad hoc* compliance framework and industry standard to stave off arrest and prosecution for selling medical cannabis. When you pay for your medicine at a dispensary, you are also paying for the work that went into growing the plant, the rent of the facility, power, lights, accounting, security, management, and staff payroll.

The misunderstanding which still persists today about dispensaries making money from selling cannabis was addressed by then retired Senator Vasconcellos in a public letter dated February 2012:

> It was certainly true that one side wanted to outlaw any profit-making, while the other side did not and would not. So right there and then—in order not to lose our coherence as a working team hoping for a broadly supported result and to hold our coalition together—we took the openly deliberated, fully appreciated compromise way out: We catered to neither side on this issue. Instead, the Task Force crafted the language that appears in Health and Safety Code section 1 1362.765(a) as follows: "nor shall anything in this section authorize any individual or group to cultivate or distribute marijuana for profit[102]."

The Senator continues:

> The language we fashioned means nothing more—nor less—than what it explicitly says. Nothing in that section prohibits profit. Nothing in that section explicitly authorizes profit, either. But I

102 Ídem 82

> must point out that nobody is required to obtain an "authorization" from the Legislature to make a profit in California.

In practice, the formal organization of a non-profit cooperative is a small price to pay for the legal protections it imbues. While the law doesn't require a formal non-profit corporation, it is one of the customs in California to insulate groups of people from prosecution over whether or not they made a "profit" from medical cannabis.

SB 420 sought to fill in the gaps left by 215. The Vasconcellos letter sought to fill in the gaps left by SB 420 but I never see it brought up or argued in court. SB 420 addressed the needs of individual patients in 11362.***765*** and the needs of collectives and cooperatives in 11362.***775***. In *.765*, the legislature explicitly says that you can't make a profit. They didn't want Johnny to have a legal job as a drug dealer selling weed. In *.775*, the legislature was explicitly silent.

Now, there are certain legal maxims regarding statutory interpretation; how to practically apply the law as put forth by a legislature. One of the basics is that if something is not prohibited, it is legal. Another is that the legislature is presumed to mean exactly what it said. If this was any other area of law, a bookstore or coffee shop, the law would have been settled in 2003 that dispensaries can indeed make a profit and that dispensaries and dispensary owners should not be raided and arrested over how much money they have in their coffers.

Since the legislature explicitly said in .765 that an individual can't make a profit and explicitly left that part out of .775, you cannot presume that the legislature meant to say it or mysteriously forgot that part in .775. The law is that you have to presume that the legislature specifically did not tie the hands of dispensaries from making a profit. Since it is not prohibited, it is allowed.

Any law student who has made it through Constitutional Law 1 knows this. However, appellate courts and the trial courts that I have been in have failed to recognize this basic issue. It is such a shame that we have wasted so many public resources prosecuting dispensaries and dispensary owners where everything else was legal other than cash sitting in their safe.

Though often used interchangeably, the terms "cooperative" and "collective" have distinct meanings in California. A cooperative is a formal entity legally incorporated and operated under State laws, usually as a non-profit corporation for the reason discussed above. A collective is not defined by statutory law, but is well understood to be a group of people that work collaboratively as patients and caregivers to produce and share medicine for one another. It is a closed system with no medicine coming in, nor leaving, the group. Bear in mind though, that a collective can also have a very fluid membership.

Common sense says that to obtain something, you can transport it or that once something is obtained, and you have the right to possess it, you can legally transport it. This was not the case pre-SB 420. Transportation of cannabis is defined as a separate crime from possessing, using, or selling. The Government likes to get as many bites at an apple as it can.

While it had been addressed in case law prior[103], SB 420 formally allowed patients and caregivers to transport their medicine. A cooperative garden would not be much use if members could not transport it to their home for use. Even though case law and now SB 420 explicitly protect the transportation of medical cannabis, they are still not an impediment against an imperious cop hassling and arresting you because he thinks in his "training and experience" that you have 'too much weed' on you. Nor

103 *People v. Trippet* (1997) 56 Cal. App. 4th 1532.

will the plain language of the law help you in court with 90 percent of prosecutors and prosecutorial-minded judges. It will be a key part of your defense in front of a jury, however. In my experience, juries actually care about following the law in cannabis cases.

The Law Of The Land

Our cannabis laws have served most Californians well over the years. Prop. 215 is an incredible foundation establishing patient rights. It has withstood federal interference, legislative tampering, and will eventually wear down the foes who continue to prosecute ignoring its very essence. Prop. 215 let the genie out of the bottle.

The additional legal protections and definitions afforded in SB 420 have extended the sphere of medical marijuana to cover wider access and cultivation. It too has survived legal challenges.

City of Garden Grove v. Superior Court settled the issue of State law enforcement versus Federal by local cops. In 2008, the U.S. Supreme Court refused to hear this case, leaving stand a lower court ruling that local police officers must enforce local laws. Cops can't bust a Californian for medical cannabis by saying, 'But it's against the law federally!'

People v. Kelly was decided by the California Supreme Court in January 2010. The ruling found that the Legislature had encroached on Prop. 215 by setting stricter standards than originally set in that initiative. This is legislative tampering, and their subsequent restrictions were invalidated.

People v. Urziceanu was decided by the Third District Court of Appeals in 2005. There, the court issued a positive decision affirming the legality of collectives and cooperatives.

Up until recent years, before the Cole Memo and federal omnibus financial restrictions (both discussed below), there were any number of federal agencies offering cash and lending resources to local cops to go after cannabis patients and caregivers.

On the federal level, in 2011, U.S. Deputy Attorney General James M. Cole released guidelines for law enforcement, which became known as the "Cole Memo."

The Cole Memo became the official position of the Federal Government under Obama. The Cole Memo represented a significant shift in the federal government's position as it de-prioritized the use of federal funds to prosecute individuals who were legally acting within their state's cannabis laws. Instead, it directed federal prosecutors to focus their attention on the following eight areas:

- Preventing the distribution of marijuana to minors;
- Preventing revenue from the sale of marijuana from going to criminal enterprises, gangs and cartels;
- Preventing the diversion of marijuana from states where it is legal under state law in some form to other states;
- Preventing state-authorized marijuana activity from being used as a cover or pretext for the trafficking of other illegal drugs or other illegal activity;
- Preventing violence and the use of firearms in the cultivation and distribution of marijuana;
- Preventing drugged driving and the exacerbation of other adverse public health consequences associated with marijuana use;
- Preventing the growing of marijuana on public lands and the attendant public safety and environmental dangers posed by marijuana production on public lands; and

- Preventing marijuana possession or use on federal property[104]."

As public opinion and favor of safe access to cannabis sweeps the nation, the Feds are finding themselves with fewer allies in Washington D.C. to fund their attacks on legal use, and local governments are realizing profits from legal cannabis that they want to protect. Even Washington, D.C. has followed in California's footsteps so boldly taken in 1996 and has recognized medical as well as adult use of cannabis. Further, The Rohrabacher-Blumenauer Amendment attached in recent years, including 2018, to Congress' Omnibus spending bill prohibits the Department of Justice from using federal funds to prevent states with medical cannabis regulations from implementing laws that authorize the use, distribution, possession or cultivation of medical cannabis. The amendment applies to medical cannabis only and not recreational cannabis. It also did not change the designation of cannabis from Schedule I[105].

Adult Use And Regulation In California

California didn't continue leading the country in progressive cannabis legislation after 1996. Washington, Colorado, Oregon, Alaska and the District of Columbia, beat California by legalizing adult use first. However, the last two years have seen a flurry of activity in this area. The California legislature put in place a new conundrum of regulations on September 11, 2015 giving long overdue recognition to the medical cannabis industry.

When it was first passed, it was called "MMRSA" for Medical Marijuana Regulation and Safety Act. However, it shared the same unfortunate

104 Cole, J. (2011). Cole Memo 1.0. Department of Justice. Retrieved 27 December 2017, from https://www.justice.gov/sites/default/files/oip/legacy/2014/07/23/dag-guidance-2011-for-medical-marijuana-use.pdf

105 Add footnote at end: Roth, F., & Rosenblum, M. (2018). Rohrabacher–Blumenauer Amendment included in omnibus FY 2018 spending bill. Thompsoncoburn.com. Retrieved 2 May 2018, from https://www.thompsoncoburn.com/insights/blogs/tracking-cannabis/post/2018-03-28/rohrabacher-blumenauer-amendment-included-in-omnibus-fy-2018-spending-bill

pronunciation with MRSA, a contagious disease and was later changed to MCRSA, pronounced "Mah-Ker-Sa." The act was composed of three different Assembly Bills: AB 266, AB 243, and AB 643. Also, in November 2016, California voters enacted another voter initiative, Proposition 64, which finally provided for the legalization of adult use.

Thus, going into 2017, California had a medical framework in MCRSA, adult use in Prop. 64, and began a whole new chapter of the state's cannabis law. Because MCRSA had directed various government agencies to craft regulations for the medical industry, the agencies were forced to acknowledge for the first time that they knew little to nothing about the industry. Various meetings were held up and down the state between the regulators (Bureau of Medical Cannabis Regulation, the Department of Food and Agriculture, the Department of Public Health) and members of the public.

Naturally, the industry, which had been around for nearly 20 years, had a lot of feedback for the state regulators. The distribution model mandated by MCRSA, was in part modeled on the alcohol industry. In fact, the head of the newly-minted Cannabis Bureau, Lori Ajax, had previously headed California's Department of Alcohol Beverage Control.

There were many aspects of MCRSA which significantly changed the way things had previously been done. For one, MCRSA by following the alcohol distribution model which inserts a middleman, a "distributor" between the growers and sellers, replaced the previous 'seed-to-sale' system where farmers could grow and sell directly to dispensaries and/or patients. It also removed medical collective protections, where groups of growers could be immune from prosecution if they grew medicine together and didn't make a profit.

As the new law stands now, small groups of family and/or friends growing, trimming, and processing as a collective and distributing the medicine amongst the group will no longer be allowed. To its credit, however, the regulatory agencies, by and large, took the public input that it received to heart and released their first draft of regulation for industry review in April 2017.

Just as the cannabis industry reacted to this first draft, Governor Jerry Brown repealed and replaced the whole MCRSA system with a new system, called the Medical and Adult Use Cannabis Regulation and Safety Act, pronounced "Mow-Ker-Sa." The process occurred more efficiently than seen anywhere else in today's politics. This new MAUCRSA, more clearly and closely integrated the regulation and licensing of adult use and medical.

Both adult use and medical will now be assigned the same license types with only an A or M to distinguish between them. MAUCRSA also allowed industry members the ability to go back to the closed loop, seed-to-sale model. What such a quick repeal and replace will do to the still-forming regulations is yet to be seen.

Prop. 64, which was conservatively packaged as the Control, Regulate and Tax Adult Use of Marijuana Act, legalized certain cannabis related behavior and promised a parallel adult use market to go along with the medical industry. In addition to the cultivation, manufacturing, testing, transportation, distribution, and dispensing license types created by MCRSA, Prop. 64 created opportunities for big agriculture.

Big Agriculture will be allowed into the adult use market five years after the passage of Prop. 64. The proposition also implemented taxes on the cultivation of both medical and adult use cannabis. Beyond the nitty gritty of the still-forming commercial industry, Prop. 64 finally carved out protections for the adult use of cannabis. Suddenly, all individuals 21 years and older were allowed to use cannabis, to possess an ounce of flower and eight grams of concentrate, and cultivate six plants. In fact, Prop. 64 said that no local jurisdiction could completely prohibit the growth of six plants indoors, something that medical never accomplished.

The act even went a step further in providing relief for individuals caught up in the Drug War by allowing their old convictions to be reviewed under the new law. It even went so far as to require the district attorney to prove, perhaps for the first time, that the behavior would be unlawful under the new laws. Finally, it reduced most marijuana offenses from felonies to misdemeanors.

Last Words

Though there are laws to protect you from arrest for medical marijuana, and guidelines published to help law enforcement understand why they must leave you alone, you can still get arrested and face prosecution. The Will of the People spoke in 1996 for Prop. 215, and again through our legislature in 2003 with SB 420 and finally in 2016 with AUMA and what would become MAUCRSA.

These laws come together in the defense of your rights, in defense of the notion that just as an adult can responsibly choose to consume wine processed from grapes, an adult can also responsibly choose to use products processed from cannabis. It will be important to keep in mind that medical use should be kept separate and distinct from adult use as the industry matures from a historically recent debut out of the shadows of prohibition.

CHAPTER ELEVEN

THE WEAPONIZATION OF BAIL

Throughout medieval and modern times bail has been used as a method of ensuring someone accused of a crime shows up for trial. Bail is a deposit, guarantee, or some other pledge backed by money or real property that the accused will appear at court. It was originally a right, a benefit, to keep evil despots from detaining someone indefinitely. The American tradition of bail, as with many of our laws, stems from English Common Law. Ensuring that someone appears for trial is good, but the process has always been ripe for official abuses. Think of the Sheriff of Nottingham, of Robin Hood fame.

Today, bail has been weaponized to punish the accused disproportionately based on their wealth. It is used clumsily by politically aspiring judges to make a statement against crime. Bail is wielded like a bludgeon by police to coerce arrestees into false witness and confessions.

The history of England is punctuated with major events precipitated by the misuse of bail by Kings and Sheriffs. In 1275, the Statute of Westminster limited the power of Sheriffs to hold detainees for bail. Sheriffs could still set bail arbitrarily, but the Statutes listed which offenses were bail-able and which were not. Part of it read "common right is to be done to all, as well poor as rich, without respect of persons;" and "excessive amercements, abuses of wardship, irregular demands for feudal aids, are forbidden[106]."

106 Statute of Westminster, The First (1275). Legislation.gov.uk. Retrieved 27 December 2017, from http://www.legislation.gov.uk/aep/Edw1/3/5/contents

The folk legends of Robin Hood memorialize this period of the people resisting the capricious whims of overreaching law enforcement.

In the 1600s bail changed the direction of England and the world again. King Charles the First ordered nobles to pay him loans, and jailed anyone who refused. Those jailed were refused bail until they paid the loans to the King. Five nobles invoked Habeas Corpus, the Magna Carta, and the English Bill of Rights to demand proof of a crime, and proof that the crime was not a bailable offense. "Excessive bail hath been required of persons committed in criminal cases, to elude the benefit of the laws made for the liberty of the subjects. Excessive bail ought not to be required." Then bail was a weapon against the rich. This was a precursor of the Eighth Amendment of our Constitution.

Grievances against bail malfeasance predated the use of the word "bail" for releasing someone from custody with a posted surety. The etymology of the word goes back to Latin and the word *bajulare* for "to carry a burden." In the case of Ancient Rome, the root of the word "bail" was a water carrier or porter, that was known as a *bajulus*. The word *bail* for scooping water out of a boat comes from this similar root via the Anglo-French word for bucket, around the 14th century. But the legal term we have today came into effect in the 15th century, also from the Anglo-French, from the verb *baillier* meaning hand over, entrust[107]. So when you bail water out of a boat, or bail a friend out of jail, you are doing the Roman equivalent of holding water for them. Both are important duties.

There are two key points for bail that occur early in the criminal process in California. The first is after arrest, where law enforcement charge you a pre-determined bail amount to ensure you return to face the first court

107 Definition of BAIL. Merriam-webster.com. Retrieved 27 December 2017, from https://www.merriam-webster.com/dictionary/bail

hearing after leaving custody. The list, known as a "bail schedule," is fixed for every crime. The bail schedule is not uniform throughout the state and is set independently in each county. The second key point for bail is at arraignment, which generally occurs at the first court appearance where the accused enters a plea, usually "not guilty." At the arraignment, the defense attorney can make a pitch to the judge for a release with no bail, known as an "O.R." and/or can argue for a lower bail. In our system, however, the innocent are punished from time of arrest, well before court or verdict.

Today, cash bail is still being used as a weapon against the poor, as a tool to punish the accused who are innocent until proven otherwise. Modern Sheriffs and self-coronated King District Attorneys abuse bail in far worse ways than the villains of old. California's cash bail system has been weaponized for use by the State against the innocent, poor, and frightened. It can coerce a confession, destroy an innocent family, or allow the law to exert undue and unconstitutional pressures on the accused.

It is interesting to note that over the past 25 years, the median bond rose from $10,000 to $25,400, according to the Bureau of Justice Statistics. Cash bail is good for cops, "tough on crime" lawmakers, and for the bail industry. It hurts everyone else.

Let's take a look at the process leading from arrest to bail to see how and where the system breaks down and hurts the most vulnerable.

When you are arrested, the police and the court want to make sure you show up to face justice at trial. Bail is the device intended to make sure someone shows up for their case. After arrest, you are booked by the police or sheriff into jail and can be held for up to 72 hours (weekends don't count, though) before they either have to bring you to court or cut you lose. At this phase, law enforcement have a Bail Schedule of listed bail amounts predetermined for the crimes for which you were arrested. The list has all crimes and all bail amounts listed, set, and approved by a panel usually composed of judges, prosecutors, bail professionals, law enforcement officials, and defense attorneys, who like to be on committees with those types of people.

The charges at arrest can be very different from the crimes the DA will charge you with, if the DA decides to proceed with prosecution at all. Many arrestees are released from jail with no charges filed, or only face lesser charges than the booking charges. The list of statutory bail amounts is one size fits all, so poor or rich, rotten or nice, upstanding figure or scoundrel, everyone faces the same bail amount during initial detention.

The District Attorney has only a few days to decide if it will formally charge you with a crime, and if so, with what crimes, before you are released from jail. The Code states 48 hours, but in practice it has been inflated to 72 hours. That is the nature of government. Sometimes the arrested are simply let go after their jail time of 72 hours has been reached, with the DA not bothering to charge them. That 72 hours can be longer if you are held over a weekend, then the clock stops running. When the DA formally charges you, you declare innocence or guilt, and bail is argued and set, this is done at an arraignment.

If you cannot afford to pay bail, you must wait in jail until your trial. Innocent until proven guilty, but jailed because you are poor. In California, 60-80 percent of those detained in jail are being held pre-trial. Of the non-convicted pre-trial defendants behind bars, 75 percent are held on non-violent charges, usually petty property or drug crimes, according to the American Bar Association's Pretrial Release Task Force.

The time between arrest and arraignment is where most bail abuses occur. It is wise to make your first call after arrest to your attorney, and to let your attorney handle the next steps after you are booked. Using a first call to ask to be bailed out leaves the accused open to exploitation by law enforcement and the bail industry.

When you post bail after arrest, you put up either the cash amount of the bail, property worth the cash amount, or pay a bail bond. A bail bond is an insurance policy ensuring you will show up. In the cash bail system here in California, Bail Bonds companies make a lot of money on the efforts of the State jailing innocent people.

The Bail Bonds company pays the entire bail for you, and you only pay them a percentage of the bail amount, usually about 10 percent. They, as an insurer, are wagering that you will return to court and that they will get their entire bail back. At the same time, they keep your bail bond amount regardless of the outcome of your case. If you are let go free the next day, if you are found innocent, or if you confess your guilt, they keep the cash deposit you or your family makes. You never get it back.

If you do not use a Bail Bond, and have the cash on hand to pay the full bail amount, that money is returned when charges are dropped, or at the completion of your trial (regardless of verdict). The only risk is that your money is tied up for the duration.

If you cannot afford the bail, either the full cash bail amount, or the 10 percent usually required for a Bail Bond, you sit in jail, innocent until proven guilty.

This is where the system breaks in terms of treating rich and poor equally. A person with cash can leave jail that day, whilst a person with no access to cash must wait until hearing or trial. The poor rot in jail pre-trial rather than going to school, work, or serving their family.

Here is a scenario illustrating the inequity of the bail system. Mr. Green and Mr. Rose are neighbors. Mr. Green owns his home, and Mr. Rose rents. One weekend they get into an argument about the plants on the property line, and the dispute turns into a wrestling match. A police officer driving by sees the two men scrapping, and arrests them both for assault. They are taken downtown and booked into jail on $50,000 bail, with arraignment scheduled for Tuesday afternoon. Mr. Green easily raises the money based on the equity in his home and is out free. Mr. Rose now has a dilemma; he must get to work on Monday morning or risk losing his job. He pays $5,000 from savings in the bank to pay for a bail bond so he can get to work. Lo and behold, the DA looks at their case on Monday when the office opens, and decides not to prosecute either for the altercation, and both men are free with charges dropped. Mr. Green gets back his cash deposit. Mr. Rose just lost his entire life savings. In this case, bail was not fair, and an innocent man lost $5,000 for a day in jail, while his neighbor lost nothing.

Bail before arraignment is set by the official bail schedule. Though law enforcement will use it maliciously to jam up a suspect. I have frequently seen bail set at over a million dollars using the "by the book" method, where law enforcement tallied up many smaller suspected crimes to make a huge bail amount. Any two-bit criminal can be branded as a menace to society by the police reporting an inflated bail amount to the press.

Then, the huge bail is made to make the suspect look bad, scare his family, and put pressure on them to give the cops what they want. There was no hearing nor did the arrestee or his attorney get to refute the bail amount. It is a tool used by law enforcement to pump up their accomplishments and mar the reputations of the arrested.

In one of my cases, the police were quick to send out a press release; the newspapers reported on the arrest and the $1.5 Million bail set by law enforcement, but the arrestee was released three days later with no formal charges filed. His name was dragged through the mud by cops hoping to crush his spirit, overwhelm him, and get him to confess to lesser crimes to justify the arrest. A high bail can be used to coerce a confession, or to get a suspect to rat on someone else.

Another scary example. The cops arrest a woman for suspected shoplifting one afternoon as she is leaving a store. She cannot find the receipt, but the woman knows she did not steal anything, and that her credit card charges will show proof of purchase. The police are holding her in jail on $25,000 bail. Her child is at daycare, and the cops threaten to call the county's Child Protective Services to put the kid in a foster home if the mom does not pick up the kid. She cannot afford bail, and she does not want to see her child traumatized by the authorities and put into the system.

The woman is offered a deal by the cops, sign this confession that she stole the items at the behest of a local crime leader, and she will go free to get her kid. The mother only has one choice, to lie about her guilt to save her child from the clutches of the government.

Cops are not the only ones to use bail maliciously. Prosecutors and judges can use bail just as unfairly.

Arraignment is where the arrestee is formally charged by the District Attorney's office for crimes. This is the first court appearance, and can be the most frightening for anyone not accustomed to it. It is also the easiest court date to get through. A Judge gives your attorney a sheet with a list of your charges. This is called a complaint. These are what are filed against you by the prosecuting DA or City Attorney based on your arrest by police. At arraignment, your attorney will plead Not Guilty for you. Then there is a hearing for the amount of bail set by the court to ensure you show up for future court dates.

Sometimes it is in the defendant's best interest to not bail out. Your attorney will give you advice on your own case. Local jail time pre-trial counts towards your sentence if you take a plea or are convicted. County jails are less frightening, and usually less dangerous, than big maximum security state prisons. Local jail is near your community, friends, and family. When someone serves time in a local county jail while awaiting trial, they are earning credit towards any future sentence if there is later a plea agreement or a guilty verdict. Because they have already earned credit towards their sentence, whatever their sentence is, it will be reduced by their credit for time served. Because they will have a reduced sentence, they can become eligible for in-home arrest or other alternatives to serve the remaining sentence.

Cash bail systems always hurt the poor and innocent. Even a low cash bail amount is only good for those with cash to pay it. A family working paycheck to paycheck cannot afford to make bail. That puts the working poor at great risk for a pre-trial jail stay, before being found innocent.

Plus, the all-or-nothing nature of the bail bond in California takes the cash deposit regardless of guilt or innocence, even in the event no charges are filed. The Bail Bonds companies are not to blame for this. They are providing a service, an insurance policy, and they deserve to get paid for the risk they assume. But, the government should not sustain the Bail Bonds industry in California by maintaining the cash system and demanding cash bail for almost every case.

The State is complicit in the travesty of cash bail. California law enforces the minimum rate a bail bondsman can charge. The California rate is 10 percent, but is reduced to 8 percent if you hire a private attorney (there are rare exceptions to this, but for the most part, 10 percent and 8 percent with a private attorney are the set percentages). The logic for the rate reduction for those who can afford a private attorney is that they are invested in their defense and will show up. Charging anything less would be a violation of the law and is called "unlawful rebate." So even if a bail bondsman wanted to give a poor client a break, they are bound by State law to charge at least 8 percent.

There are many forms of bail available, beyond the cash bail system we have here in California. The most familiar and common is to release the accused on their own recognizance (OR). That is, the accused promises to show up to court, and that pledge is accepted by the court based on that person's standing in the community, job, roots, and the likelihood they will not flee all that to dodge this trial.

Another method to release someone pre-trial is to put conditions on their release. They are released OR, but must comply with court-ordered activities to help keep tabs on them, such as an ankle monitor or required calls or visits to the police station to verify they are still in town.

Attendance at counseling like Alcoholics Anonymous or other programs is sometimes a condition. For someone with international access, the condition may be that they surrender their passport. All of these methods are consistent with treating the accused with dignity before they are tried for their alleged crimes. Jailing someone pre-trial can sometimes lead to injustice and a cash bail can be usurious.

Several states have removed the surety bond and the Bail Bondsman from the equation, having the accused pay the percentage to the courts, but then returning it after the requirements of the bail have been met.

There are many proven ways to protect people who are innocent until proven guilty. Cash bail victimizes them before a fair trial. The repercussions of the cash bail system ripple through society for years.

A 2013 study by the Arnold Foundation found that jailing people pre-trial actually increases the likelihood that the person will become a criminal in the future. Being trapped in jail knowing you are innocent can cause one to give up hope, to hate the system that wrongly jailed you, or both. Cash bail can most certainly mean locking up innocent people and releasing them primed to commit crime.

The Arnold Foundation study[108] reported that those held pre-trial were likely to be sentenced to jail, and their sentences were longer than those who were free pending trial. They also found that the longer a defendant was detained in jail pre-trial, the more likely he would be to commit a crime within two years of getting out. Finally the study found that moderate to high-risk defendants who had regular supervision were more likely to appear than those bailed out with no supervision. Further, supervision, rather than pre-trial detention or bail, resulted in lower recidivism overall.

By locking up a low-risk defendant with serious criminals, we are depriving them of liberty whilst teaching them how bad the system can be; how stacked it is against them. Rather than putting people accused of non-violent misdemeanors back home, back in school, or back at work, we punish them for not affording bail, and ruin their lives by detaining them for a few days, weeks, or even several months. Bail does not ensure public safety, nor protect us from future crimes; it only determines if the defendant has money or not.

There is a movement to abolish the cash bail system in the US. It is being led by a lawsuit filed by the group Equal Justice Under Law in San Francisco federal court. As a major county in the largest cash bail state, the verdict of this case will impact the entire state and the nation. If cash bail is ruled illegal in San Francisco, the other 58 counties in California will likely comply. A win here will bolster the cases in other cash bail lawsuits and measures that seek justice and equality under the law.

108 Laura and John Arnold Foundation releases new studies focused on pretrial detention and supervision. (2013). Laura and John Arnold Foundation. Retrieved 27 December 2017, from http://www.arnoldfoundation.org/laura-john-arnold-foundation-releases-new-studies-focused-pretrial-detention-supervision/

Equal Justice Under Law has had results in other states pushing out cash bail. In Alabama, they sued a jurisdiction for requiring cash bail for misdemeanors and traffic violations on grounds that it was unconstitutional (violating the Equal Protection Clause of the 14th Amendment). It let those with a few hundred dollars leave jail immediately, whilst all others had to sit for several days awaiting hearing. The system in Dothan Alabama has now changed, and bail is now an unsecured bond. That is, the bail amount is only assessed as penalty for not showing up for court.

Civil rights lawyer Alec Karakatsanis, the founder of EJUL, sums up the problem of cash bail up best in this quote to Slate: "Nobody should be held in a cage because they're poor. Detention should be based on objective evidentiary factors, like whether the person is a danger to the community or a flight risk—not how much money's in their pocket[109]."

Bail should only be set to make sure a defendant appears in court. Though the amount of bail can be variable (and should be, especially if we will take the means of the defendant into account), whether or not bail is offered should be binary. That is, there should be bail, or a defendant should be denied bail.

A very high bail amount should not be set as a means of protecting society. If a suspect is a danger to society, then he should not be granted bail. If the bail is $100,000 or a million dollars, a dangerous person is still dangerous. Setting a ridiculously high bail is a tactic used by cops, prosecutors, and judges to look like they are being tough on criminals. A judge with political ambitions, and wanting to be seen as anti-crime knows that simply denying bail is not as dramatic as setting high bail. This is obvious when bail is set at $25 million for a terrible, violent defendant. Bail should have been denied, not inflated for show.

109 Neyfakh, L. (2017). Is Bail Unconstitutional?. Slate Magazine. Retrieved 27 December 2017, from http://www.slate.com/articles/news_and_politics/crime/2015/06/is_bail_unconstitutional_our_broken_system_keeps_the_poor_in_jail_and_lets.html

This bail grandstanding is bad for the courts, our rights, and the system. It is unconstitutional in California to charge high bail as a means to prevent a dangerous person from harming someone on the outside. It is a dangerous fiction that courts can protect public safety by setting an inflated bail. In the case of Preventative Detention, where bail is not to be set at all [e.g. Article 1, sec. 12, para (c) California Constitution], the Government has to prove by clear and convincing evidence, following a hearing, that "no condition or combination of conditions will reasonably assure the appearance of the person…and the safety of any other person and the community."

As my law partner Jack Weiss wrote in a motion, "The reactionary police-powerists, in the Janus-faced name of 'law and order', decided to reverse [the assumption of innocence] when setting bail."

The cash bail system has shown to be discriminatory, broken, and enriching of a tiny segment of the population that sells bail bonds. It would be good to do away with it, but abolition is not the only solution. As we see above, the California Constitution insists we use "conditions or combination of conditions" to ensure the defendant appears at court.

Jailing a defendant pre-trial leaves them susceptible to law enforcement coercion, negative influences in jail, and the creeping specter of hopelessness in isolation. We have seen in Orange County, CA, that detainees in county jail were housed with police informants, paid rats, and criminals richly rewarded for delivering questionable 'confessions' from their cellmates, in direct contravention of their right to an attorney. The practice was so common that it was referred to as "putting them in the snitch tank[110]."

110 Ferrell, D., & Saavedra, T. (2015). How jailhouse informants and the 'snitch tank' put Orange County justice system in turmoil. Orange County Register. Retrieved 27 December 2017, from https://www.ocregister.com/2015/11/30/register-special-report-how-jailhouse-informants-and-the-snitch-tank-put-orange-county-justice-system-in-turmoil/

These abuses could not happen if all citizens had an opportunity to make bail via a number of conditions instead of all cash, only.

The first step to fixing the system is to not confuse bail with sentencing. Bail is not to be used as a punishment of the arrested. The goal is to get the defendant to court, not to lock them up for weeks or months awaiting trial.

Most people have plenty of "recognizance" to be released upon. They have family, homes, jobs, school, friends, and so much more that should be weighed against their likelihood to flee.

There are a number of bail conditions that work well with an OR release and that work even better than cash bail to ensure a defendant shows up for trial. Check-ins with law enforcement, weekly supervision by an officer, electronic monitoring, counseling, even phone calls, all serve to deliver the person to court to stand trial. Plus, these alternatives do not strip them of their savings, dignity, families, or livelihoods.

Bail as a weapon to punish those accused of crimes is a black eye on California's legal system. Many other states have abolished cash bail. Though there are vested interests fighting to keep the status quo, at some point, the evidence of abuses will bubble over, and a court, legislator, or citizen's ballot measure will set things right for our system of innocent until proven guilty.

While California has still not done away with the cash bail model, a new case from 2018 has taken the first step to recognizing the illogical and prejudicial nature of the system. In Re Kenneth Humphrey, 2018 Cal.App. Lexis 64, 2018 WL 550512 not only reaffirmed every defendant's right to automatic review of bail, but held that bail schedules may not be rigidly followed without consideration of "a defendant's ability to pay, as well as other individualized factors bearing upon his or her dangerousness and/or risk of flight."

The court also determined that bail schedules, “represent the antithesis of the individualized inquiry required before a court can order pretrial detention.” It held that if it is determined a defendant cannot afford the amount of cash bail necessary to ensure future court appearances, the court ”may set bail at that amount only upon a determination by clear and convincing evidence that no less restrictive alternative will satisfy that purpose. The court’s findings and reasons must be stated on the record or otherwise preserved.” In this finding, the judicial habit of creating the most cursory record before locking an individual up was finally called out.

CHAPTER TWELVE

STAND YOUR GROUND: SELF DEFENSE

California is not known as a very gun-friendly state. It sometimes feels like the Second Amendment is one of the rights that California forgot to ratify within its own borders. But one right is so primary, so fundamental, that it is even respected here in the Golden State.

The right to defend your life is as basic as it gets.

The right to protect your own life is primal, instinctive, yet also intellectually and philosophically pure. Your life is your own to defend and protect, and no one has the right to take it from you. This leads to the legal right to "Stand Your Ground" when challenged by a hostile and violent party. There is no obligation for you to retreat when met with threats of violence by a bad guy. You have every right to stay where you belong and not be forced away by evildoers.

Though California does not have specific legislation on the books protecting your right to a "Stand Your Ground" self-defense, we do have case law and precedents that are perhaps the strongest in the nation in protecting a victim's right to self-defense.

The phrase "stand your ground" came into the national vocabulary in 2008 with the George Zimmerman-Trayvon Martin case in Florida.

In that case, a seventeen-year-old boy was fatally shot by a volunteer neighborhood watchman in his Sanford Florida neighborhood. George Zimmerman was armed with a 9mm Kel-Tec PF-9 handgun patrolling his neighborhood. He spotted Martin walking through the area and followed him, thinking he looked suspicious. The two were soon involved in an altercation, and Martin was shot dead in the chest. At that time, police did not arrest Zimmerman due to Florida's "Stand Your Ground" law, as there was clear evidence of self-defense in their minds. Eventually, 44 days later, charges were filed against Zimmerman, who stood trial for Second Degree Murder.

There was national attention on the case, with supporters and outrage for both parties, and from all angles. Self-defense, gun rights, anti-crime, pro-victim, racial issues, and more. Gun rights supporters backed Zimmerman's right to defend himself, but his personal support eroded as his behavior and rhetoric turned people away.

Trayvon Martin's loss of life was mourned by many as a racist attack based on profiling and discrimination of an unarmed black teen. Ultimately, Zimmerman was found not guilty by a jury after sixteen hours of deliberation. It is interesting to note that Zimmerman's defense relied on a more traditional self-defense tactic, and not the original stand-your-ground claim at the time of the arrest. In other words, the defense tactic shifted during trial from 'Zimmerman was standing his ground' to a more traditional, 'Zimmerman and Martin were involved in a struggle and Zimmerman was about to lose his gun to Martin.'

Keep in mind, standing your ground is not the right to shoot anyone in your way. Nor can you shoot someone for yelling at you and acting obnoxiously. In every case, local laws and gun ordinances apply, so standing your ground is not a free ticket to have a concealed weapon. What the law is about is the right to defend yourself or others from death or grave harm.

Almost all states have laws or statutes stating your right to stand your ground, but most of those only recognize that right in your home. This is known as the "Castle Doctrine," which recognizes your right to defend your life within your "castle" or home. Twenty-two of those states have stronger Stand Your Ground laws that support your right to not back down from a threat anywhere you have a legal right to be.

A few states lean away from your right to defend your life, and require a "duty to retreat" before using violence to defend yourself. The specifics vary within these states, with qualifications and caveats all around. California's statutes go even further in extending 'standing your ground' to not requiring you to turn your back on danger.

The states that do not support standing your ground in public actually expect—nay, demand—that you flee if you can. Run away and live to fight another day, even when faced with imminent danger to yourself or a loved one. These laws give the belligerent, the attacker, the menace, the right to stand *their* ground whilst you must turn your back, scurry away and hide. Some of these states have "Castle Doctrine" allowances, but first and foremost, it is upon the victim to flee and find safety before being forced to use violence as a last resort against their attacker. The states least friendly to standing your ground are:

> Arkansas, Connecticut, Delaware, Hawaii, Iowa, Maine, Maryland, Massachusetts, Missouri, Minnesota, Nebraska, New Jersey, New York, North Dakota, Ohio, Rhode Island, Wisconsin, and Wyoming[111].

American law is largely derived from English Common Law which in turn was derived from Roman law. In England, the King and his officials were

111 Findlaw. (n.d.). States That Have Stand Your Ground Laws - FindLaw. [online] Available at: http://criminal.findlaw.com/criminal-law-basics/states-that-have-stand-your-ground-laws.html#sthash.YWGeweCf.dpuf [Accessed 6 Feb. 2018].

the law of the land, responsible for adjudication and punishment. But in his home, a man can expect safety and his right to protect it. "An Englishman's home is his castle." This is where the "Castle Doctrine" comes from.

This concept was formalized as English law by the 17th century. Sir Edward Coke, wrote in *The Institutes of the Laws of England*, in 1628:

> For a man's house is his castle, et domus sua cuique est tutissimum refugium [and each man's home is his safest refuge][112]

Sir William Blackstone, justice of the King's Bench in 18th century England, sums it up thusly in his *Commentaries on the Laws of England*:

> And the law of England has so particular and tender a regard to the immunity of a man's house, that it stiles it his castle, and will never suffer it to be violated with immunity: agreeing herein with the sentiments of ancient Rome, as expressed in the works of Tully; quid enim sanctius, quid omni religione munitius, quam domus uniusquisque civium[113]?

In this case, the "Tully" referred to is not one of my revered ancestors, but rather Marcus Tullius Cicero. The Latin is translated as, "What is more sacred, what more strongly guarded by every holy feeling, than a man's own home?" The Romans got it, the English got it, and we get it here in America. Perhaps we understand the right to defend yourself much better than they did, certainly here in California.

On lists of "Stand Your Ground" states, California is often omitted,

112 Coke, E., & Littleton, T. (1628). The first part of the institutes of the lawes of England. London: Printed for the Society of Stationers.
113 Blackstone, W. (1765). Commentaries on the laws of England. London: Clarendon Press.

because we do not have a specific law from the legislature. But we do have strong precedence in our statutes guaranteeing the right to stand your ground as well as jury instructions that a judge must read to a jury at the end of a case before deliberation begins. These are known as CALCRIM 3470 and 505.

CALCRIM stand for the Judicial Council of California Criminal Jury Instructions. These provide plain-language criminal jury instructions prepared by a statewide committee of justices from the Court of Appeal, trial court judges, attorneys, academicians, and lay people, and are approved by the Judicial Council as the state's official instructions pursuant to the California Rules of Court. The entire CALCRIM book[114] is almost 2,500 pages and is full of clarifications and statutes that judges provide to California juries to help them understand the laws they are hearing.

The Stand Your Ground instruction in CALCRIM 3470 and 505 reads:

> A defendant is not required to retreat. He or she is entitled to stand his or her ground and defend himself or herself and if reasonably necessary, to pursue an assailant until the danger of (death/bodily injury) has passed. This is so even if safety could have been achieved by retreating[115].

In California law, a jury instruction is considered "law" regarding standing your ground and is very favorable to the accused who was protecting his or her life and loved ones. When faced with a threat, you can stand your ground, anywhere you have a right to be: at home, on the

114 California Jury Instructions—Criminal (CALCRIM). (2017). JUSTIA. Retrieved 27 December 2017, from https://www.justia.com/criminal/docs/calcrim/100/

115 CALCRIM No. 505. Justifiable Homicide: Self-Defense or Defense of Another. (2017). JUSTIA. Retrieved 27 December 2017, from https://www.justia.com/criminal/docs/calcrim/500/505.html

sidewalk, or in the mall. Further, if you are aware of additional threats beyond yourself, you may prevent the dangerous individual from harming another person. This is called "Defense of Another." Whether self-defense or defense of another, there is explicitly no duty to retreat, even if safety could have been achieved by doing so.

Not only is California a strong Stand Your Ground state, arguably, it may be the strongest. In California, not only can you stand your ground and not have to retreat even if you could safely get away, but you can also reasonably pursue an assailant. Here is an example of how strong Stand Your Ground runs in California:

A man breaks into your house in the middle of the night. If you shoot him right then and there, you would be presumed to have acted in self-defense under the "castle doctrine." Another example, you are on your front lawn and an armed bad guy comes up and tries to rob you. During the scuffle, the bad guy drops his gun allowing you to run away and safely lock yourself inside your house. However, you stay outside and continue the fight until you are sure the bad guy is no longer a threat. As long as your continued attack was "reasonable," you were well within your rights even though you could have run away safely. That is the standard Stand Your Ground legal standard.

Both of these examples illustrate just how strong the Wild West DNA still runs through the legal heritage of California. But California goes even further. As stated in the jury instructions above, in California, you have the right to reasonably pursue your assailant. Let's take another example, you're on your sidewalk and a bad guy comes up to shoot and rob you. His gun jams. He panics, drops it, and runs away. In most states, because the danger is supposedly gone, your right to self-defense is over. However, in California, you are not required to assume that the danger is passed, you could be well within your rights to pick up the gun, clear the jam, and chase him down for the next six blocks while shooting at him in the back. As long as your pursuit was reasonable, you would be absolved in the eyes of the law from any wrongdoing.

Why is this behavior permitted? How do you know that man isn't running to go get another gun? How do you know that man isn't going to go get other bad guys and come back and finish the job or to 'take care of the witness'? You can stand your ground in the face of danger, as well as follow up on imminent threats to life and wellbeing. You are not expected to ignore or turn your back on danger.

It is interesting to note that the states with the strongest Stand Your Ground laws tend to be in the West and South. Perhaps this stems from the old days of Southern Honor and the Wild West. A famous early case was that of Doc Holliday of OK Corral fame.

John Henry "Doc" Holliday was a dentist, gambler, and gunslinger in the Wild West. He is best known for being friends with Wyatt Earp and deputized as a marshal by Virgil Earp for the gunfight at the OK Corral in Tombstone, Arizona in 1881.

After the deadly shootouts in Tombstone, Doc Holliday moved north to Leadville, Colorado where he avoided extradition to Arizona and tried to live a more quiet life gambling and dealing cards. Doc was sick from tuberculosis, broke, and in debt. Holliday borrowed $5 from a local bartender named William J. Allen (Note: for Tombstone buffs, this Billy Allen is not related to the one from the Tombstone Clanton gang).

Months went by with Allen trying to get repaid, and Holliday making excuses. Finally, Allen gave Doc a deadline of noon on August 19, 1884, to pay up, "or else," clearly stating that he would do in Holliday for the affront of non-payment, "If you don't pay it, I'll lick you, you son of a bitch." Allen spent the afternoon looking for Holliday, yelling, "I am going to hunt this party."

At 3 PM, Allen walked into Hyman's Saloon where Holliday was sitting at the bar. As Allen barged in through the saloon doors, Doc Holliday immediately pulled out his gun and shot Allen in the arm, dropping him to the ground. Doc fired again and was restrained by bystanders. History is murky but it is likely that Allen was not armed.

Holliday surrendered to the law, and was charged with "assault with intent to kill." Holliday defended his actions saying, "I saw Allen come in with his hand in his pocket, and I thought my life was as good to me as his was to him; I fired the shot, and he fell to the floor, and fired the second shot; I knew I would be a child in his hands if he got hold of me…I think Allen weighs 170 pounds…I don't think I was able to protect myself against him; I thought he had come there to kill me."

Doc Holliday stood trial by jury, and claimed self-defense and no duty to retreat. He was found Not Guilty[116].

It is interesting to note that California jury instructions CALCRIM 3470 and 505 support Doc's Wild West defense, stating, "Someone who has been threatened or harmed by a person in the past is justified in acting more quickly or taking greater self-defense measures against that person."

I have personally defended many Stand Your Ground cases at trial in California. The San Francisco Bay Area is known as a very liberal place. However, the message of protecting yourself or loved ones and not being required to turn your back to danger still resonates soundly throughout the state. One case in particular that I tried that later became known as a "landmark" Stand Your Ground case, took place in Contra Costa County,

116 Price, C. (2012). The Fading of a Legend: Doc Holliday in Leadville. Colorado Central Magazine. Retrieved 27 December 2017, from http://cozine.com/2012-may/the-fading-of-a-legend-doc-holliday-in-leadville/

just over the hills from Berkeley. The trial was in June 2014, just 11 months after the George Zimmerman-Trayvon Martin verdict.

People (read: potential jurors) were very familiar with the phrase "Stand Your Ground" from Zimmerman's defense in Florida. But it had lots of baggage from that case, burdened with politics, Zimmerman's character, and racial insensitivities.

"Stand Your Ground" took on the taint of a "shoot first, question later" mentality. In fact, the County Prosecutor played on this sentiment, claiming that my client went into the situation with intentions to shoot first. Before the trial, the prosecutor jibed me essentially saying that since everyone was still pissed off about the Zimmerman verdict, there was no way he could lose this case.

My client was the defendant in case #05-130899-8 in Contra Costa County. We'll go with the first name of "Ray" here, even though the case is widely public. Ray is a sweet little Filipino man in his 50s who lived in a humble house in a working-class suburb in the East Bay. He lived there with his disabled wife, whom he dotingly cared for. Ray was proud of his house, of being a homeowner, worked two jobs to keep up with the mortgage, and slept very little. He worked full time at San Francisco International Airport during the day and worked nights at a local market he ran with his brother.

Over the course of several years, Ray's house on Pine Street had been burglarized and vandalized repeatedly. The police would be called, sometimes they would show up and sometimes they wouldn't, sometimes there would be a minimal investigation and sometimes there wouldn't. There was never any relief for Ray or his wife from the police or anyone else and the victimization of Ray's home continued.

It was a calm, mild California autumn night. The waxing moon would be full in three days. It was this night of October 26th, 2012, at around 11

PM, Ray heard a suspicious noise outside the garage of his home. Just three nights prior, his car had been damaged by a vandal smashing a garbage bin through the rear window of the vehicle. Concerned for his property, his safety, and the safety of his sleeping wife, Ray put his handgun in his pocket and crept into his garage from the house. His garage door had to remain open because of his wife's cats and the lock to the door from the garage into the home had been damaged and not repaired since a previous burglary.

Crawling under the garage door, Ray peered into his driveway, darkened by trees and minimal street lighting. He saw the outline of three males dressed in dark clothing standing in his driveway. Ray did not crawl back into his house to call 911. The police had been unresponsive to his calls in the past and he couldn't secure his house from someone entering from the garage. As he peered out from under the partially opened garage door on his hands and knees, one of the males attacked. The attacker grabbed one of the hard plastic garbage bins, picked it up over his head and ran at Ray.

In that instant, it was fight or flight. Ray was in danger. He feared for his safety, he feared for his wife inside the house. There was no time to think, instinct kicked in, and he instinctively chose "fight." Ray quickly pulled the gun from his pocket and fired off one shot at his attacker. Ray's assailant was a 5'10" fifteen-year-old boy known to have been involved with the previous vandalisms and a one-time shooting of Ray's wife in the face with a pellet gun.

The bullet grazed the juvenile on his side. He dropped the bin and ran off into the night with his friends.

This time the police came when 911 was called.

Ray was arrested and charged with assault with a firearm and discharging a firearm with gross negligence.

In that fearful moment, before Ray was about to be crushed by the bin, he was not thinking about case law, Second Amendment rights, or his property. He was down on his hands and knees while a hooded attacker rushed at him with a garbage bin raised over his head, ready to crush Ray's head. Ray defended his life. He pulled out his gun and defended himself. That is the basis of Stand Your Ground law in California, the right to not ignore imminent danger.

Due to his arrest, Ray lost his longtime job at the San Francisco airport and he feared losing the home he worked so hard for. His trial was more than a year after the incident, during which he dangled in limbo and worried about serving years in prison and losing everything.

During the trial, the prosecutor tried to invoke Trayvon Martin sympathy and anti-gun sentiments. He portrayed Ray as "overreacting" and determined to shoot someone that evening out of revenge for the recurring vandalism, arguing that since you can't use lethal force to defend property only, Ray was guilty.

The prosecutor argued that Ray should have more carefully assessed and evaluated the situation, and not shot to defend his life or property. In some states, Ray would have been expected to flee, crawling back into the garage for safety or to keep retreating into his house. But in California we have the right, and some would say the moral obligation, to defend ourselves and loved ones from harm.

Fortunately, during the course of litigating this case, Ray had made bail and was able to spend the sixteen months between arrest and trial at home with his wife and working with his brother at their store.

I defended Ray's rights in the face of the State's claims that he was the aggressor bent on shooting a teenager out of annoyance from repeated vandalism. But the law is the law, summed up best by the judge's instructions to the jury, citing CALCRIM 3470, "A defendant is not required to retreat. He or she is entitled to stand their ground."

On June 18, 2014, Ray was acquitted of all charges. He stood his ground in California and defended himself and his wife from assault, or worse. I'm happy the jury was able to see the truth of what happened in this case. It continues to be a healing process for Ray, my exonerated client. A victim who wrongfully became the accused.

At trial, deputy district attorneys hate Stand Your Ground laws. Anything that makes a defense case clearer, or protects the rights of the accused, is usually frowned upon by prosecutors. Also, law enforcement does not want to lose its monopoly on shooting people. If you have a duty to retreat, or to dial 911, then you rely on the cops to save your life, rather than on yourself.

In fact, around the time of the Zimmerman trial, U.S. Attorney General Eric Holder questioned the need for Stand Your Ground laws. He criticized the laws as "senselessly expanding the concept of self-defense and sowing dangerous conflict in our neighborhoods."

In a 2007 National District Attorneys Association symposium, numerous concerns were voiced that the law could increase crime. These included criminals using the law as a defense for their crimes, more people carrying guns, and people not feeling safe if anyone could use deadly force in a conflict. The report also noted that the misinterpretation of body language or verbal expressions could result in use of deadly force when there was, in fact, no danger. The report specifically notes that racial and ethnic minorities could be at greater risk because of negative stereotypes[117].

117 Jansen, S., & Nugent-Borakove, M. (2008). Expansions to the Castle doctrine. Alexandria: National District Attorneys Association. Available online at www.ndaa.org/pdf/Castle%20Doctrine.pdf, Retroeved on December 27, 2017

The idea of standing your ground has been characterized as enabling vigilantism, and called "Make My Day" laws, after the line by brutal movie cop "Dirty Harry." Miami police chief John F. Timoney called the law unnecessary and dangerous in that "You're encouraging people to possibly use deadly physical force where it shouldn't be used." The Brady Campaign to Prevent Gun Violence calls them "shoot first" laws.

But in California, our Stand Your Ground laws are case law and jury instructions given by the judge to a jury right before they deliberate. They are not a guideline to "How to get away with murder" for hotheads and vigilantes. They support an "affirmative defense," meaning, if someone has been arrested and charged with a violent act, at trial the defendant has the burden to establish that they stood their ground, and that their actions were justified. It is up to the jury to then decide the fate of the defendant.

The effect Stand Your Ground laws have had on crime rates is disputed between supporters and critics of the law. Economist John Lott says that states adopting Stand Your Ground/Castle doctrine laws have reduced murder rates by nine percent and overall violent crime by 11 percent, and that was even accounting for a range of other factors such as national crime trends, law enforcement variables (arrest, execution, and imprisonment rates,) income and poverty measures, demographic changes, and the national average changes in crime rates from year-to-year, as well as average differences across states[118].

But "Stand your Ground" does not expand the concept of self-defense so much as help define it. It helps citizens, juries, and everyone in between understand justifiable self-defense. It adds context to the use of force to defend oneself. This is why California's implementation of the case law

118 Lott, J. R. (2000). More guns, less crime: Understanding crime and gun-control laws. Chicago, University of Chicago Press. Table 10.14. "Time impact of the Castle Doctrine on violent crime rates"

may well be the best way to support this right of self-defense. It was not legislated; it directly flows from our rights and Common Law and into a judge's instruction to the jury and in clear, plain language, spells it out for a jury, so it can decide.

Your right to self-defense is sacrosanct. Tautologically speaking, living is the reason for life. Any law that curtails your right to self-defense would be a blow to your rights and safety, such as any law demanding a duty to retreat. Duty-to-retreat laws give the upper hand to bad guys and force innocent people to risk turning their backs to a dangerous situation. They risk further harm by forcing some during a moment of "fight or flight," to question themselves. Human beings, by definition, do not have the cognitive skills required to logically think through the consequences of what, by definition, is a split-second decision when their life, or the life of a loved one, is in peril.

Without Stand Your Ground and Castle Doctrine laws, victims of violent crime would be made into defendants. Self-defense would be on par with assault or murder. The victim would be blamed for surviving an attack or merely for gaining the upper hand during or after being assaulted.

In California, we should consider our case law regarding standing one's ground the 'Right to Fight Back Against Evil.' We can defend ourselves in the face of violence, under the threat of violence, and even pursue a bad guy. Our case law permits not just self-defense, but the defense of others in harm's way; and not just in our homes, but anywhere throughout the Golden State.

CHAPTER THIRTEEN

THE INFINITE VARIETY OF LAWS

Molly Malloy is about to have the best day of her life.

Most of Molly's days are pretty good, but this one is about to be the best. Molly is a middle-aged suburban homemaker and mom who is active in her community. She pays her taxes, donates to charities, volunteers for organizations, and is a cheerful neighbor in her town. Everyone loves Molly Malloy.

On this day, soon to go down as one of the best, Molly wakes up from a peaceful slumber to her alarm playing an MP3 of her favorite song. Ouch! Her migraine is not going to slow her down today! Molly has too much to do, so she swallows a Vicodin from the medicine cabinet. Just in case, she drops a pill in her purse for later. Molly puts on her favorite red dress and heads downstairs to take on the day.

She pours a bowl of cereal and milk for each of her kids and packs up what she needs for her outing. Last night Molly baked a cake to share at lunch with friends, so, she puts her mother's antique cake knife in her purse to serve it later. Molly puts the cake in the back of her SUV next to her daughter's spare violin, a bag of animal food for the family's pet ferret, and her son's Boy Scout bow and arrow set from camp.

Molly backs out of her driveway on Wildflower Lane, buckles up, and heads towards the freeway. As Molly drives downtown towards her Red Frock Ladies charitable society luncheon, she gets lost amidst construction detours. Dutifully, she pulls over to the sidewalk to call for directions on her cell phone, but has no signal. After getting out and walking back and forth, she finds a weak WiFi signal and uses it to find the email with the address to the luncheon.

Unfortunately, she is lost, does not know what street she is on, or the fastest way to her destination. She waves at a passing taxi cab to ask for directions, but it drives on. Then a nice looking businessman in a nice car comes her way, and she beckons to him. He slows, glances in his rearview mirror, then speeds off. Luckily, a plain brown Crowne Victoria sedan is right behind; she waves it down and gets directions from the two men in the car on the best route to her lunch meeting.

Now armed with directions, Molly is ready to hop in the car and get going. But blocking the path to her car is a large, disheveled, homeless lady shambling up to her, asking for a ride. Molly is generally sympathetic to the needs of the less fortunate, but she is a bit frightened of this woman and is late for her luncheon, so she apologizes and demurs. The bag lady begins shouting curses and tries to get into the passenger side of Molly's car, pounding on the door and roof, yelling "Gimme a ride!"

This terrifies Molly who screams, "Get your filthy paws off of my car you crazy old loon or I will take your filthy arms off of you!" Molly feebly shoves the large woman with her purse, to no avail. Coincidently, three young men, obviously Cincinnati baseball fans, walk up and stand behind Molly. One of the men demands, "Yo, Crazy Coco, leave the lady alone and move along!"

Coco falls on the sidewalk sobbing, bawling, weeping. Molly feels terrible for losing her temper, and for the homeless woman's situation. So, Molly gets out the cake she baked for the luncheon and slices it up and apologizes. Coco, too, apologizes and thanks Molly for the slice of cake.

Molly praises each of the kind young men with some cake and with a fist-bump for helping her and then drives off. A dangerous situation turned into a chance for her to help a needy woman out, and to congratulate nice young men for doing a good deed. Life is truly wonderful and beautiful. Molly arrives at her luncheon, and is surprised by the group with the award for Red Frock Lady of the Year for her dedication to charitable service.

Driving home that evening, an ecstatic Molly sees a few deer on the side of the road and flashes her high beams to alert the deer, and the car behind her, as she slowly drives by. Once home, Molly and her husband open a bottle of wine to celebrate her award. They get into a flirty pillow fight on the couch over who will do the dinner dishes. Then the doorbell rings…

• • •

Molly is a multiple felon and a deemed a threat to society. You might not realize it, but regular citizens of California like you and Molly commit multiple crimes every day. This is another way the system colludes to make you a criminal without even knowing it.

The State of California has thousands of laws and adds hundreds of new laws every year.

Plus, the Federal Government has thousands more laws codified in almost 25,000 pages, though the specific total is almost too vast and complex to count accurately. All this, despite Thomas Jefferson specifically writing in 1798, "That the Constitution of the United States, having delegated to Congress a power to punish treason, counterfeiting the securities and current coin of the United States, piracies, and felonies committed on the high seas, and offenses against the law of nations, and no other crimes whatsoever[119]."

We are all criminals guilty of violating multiple laws every day. Legislators pass more laws every year in efforts to appear "tough on crime." In response to current events or public opinion, lawmakers make laws that are rushed, broad, and often subjective in their application. This puts too much power in the hands of police, who can choose to apply a law based on personal biases, and too much power in the hands of prosecutors, who can try to bury a defendant in charges and get a 'confession' before their attorney sorts out the truth. As Lavrentiy Beria, head of Joseph Stalin's secret police famously said, "Show me the man, and I'll show you the crime."

"Between 2.3 million and 2.4 million Americans are behind bars, roughly one in every 100 adults. If those on parole or probation are included, one adult in 31 is under "correctional" supervision. As a proportion of its total population, America incarcerates five times more people than Britain, nine times more than Germany and 12 times more than Japan[120]." The reason we have too many prisoners is that we have too many laws.

With enough laws, the arbitrary discretion of a cop or prosecutor will determine if you are a criminal, not your actions or choices.

Quoting Supreme Court Justice Breyer:

> The complexity of modern federal criminal law, codified in several thousand sections of the United States Code and the virtually infinite variety of factual circumstances that might trigger an investigation into a possible violation of the law, make it difficult

119 Draft of the Kentucky Resolutions of 1798. (1798). Constitution.org. Retrieved 27 December 2017, from http://www.constitution.org/tj/tj-ken98.htm

120 Too many laws, too many prisoners. (2010). The Economist. Retrieved 27 December 2017, from http://www.economist.com/node/16636027

> for anyone to know, in advance, just when a particular set of statements might later appear (to a prosecutor) to be relevant to some such investigation[121].

Vague laws laws delegate basic policy decisions to cops, prosecutors, and judges for application on an ad hoc and subjective basis. This will always bring the danger of arbitrary and discriminatory application of these laws.

Vague laws let cops decide if a person is a criminal or not. Are the windows too tinted on that car? Is that group being too loud? Are they a gang because they are wearing the same colors? Are they loitering in wait to commit a crime? Vague laws allow prosecutors to imagine the thoughts of a defendant when applying enhancements like those for hate crimes, or in inflating accidents into willful acts.

Unfortunately, vague laws usually err on the side of impacting the poor, powerless, and vulnerable in our society. On the other hand, laws aimed at fat cats and corporations are usually uncannily specific. The result being that the rich and powerful can find loopholes and exemptions you can drive a truck through. The rich have lobbyists who help draft those laws. The poor get scooped up in over-broad and vague crimes they were not even aware of.

Citizens have a right to know what is legal and illegal, so they can choose a path for themselves. When the lines are blurred by Government, people can no longer choose to be law-abiding. That choice is taken from them and assumed by law enforcement, which makes a mockery of the criminal justice system and the constitutional foundations of our country.

As an example, let's take something as simple as crossing the street.

121 Breyer, J. (1998). *Rubin v. United States*. Denial of petition for Writ of Certiorari to the US Court Of Appeals.. Supreme Court Of The United States. Retrieved 27 December 2017, from https://www.law.cornell.edu/supct/html/98-93.ZD.html

"Jaywalking" is a crime in California (CA Vehicle Code §21955) defined as "Between adjacent intersections controlled by traffic control signal devices or by police officers, pedestrians shall not cross the roadway at any place except in a crosswalk."

But the definition of "cross" is not defined. Does starting to cross equate with jaywalking? Or walking halfway then back? What about walking across the middle line to enter one's car on the far side, without going curb to curb? These grey areas leave the decision to enforce this law up to the officer's subjective discretion.

Disturbing the Peace is another vague crime that police often use as a catch-all to slap their cuffs on a citizen. The crime is listed as California Penal Code 415 and is triggered by a person, "Unlawfully fighting, or challenging another person to fight, in a public place. Disturbing another person by loud and unreasonable noise; if this is done willfully and maliciously. And; using offensive words in a public place . . . if the words are likely to provoke an immediate violent reaction."

A reasonable person can see that anger and obnoxiousness are part of 'Disturbing the Peace,' but the opinion of the arresting officer has wide leeway in real-life situations. A cop can claim any taunting, cursing, yelling, or amplified music was intentionally perpetrated to provoke another person. Perhaps you were the victim of a shove, or didn't realize your radio was annoying the neighbor, or your cursing was not directed at anyone in particular.

The goal of the officer is to keep the peace, so shutting down one or more parties immediately accomplishes this goal. Even though you lacked criminal intent, were falsely accused, or your actions were protected by the First Amendment; the arrest itself, enabled by a vague law, gave one cop cause to arrest you. The DA might have trouble convicting you based on the cop's subjective interpretation, but the improper arrest itself restored the peace at the expense of justice.

Vagrancy and loitering laws are also written to be vague and overbroad to make them easy to enforce, if not convict. They have traditionally been used to target unpopular or vulnerable parts of the population like migrants, sex workers, the homeless, youth, and minorities. These laws are written with selective enforcement in mind; they might ban "sleeping in a vehicle," but they mean to ban poor people from sleeping in their cars, not dad napping in the parking lot while mom shops. "Sleeping on a park bench" bans are aimed at the homeless, not grandma catching 40-winks during a park playdate with the grandkids.

Under California's vague anti-loitering laws, any woman walking down the street could be arrested for soliciting prostitution. It is up to the cop to determine her *intent* whilst walking (Cal. Pen. Code § 653.22). What can be more subjective than imagining another person's intent?

You might be in a gang and not even know it. The definition of "criminal street gang" according to section 186.22(f) of the California Penal Code states: "A criminal street gang is defined as any organization, association or group of three or more persons, whether formal or informal, which (1) has continuity of purpose, (2) seeks a group identity, and (3) has members who individually or collectively engage in or have engaged in a pattern of criminal activity."

Softball team drinks beers after games in an alcohol-free park? GANG! Girl Scout troop zig zags across the lane to sell cookies in their neighborhood? GANG! Church bowling team has a member with priors? GANG! The worst part is that the definition of a gang permits one criminal member to have the entire group branded as a member of a "criminal street gang."

So even though you only see Bob on Tuesday league bowling night, his years of embezzlement at work allow a prosecutor to label your entire bowling team a criminal gang, and you a criminal for being part of it. That makes it possible for a prosecutor to enhance any of your misdemeanors into a felony.

Other subjective enhancements used by prosecutors to arbitrarily inflate charges and sentences include: assault weapon enhancement, which can be based on the design, rather than function of a firearm; hate crimes based on the alleged thoughts of the perpetrator, knowledge about an accomplice's weapon, and "great" bodily injury.

Further confusing things is the compounding of similar crimes against one defendant. If you get into a fight, any missed punches are assaults, while those that connect are battery. But the DA will prosecute you for Assault and Battery. If you shoot and injure a bad guy who broke into your home, you can be charged with Attempted Murder, plus Assault with a Deadly Weapon, and, to add insult to injury, Discharging a Firearm. One bullet, three crimes.

Prosecutors are trained to, and will, charge as many crimes as can possibly fit a situation. Throw as many crimes at a person as you can to see what sticks, and maybe overwhelm them into taking a plea for any one of them.

Of course, a law that was too vague could be struck down as unconstitutional. Many of these laws are not unconstitutional on their face, but may be held unconstitutional as a valid defense in an individual case in court. Lawmakers argue that the vagueness of these laws is what makes them valuable for regulating society, and the instances where charges are defeated in court are the price to pay for their benefits. Meaning, just because a vague or overbroad law can be abused by subjective cops, that does not mean that we should stop enforcing them, because not all cases are proven to be abuse.

Judges will rarely go against a DA and decide a law is too vague. Unfortunately, the full and expensive trial process is used to sort out the arbitrary victims of subjectivity from the real bad guys. Luckily, we have a jury of our peers, who are hopefully sensible and will not blindly follow authority—if you can afford to get to a jury trial.

• • •

Molly Malloy is about to have the worst day of her life.

Patrol Officer Shift Log

7 PM - Wildflower Lane

My partner and I approach the subject's home after 12 hours of tailing and surveillance in our unmarked brown Crowne Vic. We are at the Wildflower Lane home of suspect Molly M. Malloy, WFA, age 49, driver of silver 2011 Acura SUV license plate CA A1U34J9.

We knock on subject's door and it is answered by Mrs. Malloy. We identify ourselves and show badges.

The subject, Malloy, still wearing her red gang clothing, is compliant, and appears overly friendly, as an attempt to cover her guilt.

Malloy states: "Oh my, it is you two! I have no idea how you found me, but I am so glad you are following up. I hope that poor homeless lady is OK. Thank you for coming. I am happy to discuss anything that will help you and her out."

We then interviewed Mrs. Malloy. Since she was in her home and not under arrest or in our custody, we did not read her her Miranda Rights.

She smells of wine. We ask her to step on to the porch to discuss the day's events. She admits that she has been drinking. PUBLIC INTOXICATION CPC 647(f)

6:50 PM - Before approaching the home, officers witness through the living room window physical domestic violence as Mrs. Malloy and her husband batter one another with large objects. Though upon inquiry, there were no signs of injury on either party. SPOUSAL BATTERY CPC 243(e)(1)

6:00 PM – Tailing subject in her silver Acura SUV, she turned onto Wildflower Lane and flashed headlight high beams. She was aiming her lights at deer near the road, though we initially assumed it to be some sort of gang signal to another member. Upon subsequent inspection of her SUV, officers saw plainly visible hunting equipment in back of vehicle. Flashing vehicle lights was apparently a form of "spotlighting" to freeze game animals in the beams to illegally poach the deer from her vehicle. FGC SECTION 2005 264(a)(2) USE OF LIGHTS WHILE HUNTING

12:25 PM – Mrs. Malloy is seen loitering and interacting with known members of the Downtown Bloods. She shares a freshly baked cake with the Bloods on a street inside the Downtown Bloods turf. Malloy is wearing red attire, the same color worn by the Bloods. She is seen exchanging "gang handshakes" with her fellow Bloods. Malloy also illegally feeds a homeless person in violation of the city's Anti-Feeding Ordinance.

GANG ACTIVITY:

- Actively participated in a criminal street gang.
- The intimidation of witnesses and victims, as defined in CPC Section 136.1.
- Threats to commit crimes resulting in death or great bodily injury, as defined in CPC Section 422.

- Gang Enhancement is 186.22(b)1A and in addition to being punished for the crimes charged, the alleged gang activity can add up to four more years prison for the same offense.

12:23 – Mrs. Malloy is seen pulling a 10" long knife from her purse. This is the weapon she mentioned in her threat to "remove your arms" from the elderly, mentally disabled transient Carol "Coco" McDuffy, BFA, age 66. FELONY CARRYING A CONCEALED DIRK OR DAGGER CPC 21310

12:20 – The subject, Mrs. Malloy, verbally and physically assaults and batters an elderly, disabled, black woman whilst yelling insensitive statements "crazy old loon." The victim of this Hate Crime is Carol "Coco" McDuffy. Officers witnessed Mrs. Malloy hit "Coco" the transient with her purse (which was found to conceal a knife) and threaten to "remove her arms."

This assault brings with it hate crime enhancements due to the offensive nature of Mrs. Malloy's thoughts and comments whilst committing the assault, and the fact that the victim is a member of elderly, economically, racially, and mentally protected populations. Backup during the assault came from three known Downtown Bloods gang members who further intimidated Coco to tears.

- CPC 241(a) ASSAULT - An assault is an unlawful attempt, coupled with a present ability, to commit a violent injury on the person of another.
- CPC 243(a) BATTERY - A battery is any willful and unlawful use of force or violence upon the person of another.
- CPC 422(a) CRIMINAL THREAT
- HATE CRIME ENHANCEMENT CPC 422.55.
    - (a) "Hate crime" means a criminal act committed, in

whole or in part, because of one or more of the following actual or perceived characteristics of the victim:

- (1) Disability.
- (2) Gender.
- (4) Race or ethnicity.

12:15 PM – Mrs. Malloy was witnessed loitering dressed in a red provocative dress, in an area known for prostitution, and controlled by the Bloods. She strutted back and forth along the sidewalk, waved and beckoned to passing cars, and approached at least one car.

CPC 653.24. LOITERING FOR THE PURPOSE OF ENGAGING IN A PROSTITUTION OFFENSE

(a) it is unlawful for any person to loiter in, on, or near any public place with the intent to commit prostitution. This intent is evidenced by acting in a manner and under circumstances which openly demonstrate the purpose of inducing, enticing, or soliciting prostitution, or procuring another to commit prostitution.

(b) Among some of the circumstances that may be considered in determining whether a person loiters with the intent to commit prostitution are that the person:

(l) Repeatedly beckons to, stops, engages in conversations with, or attempts to stop or engage in conversations with passersby.

(2) Repeatedly stops or attempts to stop motor vehicles by hailing the drivers, waving arms, or making any other

> bodily gestures and engages or attempts to engage the drivers or passengers of the motor vehicles in conversation.

12:10 PM - Police department forensic IT team confirmed that while loitering to solicit prostitution, Mrs. Malloy illegally accessed the internet of a local business. FELONY for violating the Computer Fraud and Abuse Act (CFAA) – UNAUTHORIZED USE OF AN UNSECURED WIFI CONNECTION

Mrs. Malloy's purse, in addition to concealing the knife, contained a prescription medication Vicodin tablet not prescribed to her. H&S 11350(a) - POSSESSION OF A CONTROLLED SUBSTANCE, plus B&P 4060

The back of the vehicle contained other illegal items. In addition to the weapon intended for illegal deer poaching, other items were clearly visible in the back of the SUV including a violin made with ebony and rosewood which violates the Lacey Act of 1900. The violin was confiscated and half was sent to the US Fish and Wildlife lab for testing, and the other half remains in the police department evidence room.

Mrs. Malloy was booked on 12 misdemeanors and felonies, plus Gang and Hate Crime enhancements. She is held in the county jail for $2.1 Million bail and could face many years in prison.

CHAPTER FOURTEEN

SCIENCE AND THE LAW

Science is a rational and logical system of exploring our world. The great thing about science is that it is true whether or not you believe in it. It is based upon open inquiry, peer review, experimentation, and proof. But the laws of science we experience every day are very different than the science practiced in the courtroom.

Science costs money; cancer research, space exploration, fossil dinosaur digs, observing dolphin behavior, etc. Studying and discovering knowledge is not cheap. When you are on trial, you are up against the vast resources of the government, and their talent pool of 'experts.' This enables police and prosecutors to pick, choose, and twist science and pseudoscience to demonize defendants.

Science fiction author Arthur C. Clarke one wrote that, "Any sufficiently advanced technology is indistinguishable from magic." In the Kubrick movie, based on Clarke's novel, *2001: A Space Odyssey*, the enigmatic, black monolith represented that frontier of knowledge, the intersection of truth and myth. It is important for the prosecution to make the scientific evidence seem so complex that the average juror cannot comprehend it, yet so simple that it is always infallible.

Remember that based on an AP poll, three-quarters of Americans—your jurors—believe in angels[122]. That makes it easier for them to believe

122 Poll: Nearly 8 in 10 Americans believe in angels. (2017). Cbsnews.com. Retrieved 27 December 2017, from http://www.cbsnews.com/news/poll-nearly-8-in-10-americans-believe-in-angels/

in the demons the prosecutors claim commit crimes, and the magical scientific rituals that 'prove' the prosecutor's case.

If a flat Earth supports the prosecution's theory of the crime, they will find PhDs and experts to prove we live on a disk and not a sphere. The only ways to combat these are to have an educated, free thinking jury, or a defense budget to spend more money on expert testimony. Otherwise, you cannot win against a magic black box of evidence, supported by the prosecution's air of authority imbued by the State.

Prosecutors present scientific evidence in a black box. They show off lots of bells and whistles attached to the outside of the box, but rarely let the jury or defense team look inside. They dazzle the jury with wonders of technology—the absoluteness of science—but hide the man behind the curtain who is pulling the levers.

The science presented to jurors by prosecutors is, more often than most people would think, an elaborate parlor trick that purports to put evidence in one side of the black box and truth out the other. But inside the box are variables like human error, malicious intent, unscientific conditions, faulty equipment, buggy source code, and just plain bad math.

Real science is based on the Scientific Method. The Scientific Method is a process scientists must follow in determining the workings of the universe. There are five basic components to the scientific method[123]:

- Observations to determine the nature of the phenomenon that is interesting to you (i.e. ask a question or identify a problem).
- Develop one or more hypotheses to explain this phenomenon. The hypotheses should be predictive—given a set of

123 The Scientific Method. Sciencemadesimple.com. Retrieved 27 December 2017, from http://www.sciencemadesimple.com/scientific_method.html

circumstances, the hypothesis should predict an outcome.

- Experiments to test the hypotheses. All valid scientific hypotheses must be testable.
- Analyze the experimental results and determine to what degree the results fit the predictions of the hypothesis.
- Communicate results; further modify and repeat the experiments.

So much shady evidence is backed by 'science' such as psychological profiles, handwriting analysis, DNA tests, fingerprints, medical testimony, crime scene data, drug and chemical analyses, blood alcohol levels, polygraph tests, and even hypnosis. Every type of forensic and scientific evidence can be faulty, falsified, or skewed to steer a jury one way or the other.

When the defense puts forth a shady expert, the prosecution excoriates them and blasts the faulty science. When the prosecution put up a shady expert, they can produce ten more shady experts to corroborate the State's scientific bias.

A good defense attorney anticipates the prosecution will present such experts and evidence. In fact, cognitive bias, calibration, contamination, chain of custody, statistical variance, and a number of other factors can impugn forensic evidence. All these scientific "smoking guns" are just types of evidence that a good attorney should question in court.

Blood Alcohol Levels

Driving while under the influence of alcohol is one of the most common crimes in America. Most of us drive, most of us drink, some of us drive drunk on occasion. But for cops, suspicion of DUI is a green light to pull over and interrogate any car, anytime. It is a crap shoot that sometimes pays off for the cops, but they have infinite throws of the dice. Now, it is up to you to prove you were not drinking. Your arrest for Driving Under the Influence is largely based on subjective decisions by the officer.

If you are pulled over, the officer will state a reason, like weaving, swerving, or crossing over a line. Other judgments like turning too sharply, not turning sharply enough, braking too slowly, braking too quickly, speeding, or slow driving—almost anything—can be used by an officer. "Reasonable suspicion" is all that is needed to stop or detain you. This is the first subjective test of your sobriety that has nothing to do with your actual alcohol consumption. The second covert test is the first contact with the officer. He is reading your demeanor, looking at your eyeballs, smelling your breath, and listening for slurred speech.

The fluttering movement of eyeballs can be an indication of how relaxed a person is; it is called the horizontal nystagmus test. If your focus flutters or wavers between targets, you might have been drinking. Or maybe you are on any number of safe medications that also cause rapid movement of the eyeball. Or maybe you are nervous because a cop is shining his light in your face.

Next, the officer will ask questions to get you talking, and volunteering evidence. "Have you been drinking?" If you answer "just a few beers," you have now admitted guilt. You should always be polite when interacting with police (remember, they have guns, and buddies with more guns), but you should not be lulled into thinking saying more to them will help your case.

The officer might ask you to "step out of the car," so he can informally and formally assess your coordination. This can ultimately lead to the Standard Field Sobriety Test. Stand on one foot, walk a line, touch your nose. There is no requirement in California for you to dance like a bear. If you are under arrest, always comply with a command by a cop. But until the officer decides to arrest you, there is no reason to comply with non-mandatory requests. Taking a field sobriety coordination test is entirely voluntary, entirely subjective, and never a good idea.

These observational tests are not designed to measure impairment, and are not objective. They are merely guidelines to help an officer decide whether or not to arrest you for driving under the influence—or an excuse to arrest you based on their whim.

In 1991, Dr. Spurgeon Cole of Clemson University conducted a study of the accuracy of Field Sobriety Tests[124]. The experiment involved videotaped people performing six common field sobriety tests, then showed the tapes to 14 police officers and asked them to decide whether the suspects had "had too much to drink and drive." Unknown to the officers, the actual blood-alcohol concentration of each of the 21 DUI subjects was zero! The result: the officers gave their opinion that 46 percent of these innocent people were too drunk to be able to drive.

These physical field sobriety tests are not science, they are theater. They are based on subjective observations using tests that are poorly controlled, not scientific, nor repeatable.

Then finally, we bring in technology to help the officer determine if he will arrest you for DUI: the field breath test. These tests are called PAS tests, an acronym for Preliminary Alcohol Screening test. This breath test involves a portable version of the larger Evidentiary Breath Test found in hospitals and police jails. Note, one is preliminary, and the other is evidentiary.

The PAS is just another tool to help the officer establish probable cause. For years, it was not admissible in court in California. But of course, since it is a tool for the Prosecution, it has been accepted as evidence more and

124 Cole, S., & Nowaczyk, R. (1994). Field Sobriety Tests: Are They Designed for Failure?. Perceptual And Motor Skills, 79(1), 99-104. http://dx.doi.org/10.2466/pms.1994.79.1.99

more. It is also an entirely voluntary test that you can refuse to take before being arrested. It is also very prone to error and manipulation.

It is a common trick of law enforcement to hold the portable breath analyzer near their police radio. The radio frequency interference causes the device to deliver higher readings and more false positives.

During the entire interaction, the police officer only has two options: arrest you or let you go. Everything in-between, the conversation, the sobriety test, the field Breathalyzer, are all enabled because you allowed them. If you are arrested, you will be required to give a blood or breath sample. Up until you are arrested, you should not volunteer evidence that can be used against you.

A breath test at a lab, hospital, or police station is done using a larger, more reliable machine than those used in the field. These tests are admissible as evidence of your insobriety.

According to Dr. Michael Hiastala, Professor of Physiology, Biophysics and Medicine at the University of Washington:

> Breath testing, as currently used, is a very inaccurate method for measuring BAC. Even if the breath testing instrument is working perfectly, physiological variables prevent any reasonable accuracy... Breath testing for alcohol using a single test method should not be used for scientific, medical or legal purposes where accuracy is important[125].

One study of breath tests determined that breath readings vary at least 15 percent from actual blood alcohol levels[126].

125 Hlastala, M. (1985). Physiological Errors Associated with Alcohol Breath Testing. The Champion, (19).

126 Simpson, G. (1987). Accuracy and precision of breath-alcohol measurements for a random subject in the postabsorptive state. Clinical Chemistry, 33(2).

Furthermore, at least 23 percent of all individuals tested will have breath results in excess of true blood-alcohol levels. A good defense attorney will challenge a breath test's validity, but the stigma of being a drunk driver with a high BAC level has already been attached. Blood tests for determining blood alcohol levels are more accurate than breath tests.

The evidence collected from a blood alcohol test takes juries from the realm of the officer's subjective opinion to the realm of science. The prosecutor will stand behind the measurements and readings from this complex lab equipment, and sell the results as gospel to a jury. The defense must trust this black box's results, as courts have forbidden access to the machine's workings or source code.

A number of factors can affect the blood test results. Gender, body mass, age, diet, and hydration levels are all variables that should be taken into account for a scientific measurement. But the cops and courts have a one-size-fits-all approach. Science is clinical and repeatable; DUI testing is nothing more than theater.

Fingerprints (Subjective Error-Prone 19th Century Technology)

Since caveman times, a person could leave his mark, his signature, with a stamp of their finger. The science and technology to record and identify people and their unique fingerprints has improved, but the idea is Paleolithic. The matching of fingerprints to suspects is based on subjective observations comparing prints to identify the owner of the finger.

With so many more fingerprints being taken and stored in databases, and the reliance on computers to aid in finding matches, the number of false positives is rising. Humans program computers to look for matches. Computer code is as susceptible to the biases and flaws in matching prints as is an expert in a lab.

The FBI leads the charge on inflating the infallibility and reliability of this anti-defendant tool. "The Science of Fingerprints" is the name of the FBI's manual on the subject. The FBI insists that fingerprint identification is an exact science that can be used to match prints with 100 percent certainty.

Attorney Barry Scheck of the Innocence Project says: "We have always been told that fingerprint evidence is the gold standard of forensic science. If you have a print, you have your man. But it is not an objective decision. It is inexact, partial, and open to all sorts of critics."

It is true that no two fingerprints are identical. But in many cases, the similarities can be so close that they are difficult to differentiate under the best conditions. Yet, subjective fingerprint experts believe they can look at dusted and lifted latent print fragments from a crime scene, and make a solid match to a clinically recorded print.

"After all this time, we still have no idea how well fingerprinting really works," Robert Epstein, an assistant federal public defender in Philadelphia, said. Epstein goes further:

> The F.B.I. calls it a science. By what definition is it a science? Where are the data? Where are the studies? We know that fingerprint examiners are not always right. But are they usually right or are they sometimes right? That, I am afraid, we don't know. Are there a few people in prison who shouldn't be? Are there many? Nobody has ever bothered to try and find out. Look closely at the great discipline of fingerprinting. It's not only not a science—it should not even be admitted as evidence in an American court of law[127].

127 Specter, M. (2002). Do Fingerprints Lie? The New Yorker, May 27th, 2002. Retrieved 27 December 2017, from http://www.michaelspecter.com/wp-content/uploads/fingerprint.pdf

It is doubtful that the methods used by fingerprint analysts would pass the tests of scientific rigor required by hard scientists.

In his case, seeking to invalidate fingerprint evidence, Epstein showed that standards for examiners vary widely, and that errors on proficiency tests—which are given irregularly and in a variety of forms—are far from rare. The critical evidence consisted of two fingerprint marks lifted from a car used in a robbery. To prepare for the trial, F.B.I. officials had sent the prints to agencies in all fifty states; roughly twenty percent failed to identify them correctly. A one-in-five chance of being utterly wrong on a potentially life-or-death matter. It is a shame to label that as science.

Shaken Baby Syndrome

A colleague and dear friend, the late Jaye Ryan, ardently pursued the truth to give her clients justice. As well as being a skilled criminal defense lawyer, Ms. Ryan was trained as a scientist with experience in the fields of forensic, pathology, microbiology and general laboratory science.

With her prior training and employment, Jaye Ryan had an impressive record of winning cases by challenging, excluding, and disproving forensic evidence and professional opinions that are often presented by the prosecution. One area where she excelled was in calling out the pseudoscience of Shaken Baby Syndrome. It is a pseudoscientific diagnosis that jails parents accused of savagely killing their infants.

Defending against and working to disprove Shaken Baby Syndrome is a very challenging position to assume. But the opposition to a bad medical diagnosis is not the same as condoning child abuse. Shaken Baby Syndrome is a touchstone that sets off emotions. The victims are innocent, the murder of a child is pure evil, and baby killers should be nailed to the wall. Except in the case of SBS, the "scientific evidence" of the cold blooded murder of an infant by a loving guardian is based on malarkey. An example of your bias of loving babies played up to allow a prosecutor to feather her cap with a spurious conviction.

An organization called The National Center on Shaken Baby Syndrome (NCSBS) has a mission to prevent Shaken Baby Syndrome through the development and implementation of educational programs, public policy and research; to establish networks; and to support and train families, caregivers and professionals. To justify their mission (and budget), they need to have an epidemic to advocate against. To that end, their statistics claim that in the U.S., at least one baby a day is murdered via Shaken Baby Syndrome. That is a lot of babies, and a lot of craven, violent, monstrous, murderous parents.

Prosecution-biased experts created a theory explaining certain cases resulting in injuries to children and called it Shaken Baby Syndrome (SBS). Traditionally, SBS refers to violent shaking of an infant that leads to the infant's death. Oftentimes, shaken baby syndrome results in serious injuries to the infant's head or brain. There is so much controversy surrounding this issue that whole schools of experts come to diametrically opposed conclusions reviewing the evidence surrounding the causes for victim children's injuries.

Prosecution experts believe there is a pervasive, continuing large-scale "syndrome" of babies being shaken by loved ones until they are irreparably harmed. Other, more neutral scientific experts, acknowledge that some parents harm their children, but realize there can be completely innocent explanations for how a baby was injured.

The diagnosis of SBS is defined by three internal conditions: swelling of the brain, bleeding on the surface of the brain, and bleeding in the back of the eyes. Doctors, nurses, social workers, and prosecutors are trained to seek out these cases as SBS. The diagnosis gives doctors a way to account for unexplained head injuries in babies, and prosecutors a stronger case for criminal intent when police had no witnesses, no confessions, and only circumstantial evidence.

Oftentimes, SBS is named as the cause of death, even when the infant's death may have stemmed from another medical condition. This is especially true in cases where a hemorrhage was found in the infant's brain and/or head at the time of death. When Shaken Baby Syndrome is named the cause of death, medical and legal professionals are quick to presume it was the parents or primary caregiver's fault. Once this assumption is made, parents and guardians can be charged with murder and child abuse. Even if the accused parties are innocent, they will be subjected to criminal investigation and prosecution.

In over a decade, medical scientific testing has been unable to show whether violent shaking can produce the bleeding and swelling long attributed to the diagnosis, and doctors have found that accidents and diseases can trigger identical conditions in babies. In fact, just being a baby can cause these symptoms. Coughing, crying, falling while learning to walk, and regular baby play cause the same micro-injuries that are added up to an SBS diagnosis. Post-mortem, pathologists cannot tell the child abuse deaths of infants from the ones killed by illness. Bias is the basis for charges.

The science surrounding brain injury, its causes and explanations for conditions, is complex. Child abuse is a terrible thing, but so is the false accusation of being a child abuser, or a baby killer. SBS is another example of how charged circumstances can push people to outrage before logic.

DNA Evidence—Not Foolproof

Two people are brutally murdered. Luckily the cops find a separated pair of bloody gloves soaked with the blood of both victims, plus the killer's own blood. One glove was left at the crime scene, the other was stashed behind the house of the prime suspect. On TV, this would be an open and shut case, the glove matches the glove and the DNA seals the deal.

If you haven't figured it out yet, this case was on TV, live, in the televised trial of The People v. O.J. Simpson. It was the Summer of 1994, and famous football player and movie star O.J. Simpson was on trial for the murder of his ex-wife and her acquaintance Ronald Goldman.

The science of DNA identification is pretty well developed, grounded in hard work and reviewed studies. But the Simpson case shows how the tables can be turned on "science" by exploiting bias. In this instance, celebrity, race, politics, police mistrust, and the money a defense needs to overcome the same spending presented by the prosecution.

Simpson had the wherewithal to hire two specialized DNA attorneys to his defense team. The legal "Dream Team" that represented O.J. had nine of the best attorneys in the country. You or I would have gone to jail based on just one of those bloody gloves. But the Dream Team had the resources to find flaws, errors, and inconsistencies in the LAPD Lab processes, the chutzpah to call them out on it, and the guts to back their claims.

The LAPD lab likely benefitted from the deep inspection they received by the Simpson defense, and the public scrutiny that followed. They'd be less likely to mishandle samples, break the chain of custody, enable cross-contamination, and other lazy errors going forward.

With the goal of finding where the science ends and the errors or bias begin, the questions and pushback that the defense team directed at the forensic evidence are valid for every case based on lab evidence.

Drug Lab Results—Lazy Or Corrupt Lab Work Can Ruin Credibility

A scientific lab is a lot like a kitchen. There are freezers, coolers, hot plates, and colorful chemicals. Just like in a kitchen, there are some you would eat in, and others you would rate one star and steer clear of. Analyzing DNA or chemicals requires a scientific stringency that is free from contamination. A smudge on a beaker, or the breath of the observer is enough to invalidate results. Some science labs are aware of the sensitivities of equipment, and how to nudge a result one way or another. Others may have lazy or corrupt workers who want to rush through projects and get home.

In San Francisco, the Crime Lab was scrutinized for a number of problems. From 2010 to 2015, problem after problem was revealed, exposing crimes and carelessness with evidence.

The most recent scandal revealed that the civilian lab technician and her supervisor were not properly trained or certified in handling DNA evidence. They had each failed a DNA proficiency exam and should have been barred from working on evidence. Over 1,400 cases went through the hands of these unqualified lab workers.

A few years earlier in 2010, the San Francisco crime lab was rocked when an employee was caught stealing cocaine, causing over 1,700 cases to be tossed out.

These anecdotes are big cases that made the news. Every city and county needs to be rigorous in maintaining the scientific levels of cleanliness and discipline expected from hospitals and universities. Unfortunately, as long as the lab is busting bad guys, they can avoid scrutiny.

Conclusion

Bias in the science lab invalidates any actual science. In the courtroom, bias is exploited by prosecutors to shift opinion against the defendant. Bias is used to lull a jury into accepting prosecution physical evidence as fact.

Remember that six percent of the American public believe in unicorns. 18 percent still believe the sun revolves around the Earth[128].

With so little scientific understanding, many people revert to belief in old wives' tales and superstitions. This is fun for campfire stories, but it is a disaster when fairy tales influence justice in a police station, crime lab, or court room.

A final example of bias and pseudoscience in our courtrooms and lives. The association of full moons with crime rates is a persistent myth that is perpetuated every 28 days. The Planet Earth, and humanity have a long relationship with our moon, the Moon. Luna is tied into our calendars, tides, migrations, festivals, and religions. There is no doubt that the moon has a significant impact on the Earth and its inhabitants. But we attribute much more to her influence than she is due.

A full moon is a beautiful and remarkable event, and its presence is often noted when strange things occur. When we experience something interesting, like an accident, disaster, crime, insomnia, a 'bump' in the night, a full moon gets noted—because a full moon is notable. When those things happen the rest of the month, the big notable thing is not present to influence our perception. The bright full moon creates its own recall bias in an audience.

A few studies from the '70s and '80s analyzed police reports and hospital records to look for a correlation between events and full moons. These studies are often cited. But, they involved small samples, and one neglected

128 Morford, M. (2013). 37 Percent of People Completely Lost. HuffPost. Retrieved 27 December 2017, from https://www.huffingtonpost.com/mark-morford/37-percent-of-people-comp_b_2864142.html

to note that two of the three full moons studied were on weekends, when more people were out and about at night. Statistical error. Today, with Big Data, and accurate information recorded and shared worldwide, the causation between violence and full moons has been discredited.

The influence of the moon on crime is the same as the influence of the Zodiac on crime: none. Believe me, if there were science to support a full moon "Lunacy Defense," I would use it to save a client. But there is no foundation there. On the flip side, similarly disproven pseudoscience is presented by the prosecution and strictly enforced by judges. Police and prosecutors have the same biases and misconceptions as many people.

Science and reason are as important in life as in the courtroom and in the lab. I encourage you to question things for yourself. Pseudoscience does not belong in court. Science with bias is not science.

CHAPTER FIFTEEN

MEDIA PORTRAYAL OF LAW ENFORCEMENT: PROGRAMMING AND 'MEAN WORLD SYNDROME'

On a nightly basis, the power of law enforcement is idolized in the news and on prime-time TV shows. The ′programming′ on television tells us to accept law enforcement's authority as absolute. The 'programming' on TV tells us that our neighborhoods are in a state of war, besieged by criminals. It is a 'Nightly Parade of the Bogeyman' presented by a media whose job it is to scare you, literally programming us into a perpetual state of fear and uncertainty or an unnatural fixation with violence, carnage, and bloodthirsty vengeance. The flip side of the 'fear' message is the message to blindly support those who present themselves in the guise of authority, for those are the people who can save us from all the crime and criminals.

The fact is, we live in a time when crime is statistically decreasing. Crime is not really getting worse in California; we just hear about it a lot. According to the Public Policy Institute of California[129], our state's violent crime rate dropped by one percent in 2014 to a 47-year low of 393 per 100,000 residents. Crime swelled in the '70s, wobbled in the '80s, and peaked in 1992. Since then, violent crime in the state has declined substantially.

---

129 Crime Trends in California. Public Policy Institute of California. Retrieved 9 February 2018, from http://www.ppic.org/main/publication_show.asp?i=1036

Given that crime is decreasing, why do so many people think it's on the upswing? Quite simply, it's because they believe what they see on TV. The news, crime shows, prime-time dramas, documentaries, and dark comedies they watch on TV feature a significant amount of crime and victimization—because that's what makes for an interesting show.

This wouldn't be a problem if it were just entertainment, but it's much more than that. According to a study from Purdue University, crime TV viewers believe there are 2.5 times more murders, than people who don't watch crime shows, and this has an alarming effect on their mental state. The researchers call it 'Mean World Syndrome.' Simply put, people believe the world is a fundamentally dangerous place.

Earlier research by media scholar George Gerbner associates Mean World Syndrome with paranoia about imminent victimization. When people are in a state of fear or living in a state of perpetual victimhood, it makes them come down more harshly on defendants and have less compassion, empathy, and understanding[130].

"If it bleeds, it leads!" That is the mantra of the mainstream (Lamestream) news media. The stoic days of Walter Cronkite are long gone and today's TV news needs to compete with 400 channels plus a million websites. Responsible journalism is still around, but shock, crime, and fright are what gets the ratings and revenue.

Escaped killers on the lam in Dallas. Serial rapist attacking joggers in Portland. Sniper targeting commuters in Maryland. These news stories are important, relevant, and informative to the people of Texas, Portland, and Maryland. They are not "news" to anyone else. They are shock pieces

130 Gerbner, G., & Gross, L. (1976). Living with Television: The Violence Profile. Journal Of Communication, 26(2), 172-199. http://dx.doi.org/10.1111/j.1460-2466.1976.tb01397.x

meant to scare readers and viewers around the country, and to sell ads during the news. People in California have nothing to fear from the aforementioned jailbreakers, rapist, or sniper. But the headline "Rapist targets joggers, news at 11," gets viewers who are duped into thinking the story is local and relevant, or attracts their morbid interest with the lure of a salacious story.

Evening news and daily papers portray a reality where crime is out of control and we are all doomed but for a thin blue line of heroes and federal bureaucrats that stand between us and anarchy. We are all potential victims of horrible crimes, and the police and the authority of government save the day every time. It's a mean, mean, mean world out there.

This oversimplification of law enforcement spills into prime-time TV as well. Many of the most popular TV shows are police procedurals that present a horrific crime and a miraculous conclusion before the end of the hour. The popular portrayal of crime as ubiquitous and cops as superhuman, colors the average citizen's understanding of the criminal justice system. By "average citizen," I mean jurors.

All too often, I've seen the narratives established on TV picked up by prosecutors and police in court, then regurgitated to the jury to help them get convictions. DA's frequently play to this lowest common denominator in front of a jury. Jurors seem to go right along with it as though they are part of some TV documentary or drama.

In 2003, the average local TV channel showed 3.7 hours of news per weekday. By 2013, the number of hours a day dedicated to news had grown to 5.3. Over the same period, revenue from TV station news equally increased. In 2002, news accounted for 39 percent of the average TV station's programming. In 2013, news operations accounted for 50 percent of the total revenue from a TV station. Local news viewership has been steady, it has even increased a bit over the last few years[131].

In a typical hour of television, there are 10-20 minutes of advertisements. On a network show syndicated to a station, the local station only gets a few minutes an hour to sell their own ads and generate revenue. Since local news is owned and produced by the local station, they keep all the ad revenue for the slot. The greater revenue share, combined with affordable production costs for an hour of unscripted live television, make for a big win for local TV station news.

Crime makes for great news production. There is a shocking headline to grab the audience's interest, there is the mystery of who-what-when-where-why, there is the narrative of good and evil, escape and pursuit, victims and tragedy. It's all very tidy—especially when law enforcement packages up the narrative for easy dissemination and consumption. The news bureau receives a ready-to-report story from the police, with the potential for press conferences, breaking news, alerts, and updates throughout the day.

Almost every law enforcement agency in California has a designated Public Information Officer, or PIO. This is a media savvy public relations specialist who packages police investigations and activities into media friendly nuggets.

Police control the information about a crime, the victims, the suspects, the charges, the evidence, and the entire incident. Cops release details of the crime that can outrage the public. They point to suspects or arrestees and present the 'police side' of the story to the media. The police even set the initial charges and the initial bail amounts, often intended to make the crimes look worse, and the cops look more heroic.

131 Pew Research Center. (2015). State of the News Media 2015. Retrieved 9 February 2018, from http://www.journalism.org/2015/04/29/local-tv-news-fact-sheet-2015/

One of my cases in the Bay Area involved an upright citizen who was active in local commerce, church, and community. On a tip, the police searched his home, found some firearms, and arrested him. As per usual, the police laid out all the firearms on the driveway to make it look like an amazing cache. The guns were described as "dozens of exotic semi-automatic weapons." The cops were quick to brag about the arrest, publish the name of my client, show off his guns, and set his bail at over a million dollars. He was portrayed as a menace to society, and the cops as saviors who swept an undesirable off the streets.

What the cops did not share was that my 'dangerous' client was allowed to help the police load their confiscated evidence into their van to keep any of it from being damaged. They did not mention that all the guns had been legally purchased and safely stored. The cops set the preposterously high bail, but did not mention that they let my client go, with no charges filed, as soon as the 72 hours to either file or let him go were through.

My client was named on countless news outlets. It was his turn at being the boogeyman in the nightly parade. He was branded as a dangerous nut who owned guns for a suburban army, and should be locked up. But in reality, he was a nice guy, a hardworking dad, with a legally-purchased collection that a few cops got overly enthusiastic about. He was unceremoniously released, free as a bird, with not a peep from the media.

Public opinion is swayed early on by the police and news media's collaborative efforts in presenting the 'facts' on a case. News reporters get a readymade story with all the investigative work and half the writing handed to them by law enforcement. The alleged victims are canonized, the crimes magnified, the threat to society blared to the public over thousands upon thousands of TV and radio speakers. Those accused, and their defense attorneys, often do not get to set the record straight until trial.

The bureaucratic side of government feeds the news beast as well, imposing their alerts and fear mongering into our daily lives. Statewide "Amber Alerts" for a familial kidnapping 500 miles away. Emergency Response System alerts for rising river waters on the other side of the state. Seizing control of our televisions, DVRs, and cell phones to impose their 'news' and the hope and salvation of the official solution. This State of Fear is perpetuated by the Governmental State which, according to government officials' own emails as released on Wikileaks, is in turn controlled by the Deep State.

We usually see the hyperbolic inflation of crimes and glorification of police in the mainstream news. But the brainwashing extends into prime time, where police-friendly fiction dominates.

According to Deadline[132], in the 2014-2015 TV season, the top rated (based on number of viewers) police shows were:

1. NCIS
2. NCIS: New Orleans
3. Criminal Minds
4. Blue Bloods
5. Hawaii Five-O
6. The Mentalist
7. NCIS: Los Angeles
8. CSI
9. Castle
10. CSI: Cyber

132 Full 2014-15 TV Season Series Rankings. (2015). Deadline. Retrieved 9 February 2018, from http://deadline.com/2015/05/2014-15-full-tv-season-ratings-shows-rankings-1201431167/

For the 2015-2016 TV Season[133], it was the same as it's always been, more schlagging to the authoritarian boot. Out of the top 50 Nielsen-rated TV programs, a full 24—almost half—of all the shows had to do with the executive branch; cops, detectives, crimes, or government in some way.

3 NCIS
4 NCIS: New Orleans
5 The X-files
6 Blue Bloods
11 60 Minutes
12 Criminal Minds
16 NCIS – Encore
18 The Blacklist
20 NCIS: Los Angeles
21 Hawaii Five-0
23 The Good Wife
24 Blindspot
25 Scandal
28 How To Get Away With Murder
31 Shades Of Blue
38 60 Minutes Presents
39 Elementary
40 Castle
42 Criminal Minds: Beyond Borders
43 Chicago PD

133 Full 2015-16 TV Season Series Rankings (2016). Deadline. Retrieved 9 February 2018, from http://deadline.com/2016/05/tv-season-2015-2016-series-rankings-shows-full-list-1201763189/

44 The Mysteries Of Laura

46 CSI: Cyber

47 Mike & Molly

48 Law And Order: SVU

If you think maybe something changed in 2017, take a look at positions 15-26 in the list of most watched TV programs, which includes all shows, even live sport broadcasts for the 2016-2017 season[134]:

15. **How To Get Away With Murder** ABC
16. Scandal ABC
17. Survivor CBS
18. Talking Dead AMC
19. **NCIS** CBS
20. Chicago Fire NBC
21. The Goldbergs ABC
22. **Law & Order: SVU** NBC
23. **Criminal Minds** CBS
24. Black-ish ABC
25. **Lethal Weapon** Fox
26. **Chicago PD** NBC

These cop shows garner huge ratings and viewership of 10-20 million people per week. Many of them are presented as police procedural dramas. They should more accurately be called pure fiction, or fantasy adventure.

134 Schneider, M. (2017). These Are the 100 Most-Watched TV Shows of the 2016-17 Season: Winners and Losers. IndieWire. Retrieved 9 February 2018, from http://www.indiewire.com/2017/05/most-watched-tv-show-2016-2017-season-the-walking-dead-this-is-us-football-1201832878/

But the sad truth remains, most Americans get their knowledge of the criminal justice system from these programs.

In these law-enforcement-centric shows, the heroes are the police, and they run rampant over the Constitution, and sometimes the laws of science, to catch the bad guys. The reading of a suspect's Miranda rights is often a tag at the end of an episode, a sting, an epilogue, to notify viewers that all is well and the bad guy has been captured.

In TV world, Miranda Rights are for bad guys and asking for a lawyer—"lawyering up"—is depicted as a sign of sleaziness, weakness, or guilt. When a defendant is found not guilty on TV, it is depicted as a trick or loophole exploited by a shady defense attorney, and a reason to get angry at a broken system where the bad guy gets away with murder; a reason to come to court during your inevitable jury service and vote "Guilty!" no matter what tricks the defense attorney may use.

These popular TV crime shows rarely depict police officers lying or 'shading the truth' to get their conviction, or prosecutors failing to provide exculpatory information to the defense, or judges being horribly biased in favor of law enforcement and the prosecution in order to keep their "tough on crime" reputations intact and not piss off those law enforcement unions that are so critical to their reelection.

Perhaps if the real bias against the defense that pervades the vast majority of courtrooms today were shown on TV too, people wouldn't be so misled. Americans used to believe in the phrase, "I'd rather let 99 guilty men go than hang one innocent man," but now it seems the court of public opinion is louder—and the programmed public seldom sides with the accused.

According to recent data from the state's Office of the Attorney General, only about half the felony crimes reported in California result in an arrest.

Of those arrests, the conviction (or guilty plea) rate is about 67 percent. But in TV land, every hour starts with a crime and ends with an arrest and eventual conviction. This creates a perception of hyper-efficiency in law enforcement.

In real life, you are supposed to be innocent until proven guilty. Statistically, however, you have a very low chance of being acquitted once accused. When a juror sits in the box, their expectations of guilt are informed by TV rates (100 percent guilty), which are a fantasy, or the occasional special episode where the producers want to rile up the audience and let the bad guy get away with murder based on a loophole or technicality.

A criminal investigation on a TV show is often accelerated by a witness or suspect blabbing to police. A cop asking questions will point out that the person must answer or be held for obstructing justice. People are always blabbing to cops on TV. Don't Do It! In the real world, you should never talk to cops about a crime they might implicate you in. Just ask for an attorney!

If you want to help the police by giving an eyewitness account, or background on a crime or suspect, it may help them catch a bad guy. But sometimes the cops are lying about their reason for interviewing people surrounding a crime; more often than not, they really want to talk to you about making you a suspect.

The FBI is really good at info gathering. They'll use a casual interview with a neighbor, friend, or housemate to gather background on a suspect, then coerce that interviewee into much more damning testimony.

The FBI will ask you innocuous questions about the suspect, then they will come back and point out minor errors and inaccuracies in your statements, and threaten to arrest you for lying, or worse, as an accomplice. "You claimed you were home asleep at 10AM, but then, how did you send texts to the suspect at 9AM? Tell us the truth about him being at the crime scene that morning or we will lock you up for lying to us."

The FBI, based upon judicial friendliness and the lapdog compliance of federal juries, will use the federal "Obstruction of Justice" charge to the hilt; you will talk to them and you will tell them what they want to hear or they will literally make a federal case out of it.

Here are some of the top myths that are perpetuated by many popular cop shows:

- **Cops always tell the truth, they are not allowed to lie**. In reality, the opposite is true. Appellate courts have given police the right to say anything they want to you, to get you to talk or confess. Remember it is your right to refuse to talk, but they will entice, trick, or cheat to get you to waive your right and incriminate yourself. "We have your GPS records." "Your DNA was found at the scene." "Your friend told us the truth." "There is one deal on the table for whoever squeals first." Regardless of the lie, the simplest way to avoid getting trapped is to avoid speaking to law enforcement. But on TV everyone is chatty right up to jail. Heck, even their defense attorneys bring them to the table to talk. In real life, no real defense attorney ever does that.
- **Cops can help you in your plea deal.** In line with police often lying to get evidence or incriminating information, cops on TV are sometimes shown making a deal with the person they are interviewing. If you are facing charges, the charges are filed by the prosecutor. The cops cannot make a deal for your charges or possible sentence. They do not have the authority to make deals nor do they routinely come into court and plead before a judge

for a lenient sentence. ADAs and federal prosecutors will sort out a deal in the weeks and sometimes days before trial.

- **Cops have to read you your rights**. Miranda law is actually very simple. Police only have to read you these rights during: 1. Custodial 2.Interrogation, meaning when you're actually in custody and when the cops are saying or doing something designed to make you talk. Talk about loopholes, I'm sure you can see 1,000 different loopholes enabling an officer to not read you your rights without causing any detrimental legal effects. In fact, failure to read Miranda does not make an arrest itself invalid. It simply means that any information obtained through questioning without Miranda will be excluded from admission in court until the client testifies. Also, even if an officer royally screws up the Miranda admonition, a judge will overwhelmingly rule that it was 'close enough.' Moreover, sometimes an officer doesn't need to collect a statement. If no questioning occurs, then no reading of Miranda is required.
- **Miranda warnings mean you are arrested**. Miranda warnings have nothing to do with whether or not someone is under arrest. Occasionally, I'll read a report where an officer is being thorough and reading someone the Miranda admonition even when the person isn't yet in custody or under arrest. Those times are vastly outweighed by the amount of times someone gets screwed over in the process.
- **Crimes are clear-cut**. Crime on TV is often heinous, premeditated, and conveys some sort of reward to the perpetrator. The stereotypical characterizations of criminals and their motives are a pastiche of exciting cases. The stakes are high, the crimes

are grave, and the investigation is a 'cat and mouse' thriller. But in reality, crimes are usually messy, clumsy, shady affairs. There are two sides to the story, the 'victim' is not always without involvement. There is way more he said/she said that the cops sort out by arresting people arbitrarily, then letting lawyers clear up the details. Further, most people wouldn't care if about 40 percent of the cases that I represent got lost forever, heck they might even cheer a dismissal on. I've often pondered that if all of the people who go on 'ride alongs' with law enforcement would give an equal amount of time volunteering at the public defender's office, they would probably come away thinking that at least 40 percent of the cases that are filed, that clog up our criminal justice system, are unwarranted, completely unnecessary, and merely a result of a cop's or prosecutor's personal vendetta.

- **CSI is magic**. DNA results, security camera footage, cell phone tracking; TV shows make science into science fiction. They take a kernel of truth, the theory behind a scientific technique, and make it into a parlor trick the police perform to get evidence and nail convictions. This conditions audiences (jurors) to accept the scientific evidence presented by law enforcement as gospel. In reality, science is just that, science. It is as reliable and honest as those working on it. It takes time and money. It has a margin of error, and is prone to user error. Most importantly, it cuts both ways. On TV, it is the prosecution that delivers infallible scientific evidence, but DNA and other CSI techniques can exonerate as well as falsely convict. CSI creator Anthony Zuiker admits, "We do have same day DNA results, but no one wants to watch a TV show where it takes four months to get results."

Nearly half of the top police TV shows feature an enhanced federal or State level police force; fictional FBI and federal task forces, or a mythical State Detective force. This sets a dangerous precedent that the federal government should be policing our local communities. It paints the Feds as a shadowy, yet benevolent force that is there to protect us from harm, like the paragons of efficiency and good will. It should come as no surprise that many of these shows benefit from actual funding by the government to paint them in a positive light. The programs are funded by law enforcement and are as much statist propaganda as they are entertainment, maybe more.

Using a government facility as a setting, or a real piece of equipment as a prop, can add to the realism and intensity of a show. But fighter jets and sets cost money. If your show is friendly to the government and depicts law enforcement in a positive light, they will loan you resources to aid your production.

The dodgy relationship between the media and law enforcement is not new. Way back in the '30s, J. Edgar Hoover and the FBI collaborated on the show, "Gangbusters," which ran for decades. The FBI maintains an Office of Public Affairs that reaches out to writers and producers to offer assistance. From their website: "our Office of Public Affairs is a small staff that spends a portion of its time working with domestic and international screenwriters, producers, authors, and other industry personnel associated with TV programs, documentaries, made-for-TV movies, books, and motion pictures."

They have been known to list[135] the types of services available to productions who are friendly to law enforcement:

135 A Guide for Writers, Authors, and Producers. (2008). FBI. Retrieved 9 February 2018, from https://archives.fbi.gov/archives/news/stories/2008/october/a-guide-for-writers-authors-and-producers-1

- Guidance on content regarding FBI investigations, procedures, structure, and history
- Information on costumes, props, scenery, and weapons
- Fact checks
- Liaison and coordination with local FBI field offices
- Coordination of location shots
- Access to FBI facilities for filming scenes, interviews, or b-roll footage

Millions of dollars are spent by the FBI to maintain their Hollywood relationships, and millions more are dedicated to brand placements and tacit endorsements via clandestine payments. The result is a skewed representation of FBI agents as 'salt of the earth' knights of justice. The 'white hats' called in when the local cops cannot get the job done. This is quite simply domestic propaganda to lull the people of the United States into complacency with State 'Reights' and Authority.

When people put their cash on the counter to be entertained, they want escapist fun such as animated animals, space warriors, and superheroes. The top 500 domestic box office highest-grossing movies of all time include only a handful police-centric films. Beverly Hills Cop, Rush Hour, and Paul Blart: Mall Cop are preferred by the paying cinema audience. These are broad parodies of police work that mock the status quo, not the fawning police procedurals that rule TV.

Movies, as opposed to TV, usually tend to be a little more balanced. There is cinematic work by directors and screenwriters who seek to reveal the gritty truth of police work and shine a light on misconduct. Though broadcast television is dominated by police-ist propaganda, the trend does not carry over to more thoughtful and artistic platforms like cable TV and the movies. Free pulp fiction over the airwaves feeds the masses, but cop-themed content does not figure as much in the top-grossing movie lists.

Artistic and documentary works have generated changes in society and the lives of police victims. Errol Morris' 1988 documentary, "The Thin Blue Line" showed how botched police work and a misguided prosecution jailed the wrong man in Texas; he was released soon after. More recently, the Netflix documentary series, "Making a Murderer" revealed many potential police errors and misconduct in a case in Michigan.

Looking at Best Picture Oscar nominees and the Metacritic list of highest-rated movies of all-time shows a darker portrayal of police; a grittier, more critical picture. The films include: L.A. Confidential, Serpico, The French Connection, The Departed, In the Heat of the Night, and Chinatown. Driven by the auteur, the need to sell ads and appease network execs takes a backseat to revealing institutional racism, cover-ups, brutality, and misconduct by law enforcement. These are not escapist romps, but serious, thoughtful looks at troubling themes in society. Thoughtful movies do not always equate to box office success, just like thoughtful police dramas do not fare well on free, network TV.

On cable, where art and thoughtfulness are subsidized by subscription fees, cops are less venerated than on the old free networks. "The Wire" on HBO is a realistic, naturalistic look at police work in Baltimore. FX's "The Shield" is a take on the corrupt Rampart division in Los Angeles. "Dexter" on Showtime shows the line between cops and psychopaths murderously crossed. Common themes on cable police shows include distrust of police and the conflict between ethics and political expediency, with most characters portrayed as displaying both vice and virtue. These are not the idolatrous crime-fighting fantasies of CSI and Hawaii Five-O.

Parallel to the art and social statement of paid entertainment platforms, established journalistic operations occasionally look into the real workings of the police force. The "If it bleeds, it leads" mentality sells papers and gets viewers for the news, but in-depth exposés of corruption and injustice give journalists respect and awards. Major papers like *The New York Times* have the clout, funding, and reputation to reveal the truth about the dark side of police.

The Times runs critical police stories almost every day. Edgy smaller papers like the *Orange County Weekly* (which has exposed systemic Sheriff Department and DA prosecutorial misconduct) have the chutzpah to go after challenging stories. Meanwhile, less prestigious news outlets can make money and get by reprinting what is handed to them by the local law enforcement's Public Information Officer.

The days of Andy Griffith's TV sheriff are long gone. A jovial, peaceful, thoughtful law enforcement officer does not fit with the media roadmap of glorification of police power or the Deep State demonization of police. The evening news pushes a state of crime and fear on your doorstep, replicating the narratives of law enforcement.

Scripted TV programs pick up in prime time, to show that the ends justify the means in police craft and that the cops and prosecutors have rights and privileges normal people (especially suspects and their attorneys) don't have; after all, the people with the badge are the 'good guys.'

Defense attorneys are depicted as shifty sharks who exploit loopholes and technicalities to free their otherwise guilty clients. These are plot points intended to outrage the audience and turn them against the right to a fair defense, let alone an aggressive defense. The end result is that the cops, DA's, and judges are all against you in court, with the full support of the voting public. Add to that the brainwashed jurors who are frothing to deliver TV style justice modeled on what they watch every night, and you have a recipe scientifically designed to destroy the constitutional right of Due Process, of 'Innocent Until Proven Guilty,' and ultimately, of Fairness.

While colloquially the 'American pastime' was playing baseball, nowadays it is watching TV. When TV viewers are bombarded with content intended to scare them with the boogeymen lurking around every corner, they then start to fall prey to politicians vowing to be "tough on crime." That's not necessarily a bad promise, but the pendulum has swung so far in favor of prosecutors and law enforcement that it has become financially unsustainable. Arresting and jailing people (which includes innocent people who are wrongly accused or simply awaiting trial) is a massive drain on taxpayer dollars. Shouldn't we be using that money for programs that will put an end to the cycle, like mental health care?

So, how do we fix this? We must stop relying on TV to get our information. It's up to us to correct people when they spread misinformation about the criminal justice system. When the next 'trial of the century' happens, we have to remind people that the defendant is innocent until proven guilty and that this is a deeply and firmly held American value. Instead of relying on TV writers and actors to tell us what to think, we have to take it upon ourselves to learn what is really happening in our criminal justice system.

People accused of crimes deserve a fair treatment—and they're counting on us to give it to them. Besides, one day it might be you or your loved one who is falsely accused and thrown into this lopsided jungle that is our current criminal justice system.

CHAPTER SIXTEEN

CELEBRITIES AND SPORTS FIGURES

Ancient Greece and Rome had their pantheons filled with gods and goddesses around which those societies wove copious and intricate tales. In our 'modern' culture, celebrities and sports figures fill similar roles and needs. Based upon their artistic or athletic talents, fans—which comes to us from the word "fanatic"—virtually worship these individuals. However, when those gods turn out to have feet of clay, the celebrity's foibles become a cautionary tale for the public. While I have represented many, many entertainers, professional athletes, movie and TV stars, for this chapter, I am not going to name names of my clients except where appropriate.

When our superstars succumb to hubris, envy, or wrath, cameras are there to catch them and exploit their human flaws. In the 24-hour, always-online news cycle, a 'superstar' might be a former D-lister who had a bad day blown out of proportion. But regardless of the wealth or fame of a defendant, they deserve to be treated like everyone else in the eyes of the law. An experienced criminal defense attorney can prevent a bad day from turning into a prison sentence.

I have defended celebrities, rappers, athletes, musicians, and former child actors. They are all just people with some spotlight and maybe cash, emphasis on *maybe*. Actors are accustomed to being catered to, even spoiled. Athletes can be grounded, but they can also enjoy a lavish lifestyle and have a hard time believing that they can't lawyer their own case.

Rappers may have had tough neighborhoods growing up, and often want to keep their street credibility through trial. Others just want to spread joy through their art and skills, and to put the ordeal behind them. Just like all people, celebrities and athletes can't be seen as mere stereotypes; they are all individuals, just like everyone else.

All my clients get the same treatment, regardless of their place in society. Compassion, understanding, communication, and hard work win cases. I may not have your favorite bubbly water in the office for our first meeting, but once we have our eyes on the legal prize, I will personally stock the office fridge for an actor, athlete, musician, or any of my clients. Those who lead a high-profile life don't always expect to be treated like regular people, but it is a person on trial, not the superstar image we need to defend. Justice is what matters.

Damage Control

When a celebrity gets into legal trouble, serious damage control begins. In a best case scenario, the story just goes away. When people say, "Whatever happened to so-and-so and that trouble he was in? It seemed to just disappear off the radar," the fact is it didn't vanish by accident. PR firms go into overdrive to protect their clients. The strategy depends on the person and the crime or accusation. A top-tier attorney is used to working with PR firms.

Being talented in art or a sport does not make you better prepared to face criminal charges. Vanity, embarrassment, and fear can cause a person who is normally in the spotlight to try to grab the microphone to explain. It is a normal, human reaction to want to explain yourself when you are being attacked.

That's the reason so many people make police statements, which are then twisted and used against them, instead of just saying, "I want a lawyer." But for the individuals who feel that their reputation is worth defending at the risk of a criminal conviction, celebrity is their worst enemy. They put up a YouTube video explaining their side of the story, give self-serving media or fan cellphone interviews and otherwise just dig the hole deeper. The PR firm tries to clean up the mess in the media. The legal defense is best focused on court.

The defense begins as soon as there is a chance of a problem. Criminal defense is not PR or image protection. My job is to keep my clients out of jail, to lessen the pain of any mistake they may have made or to vindicate them against false accusations. A good criminal defense attorney armed with the right resources is the best combination for a good outcome against criminal accusations.

Celebrities and athletes with an experienced criminal defense attorney on speed dial can find that the sting of arrest, bail, and incarceration processes can be expertly managed to their benefit. No case is too small, as a minor run-in with the law might permanently affect a celebrity's career. Not only do celebrities charged with or accused of crimes become the focus of national news, they often become the butt of national jokes.

The Arrest

Celebrities aren't usually arrested by having their doors broken down in the middle of the night, as happens with many defendants of lesser means. Arrangements are usually made for them to surrender themselves to authorities for an interview or arrest, of course with their defense attorney in tow. However, ordinary defendants arrested for relatively minor crimes don't face the onslaught of national and international news cameras when they leave the courthouse. Their lives don't instantly change from being admired to being treated as pariahs.

The legal advice for the famous is identical to the advice I give every client: keep quiet. Celebrities often feel they can charm their way out of a situation, or that they owe the public an explanation of the circumstances that got them into hot water. The phrase we all know applies, "Anything you say can and will be used against you in a court of law." Here's what most people don't know, anything that you say that's good, that helps your case, ***will not be allowed in court***. Only what is bad will be let into court. If something is neutral, it will only be let into court if the prosecutor can twist it into something that hurts you.

Bail

Perhaps nothing demonstrates the inequity in the criminal justice system between rich and poor like the process of bail. As I discussed in the chapter on California's broken cash-bail system, poor defendants often stay in jail for months because they can't raise even relatively low amounts of bail. That's obviously not an issue for the celebrity defendant with cash and assets to secure bond.

Poorer defendants are often considered a flight risk, while that's seldom the case with celebrities. By the way, tell that to the judge who was supposed to sentence film director Roman Polanski for engaging in unlawful sexual intercourse with a 13-year old girl back in 1978. Polanski boarded a plane to Europe just hours prior to his sentencing.

Jailhouse Suite

The rich and famous dwell in luxurious settings. But jail is jail and prison is prison for everyone. If a celebrity is put into jail, they will sometimes get 'pc' (protected custody status), meaning they don't have to spend time incarcerated with the general population. With money, a stay behind bars can become a little more bearable for those who can afford outside commissary, such as special food, toiletry items, reading materials, and snacks. In all fairness, inmates don't need fame to receive these benefits; they just need money.

Jail is undoubtedly a scary experience for celebrities no matter what special treatment they get. However, there's no comparison between their living quarters and potential interaction with dangerous inmates and what happens to the ordinary person. If the average convict is hurt by another inmate, the knowledge seldom spreads beyond the jail's walls. If a celebrity gets beaten up, jail officials know there will be a brighter spotlight on them and that can provide an impetus for giving more attention to the safety of the high-profile inmate.

On the one hand, the sheriffs running jails don't want the scrutiny that comes with a high-profile inmate getting injured on their watch. On the other hand, they view themselves as the owners of a fiefdom and no one is going to tell them what to do. The defense attorney must carefully negotiate with the jail to provide the special protection the celebrity inmate needs, whilst not offending the jail sergeant's ego.

Showbiz State

Southern California is very much an "industry town" where overnight TV ratings and pro sports' starting rosters are the talk of the water cooler. Celebrities and athletes are part of our communities, and news about them can have a large impact. When filming halts on a TV show, or a starter is benched for a game, the economic ripples affect Californians more than other Americans.

The CA Bureau of Economic Analysis reports that Arts, Entertainment, and Recreation account for four percent of our state's GDP. That is more than the yields from forestry, mining, agriculture, and utilities combined. We literally are invested in what appears as trivial industry gossip to Midwesterners[136].

Where were you when the Juice was loose? Police car chases often interrupt live TV as "Breaking News," a term that acquired a more dramatic meaning when it was San Francisco native, USC star, NFL hero, and Hollywood actor O.J. Simpson that went on a low speed chase after the bloody murder of his wife.

Before and After O.J.

Prior to O.J. Simpson going on trial for the double murder of his wife and her friend in 1995, celebrities usually received a slap on the wrist when they got into trouble with the law. Part of the fallout from the Simpson case—since so many people believed he got away with murdering two people—is that celebrities are now held to a different, tougher standard.

Prosecutors want to make an example of them, and these entertainers or athletes often end up receiving much harsher punishment than the ordinary citizen who finds himself in the same situation. It's also a great way for the head DA or trial deputy to make a name for themselves and further their careers. Don't forget—most judges in California are former prosecutors. Prosecutors Chris Darden and Marcia Clarke went on to write books and provide legal commentary on TV. Defense team attorney Robert Kardashian's family are still on TV more than twenty years after O.J.'s trial.

136 California GDP. (2015). latimes.com. Retrieved 9 February 2018, from http://www.latimes.com/visuals/graphics/la-oe-g-california-gdp-20150601-htmlstory.html

Forget it, Jake. It's Chinatown

The 1974 film, "Chinatown" by director Roman Polanski set the bar for hard-boiled detective films. Set in depression-era Los Angeles, the film stars Jack Nicholson as a private eye entangled in criminal land dealings during LA's boom growth. Just five years prior to making the film, Polanski, then already an established International director, lost his pregnant wife, actress Sharon Tate, and four friends to murder at the hands of the Manson Family. Then, in 1977, Polanski made criminal headlines of his own when he was charged with the rape of a minor.

Polanski held the attention of the nation for a decade with his tragedy, triumph, and tragedy again; famous auteur, celebrity pals, glamorous settings, a jet-setting lifestyle, tragic crimes—California style.

Roman Polanski famously fled the United States and has lived in exile since 1978, to avoid facing sentencing for his plea deal regarding unlawful sexual intercourse with a 13-year-old girl. His attorney was a star Hollywood negotiator. He worked out a plea deal that protected the minor girl from testifying in court, including some prison time and an official evaluation of Polanski's mental health.

After being locked up in Chino, and being cleared of pedophilia leanings by prison shrinks, Polanski was ready to accept his sentence. But after an inappropriate ex parte conversation with the LA District Attorney David Wells, the judge in the case, Laurence Rittenband, decided the plea deal would not be honored and promised to sentence Polanski to fifty years in jail. DA Wells had shown the judge inflammatory photos of Polanski hanging around other young starlets, and wanted him to make an example of the famous director. To avoid the prospect of decades in jail, Polanski hopped on a plane to Europe and never returned.

Roman Polanski's fame made the case a media sensation. His story has been spun to insinuate he escaped justice. In fact, with the time served in Chino pre-sentencing, and time held in the 2000's in a Swiss jail awaiting judgement on extradition, he has served a majority of what would have been the maximum at the time in 1977. His fame attracted injustice in the form of a grandstanding judge reneging on a plea deal to suit a political DA. His victim, now an adult woman, speaks out on Polanski's behalf to end the attacks on his liberty and calling out the prosecutorial misconduct that led Polanski into exile.

It will be interesting to see whether Hollywood, now embroiled in the #METOO movement, shifts its stance on Polanski. On the one hand, you have many people like Meryl Streep, an outspoken #METOO proponent, advocating for greater casting couch accountability. On the other hand, you have a room full of Hollywood insiders, including Streep, giving Polanski a rousting round of applause—and a standing ovation to boot—at the 2003 Academy Awards.

The Rap Sheet

After getting some great experience with the Fresno County Public Defender's office, my start in private practice in the Bay Area is intricately intertwined with a lot of Bay Area rappers and rap producers. I met a lot of cool Bay Area hip hop stars; some are on the charts, some are on the streets. The rap scene in the Bay is a very small community and I've either met everyone involved directly or I'm one degree away.

While Oakland, Richmond, and Vallejo are centers of musical creativity, they are also centers of poverty and violence. One of my long-term clients has seen the best of what fame can offer, and also suffered an unbelievable amount of bad luck for one lifetime.

Hit records made him a target in his home turf of East Bay. He has made some dumb mistakes, but not in proportion to the several times people have tried to kill him. I can always cut through street gossip and accusations to keep him out of jail, but his guardian angel needs to keep him out of the hospital. Well, I guess his guardian angel is doing something right, as he has been shot several times and is still a major player in the rap game.

In many ways, I have grown up with the rappers and producers I work with. We went from being young and hungry to having mortgages and families. This really hit home while hanging with Snoop Dogg and his crew after a show in Sacramento. Snoop is a machine and rocked the DJ table all night, but his entourage were just regular guys hanging out after work. Grab a bite, drink a beer, watch SportsCenter, shoot the breeze, then load the tour van, and repeat in the next town.

Groupies didn't get far with Snoop's crowd, unless they were delivering a plate of appetizers. It was surreal on one level, hanging out at a private party with Snoop as a DJ and all my NorCal cannabis clients, but it was also just a normal Wednesday for a bunch of middle-aged guys & gals appreciating music together, with none of us being excited about waking up early to have to work the next day. What's funny and unexpected about hanging out with rappers, athletes, and even media stars is that, rather than discuss the interesting work they've done, they're always curious about my cases; they ask every question under the sun about what the life of a defense attorney is like.

Sports Authority

When an actor or entertainer is arrested or faces criminal allegations, the bad behavior reflects on them. When the same thing happens to a sports figure, the behavior reflects on the whole team and perhaps even on the team's home city. Fans stay loyal to home teams through thick and thin, often forming a lifelong connection, and take a player's peccadilloes personally. Many sports figures are people of color from poor backgrounds. They're young, famous, and making more money than they ever dreamed possible. They simply aren't prepared for the type of repercussions dealt out by the media and fans for their indiscretions.

Fit, famous, and rich brings people out of the woodwork. Estranged parents pop up, stalkers try to seduce, and crooks shake down. A fake scandal can even reduce a player's net worth, and there are people who know this. Double-check the source when a celebrity is being charged with a crime, and a lawsuit is right behind to cash in. How many athletes deal with 'Extortion by 9-1-1' from lovers and martial partners?

Domestic Violence

Competition, stress, hormones, and injury can leave a pro athlete tense and on edge. Life on the road and groupies throwing themselves at you can also lead to infidelities which does not go over well at home, especially with a spouse who is undoubtedly a catch in their own right. This potential powder keg can result in allegations of spousal abuse or assault. Violence against an innocent is terrible, just like accusations against the innocent. There are two sides to every story. He said versus She said is the foundation of the domestic abuse shakedown.

Domestic violence charges, along with DUI's and drug possession, are the crimes with which athletes and celebrities are most frequently charged. Take actors Johnny Depp and Amber Heard, who were married for just 15 months. Heard accused Depp of domestic violence, and eventually walked away with a $7 million settlement, which she claims she's giving to charity. Their 2016 domestic violence and divorce proceedings are a textbook example of PR firms working to make the best out of an ugly situation between a toxic couple.

Heard submitted various photos to the court to back her claim of domestic violence, including pictures of her bruised face, a shattered picture, and broken glass on the floor. A cell phone video was leaked online, with suspicion falling on Heard, although she denied doing such leaking, under oath. During a deposition, Depp's lawyer went into considerable detail about Heard's alleged injuries and why "five concierges, two police officers as well as security guards saw no evidence of such after the incident." Reportedly, Heard maintained "she was injured and couldn't account for what others saw."

She claimed Depp was "emotionally and physically abusive." Vanessa Paradis, Depp's longtime lover and the mother of his two children, stated in a handwritten letter that Depp is a "sensitive, loving and loved person and I believe with all of my heart that these recent allegations are outrageous. In all of the years I have known Johnny, he has never been physically abusive with me, and this looks nothing like the man I lived with for 14 wonderful years."

On August 16, 2016, Heard withdrew her request for a domestic violence restraining order, with prejudice. That means the case cannot be refiled. In a joint statement, Depp and Heard wrote "Our relationship was intensely passionate and at times volatile, but always bound by love. Neither party has made false accusations for financial gain. There was never any intent of physical or emotional harm. Amber wishes the best for Johnny in the future. Amber will be donating financial proceeds from the divorce to a charity. There will be no further public statements about this matter."

At the 2017 People's Choice Awards, where Depp won as "Favorite Movie Icon," he thanked fans "who through whatever good times or bad, you know, have stood by me, trusted me." This was his first public appearance since the divorce was finalized, and many people took his remarks as a direct reference to the messy situation. Meanwhile, Heard has been busy making PSA videos on domestic violence.

Fallen Stars

We see them on TV, watch them grow up in their sitcom homes and in CGI adventures. Child stars feel like they have become part of our families over the years. But inevitably, they age out, are not as cute, are typecast, or simply burn out of the Hollywood grind. I have represented a few child actors at trial, and they are people like you and me. It can be shocking to see a former Disney Channel actor with a scruffy beard and neck tattoos. But if you had just met him, you would not have the juxtaposition of the cute TV kid with the adult man.

Growing up working in Hollywood might put a strain on young actors, but very few turn out to be felons. When one does stray to the wrong side of the law, it makes for a shock headline shared across the media.

Trust is important in any relationship. Many child actors have had expectations imposed onto them their entire lives. I am not their agent, manager, producer, or mom. My job is to help them save their life and get it back on track. One of my main goals in any case is that I never want the client to have to hire me again. I am straightforward, compassionate, explain things, listen well, establish the facts, and work very hard to let the evidence show my client is not guilty. Kid actors have grown up working hard, and they appreciate hard work when they see it. I build trust by working hard, and by not betraying it.

Beyond Redemption

Whether or not a celebrity can ever get back in the public's good graces depends on more than top legal representation and a good PR firm. It really boils down to what they are accused of doing. The public might forgive a DUI or even domestic violence arrest depending on the specific facts that come out. What doesn't get forgiven are acts that, irrespective of whether or not they are legal or illegal, are just vile. Celebrities accused of making racist or anti-Semitic comments—think Paula Deen, Michael Richards, Phil Robertson—basically commit career suicide.

There are exceptions, such as Mel Gibson, arguably the biggest star to go off the rails against an ethnic or religious group. Gibson went on an anti-Semitic tirade after a drunken driving arrest in 2006. His was a double whammy; in 2010 taped threats he made to baby momma Oksana Grigorieva became public. Gibson not only made public apologies, but in the intervening years he has "befriended rabbis, attended Passover Seders and donated to Jewish causes," according to Bloomberg News. A decade after that Malibu DUI, Gibson was back on top as the director of the commercially and critically acclaimed film, "Hacksaw Ridge."

The Brangelina Breakup and Child Abuse

The world's most famous movie star couple, Angelina Jolie and Brad Pitt, has called it quits, but not before nasty allegations of child abuse against Pitt by his wife. The couple was as well-known for their large family—consisting of three adopted and three biological children—as they were for their films. Jolie alleged Pitt and teenage son Maddox got into some sort of altercation on a flight, precipitating an investigation into Pitt's physical and verbal child abuse. After investigating, the Los Angeles County Department of Child and Family Services cleared Pitt of the allegations.

Was this a ploy by Jolie to receive sole custody of the six kids? In California, joint physical and legal custody is the rule, unless domestic violence or child abuse is involved. If that's the case, the judge decides custody under specific rules. However, it's a crime for a parent to make false claims regarding child abuse against the other parent, although I've never represented anyone with those charges, nor have I ever heard about anyone ever arrested for those charges.

Sole Custody, More Money

No matter Jolie's reasons for wanting sole custody, it's probably not about the money. She and Pitt are each quite rich. For the non-famous parent of a celebrity's child, that's often a different matter. Take Los Angeles Clipper DeAndre Jordan, who reportedly wept in court over a custody fight with the mother of his child, a woman identified as "Ashley Rose." She wanted sole custody, possibly because she would receive more child support—and a lifestyle upgrade—than if she was sharing custody with Jordan. DeAndre cried in court, claiming he wanted to be "an active parent." Presumably, the only thing standing between him and his wish was money. In December 2016, a Ventura County judge granted joint custody.

These sad stories repeat themselves every week in courtrooms throughout the country, but each family's pain stays relatively private. For the famous, their personal tragedies become fodder for water cooler and social media conversation and laugh-out-loud jokes on late night TV. Everyone has an opinion, even though they know nothing about the couple other than what they've seen on TV or read online. It's never in the best interest of any child to have the sordid details of their parents' relationship broadcast to the world.

Heading to Rehab

For many celebrities, the path to career salvation detours through rehab—It wasn't the famous person's innate bad character or poor judgment causing the crime or misbehavior, but an alcohol or substance abuse issue. In many cases, that's absolutely true. The money and fame comes with intense pressure and an unrelenting spotlight. It's not surprising that so many celebrities find temporary refuge from this unyielding strain in drink and drugs. Throw in enormous egos and toxic relationships, and the situation becomes gasoline just waiting for a match.

You probably know people who experienced a wake-up call regarding their alcohol or drug abuse due to an arrest. If they were lucky, they sought treatment and counseling and stopped drinking or using. A celebrity's situation isn't really different, except that the whole world knows of the screw-up. They deserve the opportunity to get their lives back in order. The ordinary Joe can't write a bestseller about his struggle to overcome addiction or alcoholism—maybe even have a movie or TV show made of the story—but that's how celebrities are different from you and me. After Star Wars, this kind of revelatory saga was the late Carrie Fisher's bread and butter, and she was damn good at it.

The 'Apology Tour'

Part of the celebrity and/or sports star's redemption process occurs post rehab—or post-counseling if the incident didn't involve substance abuse. That's the 'Apology Tour,' arranged by the star's PR firm. The person appears contrite on every form of media, hoping for public forgiveness.

Sometimes, the apology tour never really ends. Gibson is still asked about his DUI and anti-Semitic remarks in interviews. In November 2016, Gibson appeared on Late Night with Stephen Colbert. The host asked what Gibson would say to his younger self and he replied, "I'd tell my younger self to shut the f*** up."

Hugh Grant went on an apology tour after his arrest for having sex with an LA prostitute by the name of Divine Brown in 1995. He faced six months in jail for lewd conduct in a public place—the back of his car, parked on a public street. The charming Brit got away with a $1,000 fine and an order to attend AIDS counseling. In the meantime, he issued apologies left and right and proclaimed his embarrassment and remorse in countless interviews. His career didn't really suffer, but Ms. Brown ended up serving a six-month sentence for probation violation of previous prostitution convictions.

Never the Same

Famed lawyer Alan Dershowitz, who represented O.J. Simpson, among other famous clients, told ABC News, "Every celebrity case I've been involved in—I've been involved in a great many—the one thing you can be sure of is they don't get the same justice as everybody else. It could be worse, it could be better, it's never the same." The upside: celebrities get top attorneys. The downside: everybody pays attention and it can overshadow anything else the person ever did.

A good example from Hollywood Golden Age is the case of Hedy Lamarr. In her day, she was considered the most beautiful woman in the world. There was more to her than a string of hit movies and notable husbands and lovers. Lamarr and a friend received a patent during World War II on a radio-signaling device to reduce jamming. It was the nucleus of what later became "spread spectrum," used in countless types of technology. But in her obituary, the fact that she was twice arrested for shoplifting—no convictions—played as prominent a role as any of her accomplishments.

Lamarr's modern counterpart is Winona Ryder, arrested for shoplifting in Beverly Hills back in 2001. The career of the onetime "Face of Gen X" suffered for a while, and she didn't make another film until 2006. She's still the answer in trivia questions asking, "What famous actress was arrested for shoplifting at Saks Fifth Avenue?"

Why I Fight

This last example will always be heavy on my heart. Most people with even a passing familiarity of reggae music know of Peter Tosh. He was a contemporary of Bob Marley, a Rastafarian, and a fierce advocate for the legalization of cannabis. Jawara McIntosh is his son. Jawara is, like his father before him, a peaceful warrior who followed in the same journey in terms of social activism and the legalization of cannabis.

Through music, and Rastafarianism, Jawara continued Peter Tosh's message of Love and Justice. The elder Tosh wrote for and played with Bob Marley & the Wailers, standing up to violence from both police and outlaws. Jawara recently fell victim to violence while in custody of a local jail. Beaten into a coma by another inmate, Jawara suffered traumatic brain injury and remains in a coma nearly a year later (as of this printing).

Back in 2013, Jawara got busted in New Jersey. Stopped under very questionable circumstances, it was 'discovered' during a 'routine traffic stop' that Jawara had 44 pounds of cannabis in his truck. After a few years and several attorneys, I was brought in to either fight the motion as to the legality of the stop, settle the case making sure Jawara got the best deal possible, or go to trial.

The problem is, under New Jersey law, if Jawara was found guilty, he would have faced a mandatory 5-10 years in prison. I came in, learned New Jersey criminal law fairly quickly and with the help of my local pro hoc vici attorney sponsor, finalized a deal wherein Jawara would 'just' do another 6 months in county jail. County jail is always going to be safer than a prison sentence. Also, the judge gave him several months to finish an album that he was working on before he had to turn himself in. I was happy. I knew that I had done the best thing under the circumstances and I thought I had saved him from a violent prison, from the extreme punishment of Drug War prohibition persecution. I was even working towards getting him released after 60-90 days to serve the remaining time on home electronic detention.

However, after a little over a month of his custody time, Jawara was viciously assaulted by another inmate, which left him in a coma. This example illustrates why inmates with even some celebrity status are justified in receiving special protections while in custody. If someone is going to be a target while in custody, they should receive protection.

I felt proud that I had saved him from New Jersey's draconian mandatory prison sentence, but it turns out I didn't save him at all. I did the very best I could with his case, but my heart broke and I've felt sick ever since I got the news of the jail assault that left a beautiful, bold, and loving spirit in a coma. Even after Jawara was beaten and in the hospital, in a coma, the sheriff had him handcuffed to the hospital bed.

Imagine the family having to endure that insult after the jail had failed to provide for his safety. In fact, I had to fight with the Bergen County Sheriff's Department so he could be moved to a hospital closer to the family in Boston. It took the Bergen County Prosecutor's office over a year to dismiss the case. This despite letter after letter from Jawara's various doctors pointing out that there was very little hope of Jawara ever recovering. They got more than their pound of flesh—over a plant that grows in the ground.

Blind Justice

Justice is supposed to be blind, but it's hard for a judge or jury to be blind to a celebrity defendant. While the rich and famous shouldn't receive breaks in a court of law, neither should they suffer more than others in the same position. Too often, the judge or prosecutor want to make an example of them, a cautionary tale for the general public. That's not fair. Everyone, no matter their status in life, deserves the same treatment. Nor should someone with a media persona be used as a stepping stone for a judge for their next election or by a career-minded prosecutor for their next advancement.

There are celebrity attorneys on TV, famous for being attorneys on TV. I am a criminal defense attorney, who happens to occasionally have celebrity clients. There is an important role for other lawyers to get on camera and use their own star power to share a message about their star clients. They speak truth to power, explain legal situations, and speak up for their client when so many are calling for blood before an arraignment is even held.

My role is to be a dependable, hardworking, warrior in court, to push back against the State of Collusion, and protect my clients. The middle class, the poor and humble, as well as the rich and famous, Each case, each client, is a sacred duty that I take very seriously.

CHAPTER SEVENTEEN

RACISM PAST AND PRESENT - FROM CHINESE IMMIGRANT TAXES TO RACIAL PROFILING

California has always been a place rich with possibility, and the potential for prosperity has drawn people from all over the world. Waves of new Californians have come over the centuries, from the earliest Hispanic colonists, Russian fur trappers, and Gold Rush fortune seekers, to the Chinese and Irish railroad workers, Japanese and Mexican farmers turning the Central Valley into the world's cornucopia, Italian fishermen, Black industrial workers during World War Two, through the refugees that arrived by boat in the '70s to the steady influx of migrant workers. It was not easy getting here, but the rewards were worth the effort. Chances are you have neighbors from diverse backgrounds, representing dozens of ethnicities and traditions. Our rich diversity is part of what makes California thrive.

As a relatively young state, California somewhat avoided the entrenched societal and historical racial and ethnic divisions. Slavery, ethnic ghettos, Jim Crow, entrenched European "nobility," segregation, and other East Coast problems seem a world away here in the Golden State. Yet while opportunity has drawn migrant waves of millions of people from around the world, there is and has always been a rip-tide of racism in the criminal justice system.

Our neighborhoods and schools today are full of rainbows and moonbeams, but a few people vested with power have inflicted their biases on Californians for ages. To understand racial bias in California, it is key to learn about the current makeup of its population.

Breakdown of California's population, US Census Bureau estimates[137], 2014:

- 73.2% White
- 6.5% Black
- 15% Asian/Pacific Islander
- 1.7% American Indian
- 3.7% Mixed race

Breakdown by ethnicity:

- 8.6% Hispanic-Latino (of any race)
- 61.4% Non-Hispanic (of any race)

Largest named ancestries:

- 25% Mexican
- 9% German
- 7.7% Irish
- 7.4% English
- 5.8% Italian

Race is based on broad classifications associated with genetics (read: skin color). Ethnicity is based on cultural traditions, religion, and regional

137 U.S. Census Bureau QuickFacts: California. (2014). Census.gov. Retrieved 14 February 2018, from https://www.census.gov/quickfacts/CA

heritage. Ethnicity is not as easy to spot as skin or hair color, which makes it more subtle to detect. Biases based upon either are irrational, but racial discrimination can be triggered at a glance, whereas bigotry based on religion or country of origin requires getting to know the target of discrimination a little better.

Fear of the 'other' is an element of racism and discrimination. When bigotry becomes encoded in the law, it is usually based on protectionism: protecting economic interests, protecting power, and protecting the status quo. Going way back in California's history, fear and protectionism pop up with each new wave of immigration. A biased majority can use the law to prevent minorities from participating in legal commerce and peaceful integration.

Street level racism, individual against individual, is isolated and hard to combat. Legislative and institutional racism, from the top down, are pernicious evils of an entitled mob. From the dawn of California's statehood, racist laws targeted groups to suppress them. During the Gold Rush, there were laws aimed at Asians to keep them from fairly competing for gold, commerce, and prosperity. Other laws at the time also favored Caucasian-Anglo new Californians over the established Indians and locals, and Black residents who might have fled West to avoid slavery in the South.

We have seen how psychopaths in power inflict their will and biases on the populace. This has been going on since California became a US state. A diverse population does not equate to a diverse political class.

An 1850 California statute provided that "no black, mulatto person, or Indian, shall be allowed to give evidence in favor of, or against a white man." In 1854, the Supreme Court of California extended the prohibition to equally exclude the Chinese. Race made an easy target of the 'other,' as the populations of different races grew, lured by the promise of freedom and opportunity.

The 1850 Foreign Miners Tax placed a $20-a-month tax on all miners of foreign origin in California. The 1852 version of the law placed a $3-a-month tax exclusively for Chinese laborers. Taxes for the Chinese steadily increased with ever harsher bills passed by the California Legislature and signed into law by Governor John Bigler. One law passed by the State Legislature and signed by the Governor created a $50-per-head tax for Chinese migrants entering Californian ports, which was to be paid within three days.

In 1862, California enacted the 'Anti-Coolie Act.' Its proper title is "An act to protect free white labor against competition with Chinese coolie labor, and to discourage the immigration of the Chinese into the State of California." It was designed to protect native residents of the state from competition in the labor market from Chinese manual laborers. It aimed to discourage Chinese citizens from immigrating to California by placing a per capita tax on all Chinese laborers in the state of California. The "police tax" required a monthly work permit[138] for any worker over the age of 18 of the "Mongolian Race."

Chronology of Early Racial Discrimination in California[139]

- 1879: Voter rights [Constitution] "No native of China" would ever have the right to vote in the state of California. It was repealed in 1926.
- From 1879 to 1926, California's constitution stated that "no native of China" shall ever exercise the privileges of an elector in the state. Denying minorities the right to participate is the

138 The History of Racist Asian Stereotypes. Yellow Face. Retrieved 14 February 2018, from http://yellow-face.com/asian-discrimination.htm

139 List of Jim Crow law examples by state. Wikipedia. Retrieved 14 February 2018, from https://en.m.wikipedia.org/wiki/List_of_Jim_Crow_law_examples_by_state

most extreme form of institutional racism. It prevents a voice, a franchise, to officially dissent.

- 1879: Employment [Constitution] Prohibited public bodies from employing Chinese workers and called upon the legislature to protect "the state…from the burdens and evils arising from" their presence. A statewide anti-Chinese referendum was passed with 99.4 percent of the votes in 1879.
- 1880: Miscegenation [Statute] Made it illegal for white persons to marry Negroes or mulattos.
- 1890: Residential [City Ordinance] The city of San Francisco ordered all Chinese inhabitants to move into a certain area of the city within six months or face imprisonment. The Bingham Ordinance was later found to be unconstitutional by a federal court.
- 1891: Residential [Statute] Required the Chinese to carry with them at all times a "certificate of residence." Without it, a Chinese immigrant could be arrested and jailed.
- 1894: Voter rights [Constitution] Any person who could not read the Constitution in English or write their name would be disfranchised. An advisory referendum indicated that nearly 80 percent of voters supported an educational requirement.
- 1901: Miscegenation [Statute] The 1850 law prohibiting marriage between white persons and Negroes or mulattoes was amended, adding "Mongolian."
- 1909: Miscegenation [Statute] Persons of Japanese descent were added to the list of undesirable marriage partners of white Californians as noted in the earlier 1880 statute.
- 1913: Property [Statute] Known as the "Alien Land Laws," Asian immigrants were prohibited from owning or leasing property.

> The California Supreme Court struck down the Alien Land Laws in 1952.

These statewide measures were implemented before the federal laws pushed by trade unions to punish Asians across the continent. The American Federation of Labor (AFL) and its president, Samuel Gompers, demonized Asian workers as a threat to the American White Male way of life.

In 1882, the U.S. Congress passed the Chinese Exclusion Act, which Gompers sought to justify in the 1902 book, *Some Reasons for Chinese Exclusion: Meat v. Rice; American Manhood against Asiatic Coolieism: Which Shall Survive*[140]? Originally published by the AFL, the book was re-published a few years later by the Asiatic Exclusion League. In 1905, at its 25th Annual Convention[141], the AFL argued that the "American workingman" had enough to deal with "without being required to meet the enervating, killing, underselling and under-living competition of that nerveless, wantless people, the Chinese."

This was the scenario over a hundred years ago; fear of the 'other,' fear of competing in a free market, resulting in the enactment of anti-Asian legislation. We see this process repeated with each new race or ethnicity establishing itself in our state. Whatever the mob fears, whatever the mob does not want to work with, the mob puts in a corner using legal mob force (sometimes known as democracy).

Should the language used in these racist laws be surprising? The lawmakers were frank in their use of derogatory terms for the targets of

---

140 American Federation of Labor. (1902). Some Reasons For Chinese Exclusion, *Meat v. Rice, American Manhood Against Asiatic Coolieism- Which Shall Survive?*. Washington: Govt. Print. Off.

141 Model Minority - Dictionary definition of Model Minority | Encyclopedia.com: FREE online dictionary. (2008). Encyclopedia.com. Retrieved 14 February 2018, from http://www.encyclopedia.com/social-sciences/applied-and-social-sciences-magazines/model-minority

their laws, whether it be the "Anti-Coolie" laws or the "Greaser Act," an 1855 California law that focused on Mexicans and singled them out for subjective, victimless crimes. "Operation Wetback" was a 1954 U.S. law designed to deport a million undocumented Mexicans. This is unabashed state-endorsed racism. These laws would all be overturned by one court or another, eventually. But the fact that laws would single out "Greasers," "Wetbacks," and "Coolies" is unconscionable.

These terrible laws were passed and enforced in our Golden State, which we now associate with diversity: BBQ, sourdough, organic granola, tacos, and killer dim sum.

Today, passing overtly racist, Jim-Crow-style laws is harder to pull off. Now, when laws are enacted to target minorities, the racism is hidden behind other fears. Fear is a powerful driver, and even if race is not a primary fear of legislators, they can hide behind "protecting us" from guns, drugs, gangs, crime, etc.; with the unspoken agreement that they are fearful of minorities owning guns, or doing drugs, or socializing together. There are laws on the books that should not be there, as they are used to both prosecute and persecute minorities.

Something as American as the right to bear arms can take a back seat to racism in the hands of bigots. Great White American Cowboys ride into town with their guns on their hips. But the fear of an armed minority can whip up racist sentiments that politicians and cops then use to subjugate the 'other.'

Concealed carry of firearm laws vary from state to state. In California, we are described as a "May Carry" state, in that you "may" be allowed to carry a concealed weapon if permission is granted by the prevailing local law enforcement officer, usually the sheriff of your county or police chief of your city. This makes the decision to grant a concealed carry license a subjective choice based on the whims and biases of the sheriff or chief, Constitution be damned.

This allows a racist sheriff to prevent minorities from arming and defending themselves. It also allows the racist in charge to allow his cronies or those to whom he owes a favor, or their friends, to receive a license to carry a concealed weapon.

On July 15th, 1923, the San Francisco Chronicle reported on the passing of the Hawes Bill[142], which imposed "stringent regulations against carrying concealed firearms or explosives, and prohibition against possession of other deadly weapons," which would have a "salutary effect in checking tong wars among the Chinese, and vendettas among our people who are of Latin descent." The vast majority of citizens, and criminals, were white, but this law was drafted by law enforcement and signed by politicians to suppress 'the other.'

Similar end run racist laws have been passed more recently in California. As our large Hispanic citizenry blended in, the laws increasingly targeted those who stood out the most, and had come more recently: African Americans.

During World War II, the boom in shipbuilding and factory jobs in California supporting the war effort attracted thousands of Blacks from around the country. Port and shipbuilding cities like Oakland, Richmond, Vallejo, and Long Beach became larger industrial centers teeming with new Californians. This led to numerous laws biased against the growing Black minority in the 20th Century, and into the 21st.

We previously saw prohibitionist laws aimed at immigrant minorities, such as the ban on alcohol (Catholics, Italians, Irish, and Mexicans),

142 LEGISLATIVE HISTORY REPORT AND ANALYSIS - Assembly Bill 263 (Hawes – 1923). (2007). Hoffmang.com. Retrieved 14 February 2018, from http://www.hoffmang.com/firearms/AB263-Hawes-1923.pdf

opium (Chinese), and cannabis (Mexicans and "Hindoos"). In the 1980s, crack cocaine was the substance demonized to further suppress African Americans.

Cocaine is cocaine. Crack is a less refined and cheaper form of cocaine, associated with urban usage by black people. Cocaine was already illegal, but crack was made 'extra illegal' to punish the demographic that used it most. At its base, the substance that movie stars, athletes, and frat boys snorted was no different than the white rock fired up in a glass pipe for inhalation—except for the demographic using it.

The California Legislature overwhelmingly approved stricter penalties for crack in 1986 amid heightened national concern about its health and public safety dangers, and with the urging of then-Governor George Deukmejian's administration[143].

According to the Drug Policy Alliance (DPA), a national advocacy group that opposes the drug war, people of color account for nearly everyone sent to California prisons for the specific crime of possession of crack for sale. Sentencing enhancements for crack imposed mandatory minimums longer than those for use or sale of powder cocaine, and put restrictions on related parole.

The DPA went on to share statistics showing that from 2005 to 2010, 77 percent of those held in California prisons for possession to sell crack were Black, whilst only two percent were White. Fortunately, the California Fair Sentencing Act passed in 2014 realigned sentencing and parole guidelines lowering crack penalties to existing cocaine standards.

Another racist assault on our liberties comes in the form of "gang enhancements" that use arbitrary and subjective restrictions to single out

143 Rothberg, D. (2014). California lawmaker seeks to change 'racist' cocaine laws. The Sacramento Bee. Retrieved 14 February 2018, from http://www.sacbee.com/news/politics-government/article2601351.html

minorities in the name of 'safety.' We covered this topic earlier in the context of capricious laws, but it is important to mention it again as one of the ways racism can be hidden within legislation that sounds well-meaning. Gang enhancement and sentencing is not colorblind, and it empowers racists with badges and gavels to punish any minority they see fit for activities that a lot of people would consider normal, daily activities.

A group associating peacefully = gang. A few guys wearing clothes that have similar colors = gang. A crime that the DA can exaggerate as supporting a group = gang. These laws make targeting people easier for cops, and tacking on longer sentences easier for prosecutors and judges—all based on neighborhood and familial associations of the suspects, who are usually brown.

The Racism of Law Enforcement Institutions

Just as we expect to have a jury of our peers, our legal and law enforcement system works best when the cops, prosecutors, and judges look like the communities they serve. Institutionalized racism cannot persist when the institutions are desegregated.

As we saw earlier, about 40 percent of Californians have Hispanic ethnicity, and racially 15 percent are Asian/Pacific Islander, and almost seven percent are Black. Do our police forces and courts resemble our populace?

Of course, statistical variations will happen where law enforcement demographics are not aligned with the community. Where there is most concern is in communities that have a high minority-population paired with a mostly white police and a history of abuse and conflict between the force and the citizens.

The San Jose Mercury News ran a series of stories on the racial makeup of the Bay Area's police departments. Some were in line with their communities. For example, the affluent and leafy Bay Area suburb of Walnut Creek has a police force and population that are mostly aligned: 10 percent of the officers and 10 percent of the community are Hispanic; 1 percent of police and 1.7 percent of the population are African-American.

A few miles away, there are cities that have a majority of Hispanic and Black residents, yet the police departments are mostly white. It is no coincidence that these communities all have higher crimes and a higher tension between cops and citizens.

Examples of racial disparity between police force and residents

- Antioch: 73% white officers vs. 34% white population
- Brentwood: 72% white officers vs. 56% white population
- Napa: 81% white officers vs. 57% white population
- San Leandro: 66% white officers vs. 26% white population

At the statewide level, the California Highway Patrol (CHP) is also less diverse than the citizens they police. Of the cadets who graduated from the CHP academy, whites made up 67 percent of the class, Hispanics made up 20 percent, Asians had four percent and Blacks made up only one percent[144].

Why does the race of a cop matter to the citizenry they protect? If the cops are doing a great job, fairly enforcing the law, it matters less. Having law enforcement that mirrors the populace allows for kids to see themselves growing up to have such work, to be role models for their community. Also, when the community and police force look alike, it can reduce abuses, or perceived abuses, such as racial profiling, unfair administration of justice, and chances for white-on-black police brutality.

144 Oliver, K. (2015). Investigation: Racial diversity lost in CHP hiring process. KCRA. Retrieved 14 February 2018, from http://www.kcra.com/article/investigation-racial-diversity-lost-in-chp-hiring-process/6422651

Remember, it was not until a few years ago that California finally passed our Racial and Identity Profiling Act of 2015[145], which requires departments to log data for each stop of a citizen, including the time, date, location, and reason, as well as the "perceived race or ethnicity, gender, and approximate age of the person stopped," and whether the officer took any actions or searched the person.

Beyond arrest, the lack of diversity facing minority defendants in court stands as a bright white wall of prosecution, seeking to jail people of color arrested by white cops enforcing racist laws. Hispanics are a large and growing percentage of California's population, nearly 40 percent. But only 10 percent of the prosecutors in California are of Hispanic heritage. A report by Stanford Law School documents how minorities are underrepresented amongst prosecutors, whilst whites are overrepresented[146].

At the top of the law enforcement food chain, the judiciary, we also see an imbalance of diversity. California requires courts to report on the diversity of judges. According to a 2014 report by the Judicial Council, only six percent of California judges are Asian and only nine percent are Hispanic. Both statistics are out of balance with the diversity of California. A bright note is that Blacks are more fairly represented amongst prosecutors and judges, with a ratio that mirrors society[147].

All of this matters, and everything comes vividly into focus when we look at the population of California's prisons. The arrest, prosecution, and sentencing of defendants results in prison demographics that seem more appropriate for an apartheid nation.

145 California Cops Are Pissed About the State's New Racial Profiling Law (2015). VICE News. Retrieved 14 February 2018, from https://news.vice.com/article/california-cops-are-pissed-about-the-states-new-racial-profiling-law

146 Bies, K., Deporto, I., Long, D., McKoy, M., Mukamal, D., & Sklansky, D. (2015). Stuck in the '70s: The Demographics of California Prosecutors. Stanford Criminal Justice Center. Retrieved 14 February 2018, from https://media.law.stanford.edu/organizations/programs-and-centers/scjc/Stuck-in-the-70s-Final-Report.pdf

147 California Bench Continues to Grow More Diverse. (2015). CALIFORNIA COURTS. Retrieved 14 February 2018, from http://www.courts.ca.gov/28886.htm

The chapter on Prisons will explore the situation in more depth. The population of California's jails looks a lot different demographically than the people we see at the mall, beach, or theme park.

Your right to a jury of your peers is sacrosanct. What about the rest of the process? Minorities face arrest, prosecution, and imprisonment by government officials that do not resemble our community. In a perfect world, professionals should be able to do their job impartially. But in reality, we have decades of entrenched racism and biased application of justice that perpetuate both latent and patent racism.

Any group that has been marginalized, attacked, and minimized by the State and its agents knows best how to resist. I see in my fellow defense attorneys who fight for justice that many come from backgrounds that faced institutional adversity. Logically, racism is self-defeating because it is based on a fallacy, that human beings are different because of skin color, that we are not one, connected human race. Sadly, we still have a long way to go until our criminal justice system no longer resembles the slave ships of old.

CHAPTER EIGHTEEN

PRISONS: SYSTEMIC RACISM

For decades, California was the poster child for mass incarceration in America. In his book, "Mass Incarceration on Trial," Berkeley law professor Jonathan Simon wrote, "California is to incarceration as Mississippi was to segregation—the state that most exemplifies the social and legal deformities of the practice[148]."

Prison Demographics

In California, approximately 60 percent of adult males are non-white or Hispanic[149]. However, that's not the percentage found in the state's prison demographics, where about 76 percent of incarcerated individuals are non-white or Hispanic. Here's the breakdown of the prison population compared to the overall population[150]:

	General population	Prison population
• Hispanic	38.9%	41.6%
• African-American	6.5%	28.6%
• Non-white, other	16.9%	6%
• White, non-Hispanic	37.7%	23%

Among adult men, African Americans are incarcerated at a rate of 4,367 per 100,000, compared to 922 for Hispanics, 488 for non-Hispanic

148 Simon, J. (2014). Mass incarceration on trial: A remarkable court decision and the future of prisons in America. New York: New Press.

149 California's Changing Prison Population - Public Policy Institute of California. (2015). Public Policy Institute of California. Retrieved 10 February 2018, from http://www.ppic.org/publication/californias-changing-prison-population/

150 U.S. Census Bureau QuickFacts: California. (2017). Census.gov. Retrieved 13 February 2018, from https://www.census.gov/quickfacts/CA

whites, and 34 for Asians, according to the nonpartisan Public Policy Institute of California. The racial bias appears even more shocking when considering that one out of every 22 black men in the state is incarcerated.

Overcrowding - Cruel and Unusual Punishment

In 2001, the Prison Law Office in Berkeley filed a class action lawsuit on behalf of inmate Marciano Plata and others, alleging California had violated the "cruel and unusual punishment" clause of the Constitution's Eighth Amendment. A panel of three federal judges decided severe overcrowding was the primary cause of these Eighth Amendment violations. A later decision by the U.S. Supreme Court in *Brown v. Plata* eventually led to the early release of roughly 37,000 prisoners through various means[151].

The state's prisons have long been obscenely overcrowded. Prior to *Brown v. Plata*, inmates were basically stuck in any space available. This meant that gymnasiums, classrooms and other areas designed for different purposes became de facto cells. One toilet might suffice for 50 inmates. The overcrowding led to increased levels of assault and other violent acts.

In 2009, the U.S. Supreme Court ordered California to reduce its prison population to an "institutional design capacity" of 137.5 percent. That's still more than a third over what the prisons were created to hold. The population is down considerably from its 2006 peak of 163,000 inmates, with approximately 115,000 behind bars. At the time of the Supreme Court's order, certain prisons were at 300 percent capacity, while the average was 181 percent. The prison system is designed to hold just 85,000 people.

151 *Brown v. Plata*. (2011). OYEZ. Retrieved 13 February 2018, from https://www.oyez.org/cases/2010/09-1233

As of September 2017, California prisons are at 135.6 percent[152] of design capacity. That's the average, but some institutions are far above that. Facilities above 150 percent of design capacity include:

- California Substance Abuse Treatment Facility, Corcoran 166.5%
- Chuckawalla Valley State Prison 161.7%
- Correctional Training Facility 152.4%
- High Desert State Prison 153.7%
- North Kern State Prison 167.5%
- Valley State Prison 177.4%
- Wasco State Prison 172.0%

Only two facilities, California Health Care Facility, Stockton, and Supermax facility Pelican Bay State Prison, are under 100 percent of capacity, at 80.5 percent and 93.8 percent, respectively.

The Bill Comes Due

What led to this appalling overcrowding? Prior to the 1980s, California's prison system[153] was considered one of the nation's best, and capacity was not an issue. The entire California prison population in the 1970s consisted of approximately 20,000 inmates at any time. Then, starting in the late 1980s, state legislators began enacting ever more punitive laws designed to keep criminals in prison longer. In five years, hundreds of new laws were passed, dramatically increasing sentencing.

This new tough sentencing coincided with the elimination of education

152 *Brown v. Plata* Status Report. (2017). Cdcr.ca.gov. Retrieved 13 February 2018, from http://www.cdcr.ca.gov/News/docs/3JP-Sep-2017.pdf

153 Fuchs, E. (2013). How California Prisons Got To Be So Insanely Overcrowded. Business Insider. Retrieved 13 February 2018, from http://www.businessinsider.com/how-california-prisons-got-so-crowded-2013-8

and workforce training for inmates. Former prisoners left incarceration with no skills, causing the recidivism rate to skyrocket. At the same time, prison construction was a growth industry, but the demand could not keep up with inmate supply.

In the middle of the crack cocaine epidemic, voters approved the Three Strikes law in 1994. Designed to fight crime, Three Strikes fueled the overcrowding crisis instead. About 25 percent of all California inmates are "Strikers," and many of them are serving 25 years to life for petty theft and the like, as opposed to violent crimes, in spite of several recent voter initiatives that have addressed the issue.

Between tougher sentencing and the Three Strikes law, the prison population exploded. Three Strikes is especially liable for an older, sicker prison demographic. It's a reason the state's finances are such a mess. Although Californians' Prop. 36[154] was passed in 2012 and it rectifies some of the worst aspects of the Three Strikes law, it is too little, too late. The bill has come due, and state residents must pay it.

An Aging Population

People on the outside probably think of the inmate population as young and relatively healthy. That's not the case. More than one-fifth of all California inmates are over age 50, and only 13 percent are age 25 or less. A substantial percentage of the over-50 population is actually over age 65. An aging inmate population means greater costs for health care, but the state isn't providing this mandate. Many prisons are now serving as de facto nursing homes or hospices for considerable numbers of inmates. Prisoners don't receive Medicaid, so the facility must pay for all hospital bills.

154 California Proposition 36, Changes in the "Three Strikes" Law (2012). Ballotpedia.org. Retrieved 13 February 2018, from https://ballotpedia.org/California_Proposition_36,_Changes_in_the_%22Three_Strikes%22_Law_(2012)#Text_of_measure

Some famous California prisoners personalize the problem. The 1969 Tate-LaBianca murders, carried out at the behest of Charles Manson, spelled the end of the optimistic late 1960s ethos virtually overnight. You have probably seen photos of Manson's "family" at their trial, young women with X's carved into their foreheads in imitation of Charlie. Now, the surviving members of Manson's crew are old ladies, still in prison. No one suggests that granting parole to Charlie, now deceased, would have been a good idea, but two of the aged Manson Family members are a different story.

In 2017, Manson family member Patricia Krenwinkel[155], California's longest-serving female inmate, was again denied parole. Now 70, Krenwinkel took part in the killings at age 21. Her disciplinary record is clean, and she has earned a bachelor's degree. Krenwinkel worked training service dogs and counseling fellow inmates, according to an earlier parole hearing. She has expressed deep remorse for her actions, and doctors say she doesn't pose a threat to society.

Leslie van Houten[156], 68, was granted parole in 2016 and 2017, but was denied each time by Governor Jerry Brown despite being a model prisoner for the majority of her life. While the notoriety of these crimes will likely keep these women in prison, there are many others convicted of less publicized crimes whose behavior and age mean they currently pose little threat to society, but a great cost to its prison system.

Deplorable Health Care

For too many California inmates, prison resulted in a death sentence even if they weren't incarcerated for a capital crime. They are dying for lack of

155 Hamilton, M. (2016). This Manson family member is the longest-serving woman in California prisons. Will she get parole?. LA Times. Retrieved 13 February 2018, from http://www.latimes.com/local/lanow/la-me-ln-manson-parole-hearing-20161229-story.html2)#Text_of_measure

156 California board grants parole to Manson disciple Leslie Van Houten. (2017). USA TODAY. Retrieved 13 February 2018, from https://www.usatoday.com/story/news/2017/09/06/california-board-grants-parole-manson-disciple-leslie-van-houten/640101001/

kidney dialysis, chemotherapy, and other treatments that save or prolong lives, or because they aren't diagnosed with diabetes, high blood pressure, and similar conditions until it is too late. No one made sure patients kept the doctor's appointments they did receive or took their medication as needed, or even dispensed them the medication as prescribed.

As California Healthline[157] notes, "For years, California's state prison health system served inmates so poorly that many died for lack of medical care." In 2011's *Brown v. Plata*, the Supreme Court noted that every five to six days, "a preventable or possibly preventable cause of death" occurred in the state's prison system. Doctors weren't seeing inmate patients in clean, safe medical facilities. Instead, when physicians did examine patients, it was often in "converted showers and closets[158]," according to one prison doctor.

In 2005, U.S. District Judge Thelton Henderson[159], saying the state's prison medical system involved "at times outright depravity," ordered a receiver to take over the prison health care system. In his decision, Henderson referred to the "deplorable" conditions in California's prison health system. He issued his decision after hearing weeks of testimony regarding the needless deaths and injuries resulting from medical negligence.

Plata revealed that the reported position vacancy rates included 25 percent for physicians and 54 percent for psychiatrists. Overcrowding, including huge caseloads and the threat of violence, made hiring and keeping competent doctors "challenging." The three-judge panel actually accused the California prison system of hiring any doctor possessing "a license, a pulse,

157 More Prisoners Die Of Old Age Behind Bars. (2016). California Healthline. Retrieved 13 February 2018, from https://californiahealthline.org/news/more-prisoners-die-of-old-age-behind-bars/

158 Bursting at the seams: how did California's prisons become so crowded? (2010). KALW. Retrieved 13 February 2018, from http://blog.sfgate.com/kalw/2010/11/30/bursting-at-the-seams-how-did-californias-prisons-become-so-crowded/

159 U.S. seizes state prison health care / Judge cites preventable deaths of inmates, 'depravity' of system. (2005). SFGate. Retrieved 13 February 2018, from https://www.sfgate.com/health/article/U-S-seizes-state-prison-health-care-Judge-2658768.php

and a pair of shoes." Doctors willing to work within the prison system often had "issues" with their medical licenses. They probably couldn't get work in a public hospital, but a prison facility welcomed them with open arms.

One may think, "Good! Good riddance!" but that knee-jerk reaction to the peril of prisoners is off the mark. Remember that many in prison are there for non-violent, victimless crimes, or they may have been wrongly convicted in the first place. Incarceration should never be a death sentence in and of itself. The function of a prison is to make sure people pay their debt to society, not to grind the souls and bodies of the inmates to dust.

Mental Health Care

The mentally ill make up nearly one-quarter of the California prison population. Even as the sheer number of inmates has declined, the percentage of those battling mental illness[160] has increased. In 2013, the California Department of Corrections and Rehabilitation (CDCR) reported an even higher percentage of mentally ill inmates—37 percent—while acknowledging that many of these patients have less severe conditions which don't require "enhanced" treatment.

Suicide rates have risen to 24 per 100,000 inmates per year, a figure that surpasses the national average by 48 percent, according to *The New York Times*[161]. Up to 70 percent of these suicides may have been averted, had the inmates received adequate mental health care. In 2009, officials agreed that any prisoner with a life-threatening psychiatric issue would receive help within 24 hours, and that other seriously mentally ill inmates would receive care within 30 days.

160 Mentally ill inmates are swamping the state's prisons and jails. Here's one man's story. (2016). LA Times. Retrieved 13 February 2018, from http://www.latimes.com/local/california/la-me-mentally-ill-inmate-snap-story.html

161 Mental Illness in California Prisons (2013). New York Times. Retrieved 13 February 2018, from http://www.nytimes.com/2013/04/11/opinion/mental-illness-in-california-prisons.html

In a 2013 decision regarding a motion by the state to end CDCR oversight, Judge Lawrence Karlton of the Federal District Court in Sacramento wrote, "Systemic failures persist in the form of inadequate suicide prevention measures, excessive administrative segregation of the mentally ill, lack of timely access to adequate care, insufficient treatment space and access to beds, and unmet staffing needs."

Fast forward four years. In April 2017, U.S. District Judge Kimberly Mueller[162] threatened to fine California prison officials hundreds of thousands of dollars *per day* if they didn't comply with the new mental health care protocol. Approximately one-quarter of all mentally ill inmates needing acute care were still not receiving treatment within 24 hours. Mueller determined the problem wasn't a lack of mental health crisis beds, rather, it was a shortage of professionals to tend to them. Insufficient staffing results in many mentally ill prisoners being placed on a long waiting list to receive treatment.

The disgraceful treatment of the mentally ill was one of the catalysts behind the reform[163] of California's criminal justice system. While many of these changes are coming to fruition, treatment of the mentally ill is not improving. Why is this? Many of the reform stipulations focus on inmate behavior, and the number of prison rule violations is a major consideration for the officials in charge of making early release decisions. Inmates suffering from mental illness are likely to take a turn for the worse merely because of the prison environment.

---

162 Pickoff-White, L., & Small, J. (2017). Judge Threatens to Fine California Prisons for Delayed Mental Health Treatment. KQED News. Retrieved 13 February 2018, from https://ww2.kqed.org/news/2017/04/20/judge-threatens-to-fine-california-prisons-for-delayed-mental-health-treatment/

163 The Prevalence And Severity Of Mental Illness Among California Prisoners On The Rise. (2017). Stanford. Justice Advocacy Project. Retrieved 13 February 2018, from https://www-cdn.law.stanford.edu/wp-content/uploads/2017/05/Stanford-Report-FINAL.pdf

Out-of-State Imprisonment

Defendants sentenced in a California courtroom will not necessarily serve their sentences in a California prison. California's prisons are so overcrowded, even after the 2006 overcrowding state of emergency declaration, that the state spends money sending inmates to out-of-state facilities.

The system often relocates the prisoners[164] with the fewest disciplinary issues, and they are sent to locations as varied as Arizona, Florida, and Mississippi. The prisons they end up in are private, not state facilities, such as institutions run by the Corrections Corporation of America.

California is one of just four states that contracts with private prisons to ease overcrowding. Ironically, for the inmates sent to such out-of-state private facilities, the reward for their good behavior is usually a complete loss of personal visits from family and friends. In addition, private prisons do not have the experienced staff and various services that are available at California facilities. Rates of assault and other inmate on inmate crime are higher in private prisons.

Death Row

The United States has more people in prison than Russia, Iran, and Iraq combined. The U.S. has the death penalty even though most other countries have banned it, with the exception of China, Iran, Saudi Arabia, and a few Third World nations in Asia and Africa; look at the company we're in! Currently, 747 people await their fate on California's Death Row[165]. Although it's been a decade since the state last executed a Death

164 Schumacher, K. (2016). Shipping Inmates Out of State. Go Big Read. Retrieved 13 February 2018, from https://gobigread.wisc.edu/2016/04/shipping-inmates-out-of-state/

165 These are the 747 inmates awaiting execution on California's death row. (2017). LA Times. Retrieved 13 February 2018, from http://www.latimes.com/projects/la-me-death-row/

Row inmate, a spate of executions are likely to be scheduled in the near future, thanks to the passage of Proposition 66[166] in the 2016 election.

Passed by a narrow 51 to 49 percent, Prop. 66 is intended to speed up the capital trial and execution process. It establishes strict timelines for inmate death sentence appeals, among other procedures to expedite the execution process. What all of this really means is that more inmates will lose their rights, and it's a virtual certainty that innocent people will end up being executed by the state.

In November 2017, Californians also had the opportunity to vote on a proposition to abolish the death penalty. Unfortunately, 53 percent voted down this proposition. Had it passed, Prop. 66 would not have gone into effect. I suspect another attempt to abolish the death penalty in California will eventually pass. But the impetus behind that will probably have to be the execution of someone whose guilt is truly questionable. Californians pride themselves on being a more 'civilized' people than those in other execution-mad states. That's not something we can take pride in much longer.

Proposition 57 – A Bit of Sensibility

In November 2016, California voters approved another ballot initiative, Proposition 57[167]. The proposition changed policies on juvenile prosecution, authorized sentence credits for rehabilitation, good behavior, and education, and most notably, allowed for parole consideration for nonviolent felons. In short, it bravely stood up to the maniacal cries of "Get tough on crime!" and swung the pendulum slightly back towards reason.

166 California votes to speed up 'broken' death penalty system. (2016). The Sacramento Bee. Retrieved 13 February 2018, from http://www.sacbee.com/news/politics-government/capitol-alert/article116588753.html

167 Proposition 57 – Public Safety and Rehabilitation Act of 2016. (2017). CDCR. Retrieved 13 February 2018, from http://www.cdcr.ca.gov/proposition57/docs/prop-57-fact-sheet.pdf

Proposition 57 added the following provisions:

- Shortened prison stays for nonviolent felony offenses by making it quicker to get paroled.
- Gave the Department of Corrections and Rehabilitation the authority to award credits earned for good behavior and approved rehabilitative or educational achievements.
- Gave the Department of Corrections and Rehabilitation the mandate to adopt regulations to make the goals of Prop. 57 happen, with a review by the Secretary of the Department of Corrections and Rehabilitation to make sure that the regulations protect and enhance public safety.

The new legislation establishes shorter prison stays when a prisoner has been convicted of multiple nonviolent offenses. Under Prop. 57, they may be eligible for parole once they have served the full term of their primary offense. For example, if a prisoner was convicted of three different nonviolent felonies and was sentenced to four years on the first felony, and one year each for the remaining two for a total of six years, once the inmate has served just four years, they may be eligible for a release on parole.

A lot of questions surfaced after Prop. 57 was passed, including what convictions qualify as nonviolent, when would inmates start getting released, and how exactly the process would work. The text of the proposition lacks many details on the implementation of its overarching goals, but it did leave it up to the CDCR to adopt regulations.

The CDCR has already implemented some regulations which clarify these ambiguities, stating that the nonviolent parole process began on July 1, 2017, and that if an inmate is determined to be an eligible nonviolent offender, he or she will be screened for possible referral to the Board of Parole Hearings[168] no later than 35 days prior to serving the full term of their primary offense.

However, this does not mean that inmates are automatically granted parole; rather, the inmate's behavior will be reviewed and considered by the parole board and may be denied if they pose a current threat to public safety. Additionally, the CDCR has clarified that a "nonviolent felony offense" is an offense that is not listed in Penal Code section 667.5, subdivision (c), which includes many obvious violent crimes such as murder, mayhem, and rape, but also crimes such as carjacking, extortion, and threats to victims or witnesses.

Three Strikes are Still Out

Although Prop. 57 shows promise, it doesn't affect inmates sentenced from 25 years to life under Three Strikes. In July 2017, the California Supreme Court ruled in a 4-3 decision that judges have considerable leeway when it comes to reducing the sentences of Three Strikes inmates. Prop. 36 proposes the revision of the Three Strikes law to impose a life sentence only when the new felony conviction is "serious or violent." It also authorizes re-sentencing for offenders currently serving life sentences if the third strike conviction was neither serious nor violent, and if the judge determines that resentencing does not pose unreasonable risk to public safety.

In 2014, the state passed Prop. 47[169]. This legislation "reduces certain drug possession felonies to misdemeanors. It also requires misdemeanor sentencing for petty theft, receiving stolen property and

168 Proposition 57: Nonviolent Parole Process Frequently Asked Questions. (2017). CDRC. Retrieved 13 February 2018, from http://www.cdcr.ca.gov/proposition57/docs/FAQ-Prop-57-Nonviolent-Parole-Process.pdf

169 Proposition 47 - What CDCR inmates and their family and friends need to know (2017). CDCR. Retrieved 13 February 2018, from http://www.cdcr.ca.gov/News/prop47.html

forging/writing bad checks when the amount involved is $950 or less." California was the first state to make drug possession, even of 'hard' drugs, a misdemeanor rather than a felony; a flashback to California's pioneering innovation.

The California Supreme Court's July 2017 decision allows judges to "freely decline" sentence reductions for those eligible for such reductions under Prop. 47. The court ruled that the definition of who poses an unreasonable risk to public safety did not apply to Three Strikes inmates, and that the ballot question for Prop. 47 did not include any references to Three Strikes.

In his dissent, Associate Justice Goodwin Hon Liu wrote, "Today the court departs from plain meaning in deciding whether the terms of a recent initiative broaden a statutory entitlement to resentencing for certain inmates whose third strike was neither serious nor violent. This turnabout is as unorthodox in its methodology as it is unsettling in its implications for the initiative process and the limited role of courts in interpreting statutes."

As to the ballot's language, Liu observes, "Ballot materials may help illuminate the purpose of an initiative statute. But the fact that ballot materials do not speak to the application of the statute in a particular case is not a reason to disregard the plain meaning of the enacted text. Ballot materials are necessarily incomplete and serve as summaries. The summary must yield to the statute, not the statute to the summary."

When it comes to reasonable sentencing and the reduction of prison overcrowding in California, it seems like it's always one step forward and two steps backward.

Some Good News

It's not time to abandon hope, all ye who enter the California prison system. The mass release[170] of 30,000 plus prisoners due to reform through voter initiative and a rare enlightened high-court decision within the past few years has not created a huge rise in crime. In fact, California's crime rates have declined, aside from a spike in automobile theft.

Recidivism rates have also dropped significantly. County criminal justice systems were charged with post-release management, and they have stepped up to the plate with drug addiction and mental health treatments, as well as other needed programs. Now, it's time for state officials to take a cue from their county counterparts and work to address the root problems of those still incarcerated!

---

170 What happened when California released 30,000 prisoners. (2015). Time. Retrieved 13 February 2018, from http://time.com/4065359/california-prison-release-department-of-justice/

CONCLUSION

HIGH COURTS, HIGH TREASON

In courts today, we practice 'F**ck you' law. Please forgive the vulgarity that is otherwise not present in this book, but it's the best way to get the reader to understand the baseness of the legal system that is in play every day in courts up and down the state and across the nation.

For the last 40 years, appellate courts have been obliterating our civil freedoms and constitutional rights. A 40-year track record does not happen by accident. It happens as a result of a carefully thought-out and meticulously followed plan of action. More than any other institution, appellate courts are front and center to the corruption of our country. What's even more frightening than the power they wield is their relative obscurity and unaccountability.

For example, if the President does or says something debatable, he is called out by the press, just like any other politician. However, in the case of courts, the public tends to take their opinion as 'the word of God'. The public believes the fallacious premise that courts always follow the law. They believe that if a court did it, it must have been the legal, lawful, and right thing to do.

Furthermore, appellate courts such as the 9th Circuit Court of Appeals, and the U.S. Supreme Court are relatively anonymous institutions that shield its members from direct and personal public scrutiny. A headline might talk about a 'California Court of Appeals' but refrain from naming names. That's going to change with this chapter.

Appellate courts are dangerous because they create law. They rewrite the Constitution and legislate without any accountability for their decisions. By defining statues and ruling on Constitutional matters, appellate courts have actively eroded our rights.

In under a minute, anyone can become an expert in constitutional law as it applies to someone accused of a crime. You think you have rights? Well, the appellate courts say, 'F**ck You':

> Cops unlawfully searched your home or car and then arrested you based on that unlawful search? Well, let's see what appellate courts have said about that situation… Oh, here, it's – F**ck you!
>
> You were arrested and the officer didn't read you your rights? You want your case dismissed? Hmmm… The Constitution says, 'Can't force someone to incriminate themselves,' long history of this, then… okay, the appellate law on the books on this point says – F**ck You!
>
> The jail violated your constitutional right to an attorney? You know, I just read a ruling on that issue by an appellate court, yeah, here it is… the court said, F**ck You!

The local courts in your cities and towns are called 'superior courts.' They have jurisdiction over things that happen in the county. To appeal something that may have gone wrong in a county superior court, you would appeal to an appellate court. The people in black robes in superior courts are called 'judges.' The people in black robes in appellate courts are called 'justices.'

To appeal something that may have gone wrong in an appellate court, you would appeal to the California Supreme Court. Those black robes are also called 'Justices.' However, if an appeal touches on constitutional matters, it can be appealed to a federal court, most often the 9th Circuit in California. From there, a 9th Circuit decision can be appealed to the highest court in the land, the United States Supreme Court.

Unlike what you see on TV, you would have to wait a long time in a superior court to hear a judge rule in favor of a significant motion filed by a defendant. Superior courts know they can f**ck you, because they know they have a safety net from the appellate courts—if a superior court's decision goes against the defendant or results in a conviction, the appellate court will overwhelmingly approve it.

Appellate courts know they are the safety net for the superior courts. They also know that their decisions are unlikely to ever undergo scrutiny by the Supreme Courts. On average, the California Supreme Court[171] only hears 83 cases each year. The U.S. Supreme Court reviews about 100 cases a year and that's for all 50 states.

There are two main ways to get to an appellate court, through an appeal or through a writ. An appeal is used after a case is done, and the lower court's decision is reviewed by a higher court. Generally speaking, a writ is like an appeal, but it's used while the case is still being litigated.

Under California law, writ petitions are the only method for obtaining appellate review of specific types of trial court decisions. A writ denial generally takes a 'summary' form—pretty much one sentence. Defense attorneys call it the "F**ck You postcard."

That's because 99 percent of the time when you take the immense

171 2015 COURT STATISTICS REPORT Statewide Caseload Trends. (2015). Judicial Council of California. Retrieved 13 January 2018, from http://www.courts.ca.gov/documents/2015-Court-Statistics-Report.pdf

time and effort to 'writ' an issue, the appellate court sends back a letter simply stating 'The petition is DENIED.' There's no explanation, no case law, no nothing. The petitioner can only guess at the reasons for the denial. For a minimum of 80 hours of work by the defense researching, writing, formatting, and filing pages and pages for a writ, we most often get a 'F**ck You' postcard in return.

A private citizen or company could spend tens of millions of dollars litigating an appeal all the way to the U.S. Supreme Court. The Government can defend its stance, attacking your appeal, using your, and everyone else's, tax dollars. Someone facing criminal allegations or a wrongful conviction has the deck equally stacked against them within the appellate process.

True, lasting change in society must come about from peaceful acts and demonstrations. As a society, we will be better off if we commit to being virtuous, if we base our society on justice, compassion, and love. However, in terms of real change, of revolution, there is no area more ripe for attention than the relatively anonymous and unaccountable appellate courts. More powerful than impeachment, more potent than a recall or 'voting the incumbent bums out' at the next election cycle, no act would cause a more direct and immediate change in any country across the world as the act of peacefully and calmly rounding up the members of a corrupt appellate court and marching them out of their lair onto the steps of their very own courthouse, where the justices could be seen in the light of day and face the public whom they have betrayed so deeply.

A lot of the bad behavior by officers, including the 'shoot first, lie about it later,' shootings by cops against citizens, are a direct result of appellate court 'justices' empowering psychopathic cops to do whatever they want, whenever they want. Think about it, if you are on a BART train and all four kids belonging to a mom and dad are acting horribly, bullying other passengers, stealing, and picking fights, you'd look at the parents and think that, because it's their responsibility to oversee their children, the kids' bad behavior is their fault.

When psychopathic officers take the stand and are caught red-handed in a lie, yet the superior court does nothing about it, and then denies the defendant's motion, the cop feels emboldened to do it again. We know superior courts are rarely overturned by appellate courts if their decision cuts against the defendant. Thus, it should be a real discussion when a bad cop is exposed, to what extent that officer's behavior was overlooked or sanctioned by judges.

Unwarranted officer shootings or beatings of people, the responsive violence by citizens against innocent, unrelated officers, Black Lives Matter, Antifa, Blue Lives Matter—how much of this social narrative has been given life by appellate court 'justices' playing the 'F**ck You' game in courts of law?

As we have seen, psychopaths seek power, they seek promotion. Thus, it's axiomatic that the psychopaths in the court system would also seek power and promotion, first, to become a judge in superior court and then to be elevated to an appellate court. But murderers such as Charles Manson or the Son of Sam aren't the most evil people in the world. That designation goes to those cold-blooded psychopaths that carry out calculated plans for the systematic murder of thousands or millions; think Stalin, think Mao. Also, think about the engineers in their offices who calmly designed the death camps at Dachau using the knowledge they learned in schools.

When Charles Manson facilitates the murder of seven people, it's a tragedy. When U.S. Government officials enact a false flag in the Gulf of Tonkin which leads to the Vietnam War and the loss of over 58,000 American lives alone, that is a mere statistic. Appellate courts at their worst are no different than the Ford executives who coldly calculated the cost of the retrofitting needed to make their Pintos safe versus just paying the wrongful death lawsuits. After all, the U.S. Supreme Court, in *McCleskey v. Kemp*[172] (1987) 481 U.S. 279, *recognized* that there was rampant racial discrimination in the application of the death penalty, but sustained the practice.

The Constitution and Criminal Law

The Bill of Rights consists of the first ten amendments to the Constitution. Criminal law is mainly governed by the Fourth, Fifth, and Sixth Amendments.

The Fourth Amendment is *supposed to* safeguard us against unreasonable searches and seizures by the government.

The Fifth Amendment is *supposed to* safeguard us from the government forcing and/or coercing us to make self-incriminating statements, it's *supposed to* safeguard us from the government going after us or convicting us twice for the same offense (double jeopardy), and it's also *supposed to* safeguard us from the government taking away our rights or property without due process of law—a fair legal procedure.

The Sixth Amendment is *supposed to* guarantee us the right to a speedy trial, the right to an attorney, the right to know the accusers and the charges against us, and, more importantly, the right to confront your accusers and present evidence on your behalf.

All three of these amendments have been gutted by appellate courts over the last 40 years, and it's no mistake. It's deliberate; it's systematic and systemic. You would assume that the progressive 'liberal' and 'caring' California Supreme Court, or the 'hallowed' and 'above-reproach' United

172 *McCleskey v. Kemp*, 481 U.S. 279 (1987). (1987). Justia Law. Retrieved 13 January 2018, from https://supreme.justia.com/cases/federal/us/481/279/case.html

States Supreme Court would uphold these three sacred amendments but, alas, they do not. In reality, that is far from the case. Here are some examples of relatively recent egregious decisions from these high courts.

Fourth Amendment

Have you seen the headlines about government surveillance lately? It's happening illegally right now and we all know it. In fact, we even know about the NSA center in Utah where all of our emails, texts, and phone calls are recorded and stored illegally. But not one cop, prosecutor, judge, justice, or politician has stopped it. This illegal government surveillance is but one example of our rights being systematically eviscerated.

People v. Diaz

California Supreme Court

350 McAllister St, San Francisco, CA 94102

Majority opinion by Ming Chin, joined by Marvin Baxter, Carol Corrigan, Ronald George, concurrence by Joyce Kennard

In *People v. Diaz*, the California Supreme Court ruled that a warrantless search of text messages on a defendant's phone was not unconstitutional, meaning the search was just fine under Chin, Baxter, Corrigan, George and Kennard's reading of the Constitution.

The case involves Gregory Diaz, an accused drug dealer arrested for the sale of the club drug Ecstasy. The police seized and searched his cell phone without a warrant, and his text messages contained incriminating evidence. Diaz attempted to suppress the text messages, stating that warrantless seizure of the phone violated his Fourth Amendment rights.

He argued cell phones "contain quantities of personal data unrivaled by any conventional item of evidence traditionally considered to be immediately associated with the person of the arrestee, such as an article of clothing, a wallet or a crumpled cigarette box found in an arrestee's pocket, and therefore implicate heightened privacy concerns." The superior court said 'f**ck you' to this argument. Thereafter, Diaz was convicted. His attorney appealed to the appellate court. The appellate court said 'f**ck you' to the appeal.

The California Supreme Court also answered 'f**ck you' to this important constitutional issue. Chin, Baxter, Corrigan, George, and Kennard reasoned that defendants give up a certain amount of privacy upon arrest. The two dissenting justices, Kathryn Mickle Werdegar and Carlos Moreno, noted the majority decision permitted police to go through all the personal and business information found on cell phones 'carte blanche' and pointed out the unique qualities of a cell phone compared to other articles a person might carry. Yep.

It's obvious that James Madison could not envision the complexity of a cell phone when working on the Bill of Rights. In his day, though, he understood the importance of protecting personal information, whether it was carried in the pocket, saddle bags, or a valise. The California courts didn't care about these values, they were happy to create law mandating that if a cop wanted to look all through your cell phone, any app, any data, any pictures, that was just fine with them. If you didn't like it, f**ck you.

In a rare example of a higher court righting a wrong, the U.S. Supreme Court thankfully overturned this decision in *Riley v. California*, (2014) 134 S. Ct. 2473, noting the obvious: that a search of a personal device that has loads of personal and confidential information on it without a warrant is a violation of the Fourth Amendment.

Utah v. Strieff

U.S. Supreme Court

1 First St. NE, Washington, DC 20543

John Roberts, Clarence Thomas, Samuel Alito, Stephen Breyer, and Anthony Kennedy

In *Utah v. Strieff*, (2016) 136 S. Ct. 2056, the U.S. Supreme Court ruled that even if a police stop and search of an individual was unconstitutional, as long as there was no 'flagrant' police misconduct and there was a pre-existing, valid warrant for someone's arrest, any evidence seized was admissible. In other words, when a police officer unconstitutionally stops someone and unconstitutionally seizes evidence, but there is a warrant for the person somewhere, then everything is fine and the fruit of the illegal search—the evidence—will be admissible.

The case involved police surveillance[173] of a Salt Lake City house, which started when police received an 'anonymous' tip about illegal drug activity. A SLC detective watched the dwelling intermittently for a week. He saw many visitors to the house, who stayed for just a few minutes. At one point, the detective saw Edward Strieff leave the house and walk to a nearby store. The detective then stopped Strieff without any legal justification and demanded his identification. He then used the identification to have dispatch search for any outstanding warrants.

The detective was informed by dispatch that Strieff had an outstanding arrest warrant for a traffic violation. The detective then arrested Strieff and searched him, discovering illegal drugs. Streiff was charged with possession of methamphetamine and drug paraphernalia. Strieff's attorney

173 FOURTH AMENDMENT *Utah v. Strieff*. (2016). Harvard Law Review, 130(1).

moved to suppress the evidence because it was obtained by an illegal stop. Although the State agreed the detective did violate the Fourth Amendment by detaining Strieff without 'reasonable articulable suspicion,' it argued the evidence was admissible because discovery of the arrest warrant created valid cause for searching Strieff, despite the illegal stop. Of course the judge agreed with the prosecution, denied the defense's suppression motion, and admitted the evidence. Strieff pled guilty but reserved the right to appeal.

On appeal, the Utah Court of Appeals affirmed the suppression motion denial. When that was appealed to the Utah Supreme Court, they actually reversed it. Since it looked like a low level drug user might get off scot-free, the state used its resources to appeal to the highest court in the land—the U.S. Supreme Court. Unsurprisingly, the U.S. Supreme Court found against the defendant, reversing the Utah Supreme Court decision. "The unlawful stop was sufficiently attenuated by the pre-existing arrest warrant," according to the majority.

In America, we decided that we didn't want armed thugs for the government harassing us because we visited a house they might not like or about which they had received an 'anonymous' tip. For that reason, we have the Fourth Amendment. For that reason, we have had a long standing legal doctrine called the 'Fruit of the Poisonous Tree'[174] going back to the 1920s and 1930s.

If the police break the law, then a search is a 'poisonous tree.' The fruits of that poisonous tree are not consumed, they are rejected in court – or they should be. Think about it, the initial stop was unconstitutional. This was admitted even by the prosecution and wasn't an argument in court. The cop used the illegal stop to acquire Strieff's identification.

174 *Fruit of the Poisonous Tree. The Free Dictionary.* Retrieved 12 January 2018, from https://legal-dictionary.thefreedictionary.com/Fruit+of+the+Poisonous+Tree

Then, using the identification, he obtained information that Strieff had a warrant. He then arrested Strieff and, based upon a 'search incident to arrest,' which is lawful, found the meth and pipe. None of this would have been possible without the illegal stop! So, our modern day U.S. Supreme Court found a way to demolish nearly 100 years of Fruit of the Poisonous Tree jurisprudence!

Justice Sonia Sotomayor, one of the dissenters, said it best in writing, "it's no secret that people of color are disproportionate victims of this type of scrutiny… this case tells everyone, white and black, guilty and innocent, that an officer can verify your legal status at any time. It says that your body is subject to invasion while courts excuse the violation of your rights. It implies that you are not a citizen of a democracy but the subject of a carceral state, just waiting to be cataloged[175]." Sotomayor's dissent also stated that the finding of the warrant was part and parcel of the officer's illegal 'expedition for evidence' in the hope that something might 'turn up.' In other words, the warrant would not have been found but for the illegal stop!

The Supreme Court may have been happy to go one step forward in *Riley* as long as they could go three steps back in *Strieff*. Why would the U.S. Supreme Court erase decades of well-established law and doctrine? Because 'F**ck you,' that's why.

Fifth Amendment

Berghuis v. Thompkins

U.S. Supreme Court

175 Stern, M. (2016). Read Sonia Sotomayor's Atomic Bomb of a Dissent Slamming Racial Profiling and Mass Imprisonment. Slate Magazine, June 20, 2016. Retrieved 12 January 2018, from http://www.slate.com/blogs/the_slatest/2016/06/20/sonia_sotomayor_dissent_in_utah_v_strieff_takes_on_police_misconduct.html

1 First St. NE, Washington, DC 20543

Anthony Kennedy, joined by John Roberts, Antonin Scalia, Clarence Thomas, and Samuel Alito

Most people in America know that the Fifth Amendment guarantees the "right to remain silent" by "pleading the Fifth." Well, this is not true anymore in our 'F**ck You' legal landscape. The U.S. Supreme Court in *Berghuis v. Thompkins*, (2010) 560 U.S. 370 held that the right to remain silent doesn't mean the right to remain silent. The Court held that a defendant must explicitly invoke the right under questioning by police. In other words, when an officer says, "You have the right to remain silent," you have to say, "Yes, please, nice officer, I would like to remain silent and not be questioned further." That means, you actually *didn't* have a *right to remain silent* because you had to say something first, before being able to remain silent.

Trying to find logic in this is sheer torture. Police officers don't say, "If you want to be silent and don't want us to question you further, then you have to let us know." But officers do say, "You have the right to ***remain*** silent." The only logical, rational interpretation of this is that, when someone is silent as the officer is reading him or her their rights, they can ***remain*** silent without saying or doing anything further. In fact, a legal scholar noted that the *Berghuis v. Thompkins* decision 'effectively gutted' *Miranda* rights[176]. Other critics agreed that the decision turned back the clock on previous safeguards.

Again, one of the dissenters, Justice Sonia Sotomayor, put it most eloquently, "A suspect who wishes to guard his right to remain silent must,

176 Weisselberg, C. and Bibas, S. The Right to Remain Silent, 159 U. Pa. L. Rev. PENNumbra 69 (2010), Available at: http://scholarship.law.berkeley.edu/facpubs/2181 (January 10, 2018)

counterintuitively, speak... At best, the court today creates an unworkable and conflicting set of presumptions. At worst, it overrules sub silentio an essential aspect of the protections *Miranda* has long provided."

Tortured logic, decades gutting long-standing legal protections, counterintuitive, unworkable, and conflicting are just some expressions to use to describe the ruling in this case. This is what happens when we veer away from the rule of law and adopt the new rule of 'F**ck you.'

People v. Superior court (Ward)

Court of Appeal of California, Fourth Appellate District, Division Two

3389 12th St.

Riverside, CA 92501

Douglas Miller, Manuel Ramirez, and Betty Ann Richli

The California Legislature passed Assembly Bill 109, "The Public Safety Realignment Act of 2011[177]" and Governor Jerry Brown approved it in April, 2011. "AB 109" shifted responsibility from the California Department of Corrections and Rehabilitation to counties to manage some of the individuals convicted of crimes that AB 109 classified as non-serious, non-violent and non-sexual felony offenses.

The bill granted the state Division of Adult Parole Operations (DAPO) the authority to impose flash incarceration—a sanction of up to 10 days in county jail for violation of parole terms. Yes, you read that right, AB 109 gave parole officers the power to put someone in jail if the parole officer thought the person violated probation. This clearly contrasts with the Fifth Amendment's due process clause of the U.S. Constitution

177 The Cornerstone of California's Solution to Reduce Overcrowding, Costs, and Recidivism. (2011). California Department of Corrections and Rehabilitation. Retrieved 13 January 2018, from https://www.cdcr.ca.gov/realignment/

prohibiting anyone "be deprived of life, liberty or property, without due process of law."

By foregoing the constitutionally-mandated procedure of due process, the California legislature left it up to the mere whim or mood of a parole/ probation officer whether or not someone under their supervision could find their home raided, a gun stuck to their head, and be marched off to jail for ten days. Even more shocking: numerous Americans have died as a result of neglect and abuse during this type of flash incarceration.

But our California Appellate Courts are there to correct this type of mistakes, right? Our brave and honorable Appellate Court Justices are there to take a stand and enforce our constitutional rights, aren't they? Once again, you'd be mistaken if you thought so. Check out what Justices Douglas P. Miller, Manuel A. Ramirez, and Betty Ann Richli said:

"Given the routine delays involved in bringing the matter to the court or parole board for resolution, the Legislature could logically find that authorizing flash incarceration represented no significant comparative infringement on the offenders' rights[178]."

In other words, getting a gun pointed at you and being forcibly taken to a concrete cell for 10-days at the whim of a government official with no judicial oversight whatsoever represents no "significant comparative infringement" on someone's constitutional rights.

"And although the People argue that the written waiver is unnecessary because the right to a hearing is statutorily waived, we are not at all convinced that it was inadequate if it was necessary. It clearly informed Ward that the flash incarceration would count as a custodial sanction and that if he wished to contest it, a formal revocation petition would be

---

178 *PEOPLE v. Thomas* Robert Ward, Real Party in Interest.. (2014). FindLaw - California Court of Appeal case and opinions. Retrieved 12 January 2018, from http://caselaw.findlaw.com/ca-court-of-appeal/1686675.html

filed with the court. We are not persuaded that counsel was required to be appointed before this decision was made."

Basically, the prosecution piped in and argued that this procedure was legal even if the defendant didn't waive the right to due process because the legislature had passed AB 109 which "statutorily waived" the U.S. Constitution's due process clause. Huh? Can a state waive the Bill of Rights by passing a state law? No! Even a third grader knows this isn't true.

However, this court wasn't "convinced" whether a waiver was necessary because if the defendant wanted a hearing, he could apply and get one after the fact, probably after the ten days was already completed. How convenient this is for these 'Justices.' Imagine the smiles on these Justices' faces as they were discussing this case behind closed doors and what they were going to do, 'Haha, these people think they have Due Process rights? They think they have the right to a fair court proceeding before being 'sentenced' by a parole officer? Let's tell them what they really have – F**ck you.'

Sixth Amendment

Kaley v. the United States

U.S. Supreme Court

1 First St. NE, Washington, DC 20543

Elena Kagan, Clarence Thomas, Ruth Bader Ginsberg, Samuel Alito, Antonin Scalia, and Anthony Kennedy

New York residents Mr. and Mrs. Brian and Kerri Kaley were indicted[179]

179 Opinion analysis: No right to challenge probable cause finding underlying asset freeze – even to pay your lawyers. (2014). SCOTUS blog. Retrieved 12 January 2018, from http://www.scotusblog.com/2014/02/opinion-analysis-no-right-to-challenge-probable-cause-finding-underlying-asset-freeze-even-to-pay-your-lawyers/

in 2007, charged with planning to re-sell "surplus" prescription medical devices. Kerri worked as a sales representative selling prescription medical devices to health care providers. When these providers received newer models, the old models became surplus devices[180]. Along with her husband and other sales reps, Kerri sold the surplus to a company in Florida. Their activity caught the eye of investigators. The Kaleys argued that the "medical devices at issue were unwanted, excess hospital inventory, which they could lawfully take and market to others."

The Kaleys were indicted by a grand jury. Keep in mind, a grand jury is conducted in secret, by a prosecutor only with no judge and no defense attorney allowed. Also, the legal standard to get someone indicted is "probable cause," a laughably low standard that might as well amount to a rubber stamp for the prosecutor. After the indictment, the prosecutor froze all of the Kaley's assets, claiming they were gained illicitly from the sales of the medical devices and had the district court issue an order preventing them from transferring or disposing of any property relating to the accusations.

The Kaleys did not dispute that these assets were related to their alleged crimes, but their whole point was that the charges were baseless, since they had committed no crime by selling inventory that no one had wanted. Of course, they needed attorneys to prove this point in court and to exonerate them. The couple petitioned a district court to lift the freeze on their assets, so they could afford a legal defense as the couple had already tapped their savings and home equity.

After what was no doubt a few very expensive rounds of legal motions and appeals, reversals and remands, the Kaleys ended back before the same district court that had frozen their assets in the first place. The court

180 *Kaley v. United States*. (2014). Harvard Law Review. Nov 2014,, 128(1), 261-270.

was forced to grant a hearing, but it limited the hearing to the question of whether the property in the forfeiture count was traceable to the Kaleys' conduct that they were being prosecuted for. Again, the Kaleys were not arguing that the money did not come from the selling of the defunct, surplus equipment, they were arguing that the conduct was not criminal and that they could prove it, if they could just hire an attorney to present their argument in court. If their conduct was not illegal, the fact that the source of their money was from the lawful sale of property shouldn't have been an issue in court.

Of course, the district court refused to hear any of that and sat there, listening straight-faced to the Kaleys, and then demanded, "Can you prove that the money isn't related to the sale of equipment that the prosecutor says is bad?" When the Kaleys could not show that the money was not traceable to the equipment, the district court kept the order in place. The Kaleys appealed again, arguing that they should have been allowed to challenge the validity of the indictment in the pretrial hearing, to counter the prosecution's theories, which could have refuted any illegality of their money. The appellate court disagreed and affirmed the lower court's decision. Their assets remained seized[181].

In 2014, the Kaleys took it up to the U.S. Supreme Court. Unsurprisingly, the SCOTUS agreed with the lower courts' decisions and issued a 'F**ck you' to the Kaleys and all Americans. It didn't matter that the government took the Kaleys' assets with only a probable cause hearing via a secret grand jury indictment with no defense, that was good enough. Whether or not there was evidence or argument that their conduct was lawful did not matter. Justice Elena Kagan, writing for the majority, stated that "with

181 *Kaley v. United States*. (2013). Oyez, Supreme Court Resources. Retrieved 12 January 2018, from https://www.oyez.org/cases/2013/12-464

probable cause, a freeze is valid," and that held true even if the frozen assets were needed to pay for legal representation.

Chief Justice Robert's dissent exemplifies why the *Kaley* decision was a bad one. He wrote that the right to counsel was "the most precious right a defendant has, because it's his attorney who will fight for the other rights the defendant enjoys."

Needless to say, this tactic of seizing the assets of defendants to stymie their ability to hire adequate defense is used by prosecutors, state district attorneys, and assistant U.S. attorneys alike. You think you have a right to hire an attorney? A prosecutor can take that away from you pretrial with only probable cause. Try fighting the charges with no money. If you disagree with that, the highest court of the land says, 'F**ck you.'

Moran v. Brisbane

U.S. Supreme Court

1 First St. NE, Washington, DC 20543

Sandra Day O'Connor, Harry Blackmun, William Rehnquist, Warren Burger, Byron White, and Lewis Powell

In 1977, after an arrest for burglary in Rhode Island, Brian Burbine[182], then 20, was suspected of involvement in a murder in Providence that had taken place a few months earlier. At first, Burbine refused to waive any of his rights, but after further pressure from the police, Burbine signed forms waiving his rights to an attorney.

Meanwhile, Burbine's sister called the local public defender's office to obtain legal representation for her brother, but she was unaware of the

182 *Moran v. Burbine*. (1985). Oyez, Supreme Court Resources. Retrieved 12 January 2018, from https://www.oyez.org/cases/2013/12-464

murder charge. When the public defender called the police department, he was told that Burbine was not available and that no questioning would take place until the following day. The police also failed to inform the attorney that Burbine was now a murder suspect[183]. Within an hour of telling the public defender no questioning would take place that night, police questioning began. Furthermore, police purposefully kept from Burbine that a lawyer had tried to contact him.

Upon questioning, he admitted his role in the murder and signed three statements to that effect. At Burbine's trial, the judge denied a motion to suppress the statements he made the night of his arrest at the police station. The judge held that Burbine made the statements knowingly, voluntarily waiving his rights to self-incrimination and an attorney. Burbine was convicted of first-degree murder.

The Rhode Island Supreme Court affirmed the decision, rejecting the defense's contention that the Constitution required Burbine's statements to be suppressed. The Court of Appeals reversed the decision, finding that law enforcement's failure to inform Burbine of the attorney's call "fatally tainted" his Sixth Amendment waivers of right to counsel and Fifth Amendment privilege against self-incrimination.

Supreme Court Justice Sandra Day O'Connor, writing for the majority, stated: "Events occurring outside of the presence of the suspect and entirely unknown to him surely can have no bearing on the capacity to comprehend and knowingly relinquish a constitutional right." In his dissent, Justice Stevens wrote that the decision "trampled on well-established legal principles and flouted the spirit of our accusatorial system of justice[184]."

183 *Moran v. Burbine*, 475 U.S. 412 (1986). (2018). Justia Law. Retrieved 12 January 2018, from https://supreme.justia.com/cases/federal/us/475/412/case.html

184 Flynn, M. (1988). Police Deception of a Criminal Suspect's Attorney: An Analysis of *Moran v. Burbine* Under the Alaska Constitution. Alaska Law Review Volume:5 Issue:1 Dated:(June 1988) Pages: Date Published: 1988, 5(1), 161-192.

This decision permits police deception of a criminal suspect's attorney. It is appalling. As Stevens wrote, "In my judgment, police interference in the attorney-client relationship is the type of governmental misconduct on a matter of central importance to the administration of justice that the Due Process Clause prohibits. Just as the police cannot impliedly promise a suspect that his silence will not be used against him and then proceed to break that promise, so too police cannot tell a suspect's attorney that they will not question the suspect and then proceed to question him. Just as the government cannot conceal from a suspect material and exculpatory evidence, so too the government cannot conceal from a suspect the material fact of his attorney's communication."

Apparently, the majority believed the defendant's Sixth Amendment right to counsel stops if the police decide to lie to the attorney. Once again, courts back the bad behavior of cops in giving us the finger with a loud, 'F**ck you!'

Bad California Rulings

Our California appellate court system doesn't limit itself to eviscerating our constitutional rights. Every day, in every way, it seems that appellate courts are doing whatever they can to extend the power of the state and in doing so, handing our lives over to the psychopaths that wantonly inhabit our justice system. You don't have to look too hard to find cases that torture themselves to find against the defendant. Below are just a few random cases that I've encountered over the years.

People v. Rubalcava

California Supreme Court

350 McAllister St, San Francisco, CA 94102

Opinion by Janice Brown, with Ronald George, Joyce Kennard, Marvin Baxter, and Ming Chin, concurring. Concurring opinion by Stanley Mosk. Concurring opinion by Kathryn Werdegar.

Rubalcava revolved around whether or not intent is relevant regarding concealed weapons charges. In deciding that intent is not relevant to a concealed weapons charge, here's what the California Supreme Court said:

"Rubalcava argues that the Legislature could not have intended to make a felon out of 'the tailor who places a pair of scissors in his jacket... the carpenter who puts an awl in his pocket, the auto mechanic who absentmindedly slips a utility knife in his back pocket before going out to lunch... the shopper who walks out of a kitchen-supply store with a recently purchased steak knife 'concealed' in his or her pocket... the parent who wraps a sharp pointed knife in a paper towel and places it in his coat to carry into a PTA potluck dinner, or... the recreational user who tucks his throwing knives into a pocket as he heads home after target practice or a game of mumblety-peg.' Although the potentially broad reach of section 12020 [now 21310] in the absence of a specific intent element is troubling, these concerns do not render the statute unconstitutional[185]."

In other words, F**CK YOU honest, hardworking tailor who put a pair of scissors in his jacket pocket. You're a felon, you will be on felony probation. F**CK YOU carpenter who put an awl in his pocket, you're not going to vote and with the two DUIs on your record and now this felony, you are going to prison! Hey shopper who purchased a steak knife at the store and wanted to be environmentally friendly and put the knife in your pocket, do you know what you just bought? A one-way ticket to losing

185 *People v. Rubalcava*. (2000). Findlaw, Supreme Court of California case and opinions.. Retrieved 12 January 2018, from http://caselaw.findlaw.com/ca-supreme-court/1299695.html

your Second Amendment rights and a permanent felony on your record.

As a matter of fact, any shopper who purchases a knife in any store and carries the knife in a shopping bag is also guilty of this code section; when you buy any knife at any store, unless you carry it openly, and not concealed, you are committing a felony punishable by three years in prison! But beware of how 'openly' you carry it, because brandishing the knife (PC 417) is also a crime, although that's only a misdemeanor and 'only' carries a minimum of 30 days county jail. F**CK YOU either way, knife buyer. Lastly, you PTA parent going to a potluck dinner, you're going to jail instead. F**CK YOU.

What the *Rubacalva* decision said to the tailor, the carpenter, the shopper, and the PTA parent was, 'You will be found guilty of a felony. You will do jail time. You will probably lose your job, if not from the conviction, then from the jail time. But even if you do lose your job, you will still pay our fines and fees or be held in violation of probation.'

I have a fantasy about this California Supreme Court. I'd love to give them a special award of letter openers from all the citizens of the state for their hard work. The letter openers would be beautiful sterling silver and come in a nice gift box. To commemorate the occasion, there would be a photographer outside to take their picture. The Justices in their flowing black robes would be given the knife-shaped letter openers and the gift boxes outside in the sunshine in a nearby park where the photography would take place in order to have a nice background.

Of course, the photographer would take a few photos here and a few photos there, instructing the Justices to move from this location to that location. Of course, the Justices would naturally, out of human instinct, put the letter openers, dirk or daggers by the legal definition, somewhere under their robes while they're moving from shot to shot. Then, a group of citizens would come up and place them under citizen's arrest for a violation of PC 21310 followed by a cop arresting them all for a felony which carries a three-year prison sentence. F**ck you.

A Very Bad Cannabis Case

California voted to legalize medical marijuana back in 1996; the first state to do so. Twenty years later, voters approved Proposition 64, legalizing adult use cannabis, although several states were ahead of us on the adult use or 'recreational' issue. While most California citizens would tout our state as being progressive and on the forefront of ending the prohibition of cannabis, they would be surprised to learn how our 'High Courts' have broken bounds of logic and reason in their rulings on cannabis cases in their ever present quest to help prosecutors 'secure the conviction.'

While there have been many, many really bad decisions regarding cannabis, I'll pick one out here to focus on so you can see how our 'High Courts' violate the law by issuing rulings that break it. What does our society call people who violate the law? Criminals. When appellate court justices issue rulings that flagrantly fly in the face of established law, what should we call them? Criminals.

How does our society handle criminals? How does our society treat low level criminals versus high level offenders? How does our society treat someone who steals a candy bar one time versus someone who runs a Ponzi scheme that deprives hundreds of thousands of their rightfully-earned savings? How should society treat a 'High Court' that willfully violates legal principles in its very own ruling which affects every citizen in our state? Like criminals. Except, we don't. The below case is an example of what we get for not doing so.

People v. Skytte

California Court of Appeal, Third Appellate District

914 Capitol Mall

Sacramento, CA 95814

Justices Elena Duarte, Louis Mauro, and Vance Raye

In December 2010, Timothy Skytte[186] made cash deposits into his bank account on three consecutive days. Each deposit was under the federal reporting limit of $10,000. A bank official noted one cash deposit reeked of marijuana. Skytte had also recently received a settlement of $24,000 in an auto accident case.

Skytte was a member of the 30th Street Patient Collective, a San Diego dispensary "providing good quality medical marijuana to patients in compliance with Proposition 215 and SB 420 since 2008." He grew medical grade marijuana for the collective and was paid for transporting it to San Diego during the timeframe of his deposits. Note: getting paid a reasonable compensation for medical marijuana is permitted under the law.

In August 2011, officers from the Butte County Sheriff's Department searched Skytte's property and found two fenced gardens. One contained 24 medical marijuana plants and the other contained 30. On another property owned by Skytte and rented to another person, police found 369 marijuana plants.

Mr. Skytte was charged with felony counts of 1.) cultivation (growing and processing plants), 2.) possessing for sales (possessing cannabis with the intent to *illegally* sell) and 3.) money laundering (depositing money into a bank knowing that it comes from *criminal* activity). After trial, a jury

186 *People v. Skytte* CA3. (2015). CourtListener. Retrieved 12 January 2018, from https://www.courtlistener.com/opinion/3157320/people-v-skytte-ca3/

in Butte County found Skytte not guilty[187] of cultivation and possession for sale. However, the judge allowed the prosecutor to argue that, because cannabis is illegal federally, Mr. Skytte knew that the money that he received from (lawfully!) donating cannabis to a dispensary was from criminal activity. Note again, it is perfectly legal to receive money which offsets costs of legal cultivation. Because here the jury acquitted Mr. Skytte of cultivation, that logically meant that the cultivation was legal.

Based on this argument by the prosecutor and backed up by the jury instruction given by the judge, the jury found Skytte guilty of money laundering. Skytte was sentenced to two years hard time in prison, but was granted bail pending appeal. In his appeal, Skytte argued that since medical marijuana is legal in the state, depositing money from the proceeds of sales does not constitute money laundering.

it is important to note here that there is a long lineage of seminal California cases which recognize the distinction between legal state activity and the fact that that same legal state activity would be illegal federally. *Skytte* was decided in 2015 but the seminal cases of *People v. Tilehkooh* (2003) and *City of Garden Grove v. Superior Court* (2007) had long established that if someone was complying with California state law, a prosecutor couldn't do an 'end-around' by arguing that the person was guilty of something because marijuana was illegal federally.

Tilehkooh reversed a probation revocation for marijuana possession for "failure to obey all laws." There, the prosecution had argued that a patient's use of cannabis, legal under California law, was nonetheless a violation of California probation because it was not in compliance with federal law. Same thing with *City of Garden Grove*. That court held that federal law did

187 Jury acquits man of pot charges. (2015). Chicoer.com. Retrieved 12 January 2018, from http://www.chicoer.com/article/zz/20111220/NEWS/111229987

not preempt state law on the issue of medical marijuana and probation, so the defendant was entitled to have his marijuana, which had previously been held as evidence, returned to him after state criminal charges had been dismissed because he was in compliance with California state law.

Tilehkooh and *City of Garden Grove* reached the right decisions because, if a district attorney could argue that a patient was guilty of something because they were in violation of federal law, our California medical cannabis laws would be rendered meaningless.

However, true to form, the California Court of Appeals, Third Appellate District, Butte, 'secured the conviction' for the prosecutor against Skytte. The prosecution's position was that "regardless of applicability of the medical marijuana defense, money laundering could be based on using money obtained from activity that is illegal under federal law." Because Skytte made the three cash deposits in amounts just under the federal minimum reporting requirement, the appellate court stated he must have known the cash came from an illegal activity.

Skytte's appellate lawyer logically and reasonably argued that Skytte's deposits did not constitute money laundering because, "If immunity directly applied to growing and providing marijuana, then the funds derived as reimbursement are protected in the same way." The justices demeaned and brushed aside that argument by stating that it relies on "logic, not law." Again, they ignored the legal precedents long since set by *Tilehkooh* and *City of Garden Grove,* so perhaps their argument was not only illogical, but also criminal.

The cowardice of the individuals that issued this decision, Elena Duarte, Louis Mauro, and Vance Raye, is evidenced by the fact that they ordered their opinion not to be published. This group, this clique, this 'appellate court' was willing to screw the defendant but they didn't want to take the step of making this an official case, to be published and therefore become a valid legal precedent. Talk about trying to conceal a crime!

Because the jury acquitted Skytte of cultivation and possession for sales, they acknowledged that he was acting lawfully under California law! Pure and simple, the judge should not have permitted the prosecutor to argue that the technical violation of federal law could be used in considering a California state violation of "money laundering."

But this is how prosecutors and their familiar lackeys, judges, like to stick it to people fighting for their rights in court. They love to remove obvious and justifiable defenses in order to 'secure the conviction.' To a psychopath, shooting fish in a barrel is much more gratifying than having to fish. Utter domination in a 'fixed' situation allows them to take delight in how powerful they believe they are.

Another point against the *Skytte* court decision is that state law, Health and Safety Code section 11362.775, written by our legislature itself, signed by our governor, and which became law in 2003, permits payment to individuals for supplying collectives with medical marijuana. Does this mean that Duarte, Mauro, and Raye would consider the 2003 California state legislature as co-conspirators or aiders and abetters of Skytte? After all, Skytte wouldn't have gotten paid if the legislature hadn´t enacted that law.

Skytte's 'crime' was putting legally earned cash in the bank. There are now thousands of people working in the legal marijuana industry in the state. Because of marijuana's federally illegal status, banks do not provide the services to this industry that they do to other industries.

Marijuana businesses must already hire security firms to oversee the large amounts of cash that come in. However, based on the Third Appellate District court's decision in *Skytte*, making a bank deposit from a marijuana-related business will land you with an arrest, charges, conviction, and prison time for money laundering. Are you following California laws regarding medical cannabis? It doesn't matter, according to the prosecutor, judge, and appellate court in *Skytte*, F**ck you.

Last But Far From Least

California v. Trombetta

U.S. Supreme Court

1 First St. NE, Washington, DC 20543

Warren E. Burger, William J. Brennan, Jr., Byron R. White, Thurgood Marshall, Harry A. Blackmun, Lewis F. Powell, Jr., William H. Rehnquist, John Paul Stevens, and Sandra Day O'Connor

California v. Trombetta was a California case that made it all the way to the U.S. Supreme Court. It dealt with whether or not the government has a duty to preserve evidence that could potentially be useful to a defendant, in other words, could the state destroy evidence that a defendant could potentially use to prove his or her innocence? *Trombetta* got a lot right. The court rightfully concluded that:

- Due process clause of the Fourteenth Amendment does require the state to disclose to criminal defendants favorable evidence that is material to either guilt or punishment.
- Under due process clause of Fourteenth Amendment, criminal prosecutions must comport with prevailing notions of fundamental fairness.
- A defendant has a constitutionally protected privilege to request and obtain from the prosecution evidence that is either material

to guilt of defendant or relevant to punishment to be imposed. (This was already established in *Brady v. Maryland.*)

- Even in absence of a specific request, the prosecution has a constitutional duty to turn over exculpatory evidence that would raise reasonable doubt about defendant's guilt.

But, even in concluding the above, the court unanimously ruled that **the Fourteenth Amendment due process clause does not *require* the government to preserve evidence that could potentially be useful to a defendant**. So, while the prosecution has a constitutional duty to turn over exculpatory evidence that would raise reasonable doubt about defendant's guilt, if the prosecution ***destroys*** the evidence, that's okay.

Of course, out and out destroying exculpatory evidence isn't allowed, but to win a motion under Trombetta, the defense has to prove that the evidence 1.) would have been exculpatory, 2.) the exculpatory value was apparent before it was destroyed and 3.) the defendant is unable to obtain comparable evidence by other reasonably available means.

The sick joke of this ruling is, how do you prove something would have been helpful if it's destroyed? How do you prove that a video would have shown that the officer brutalized your client while your client was already down if it has been deleted? How do you prove that dispatch calls would have shown that an officer stopped your client due to racial motivations if they were allowed to be purposefully written over? How do you prove that an officer's raw notes would have been materially different than his or her official report and therefore that the final report should not be trusted, if they were destroyed per department policy? You can't. F**ck you.

Treason?

These rulings provide ironclad proof that what goes on in courts nowadays is 'F**ck you' law. it's not a 'conspiracy theory' to say that appellate courts—at all levels—have been systematically eradicating decades of our well-established constitutional rights, because it's true. If a group devotes itself meticulously and thoroughly to destroying our Constitution and its safeguards, isn't that treason?

Time to Reveal the Psychopaths

It's Time to Reveal the Psychopaths. In all trades and spheres there are people who behave badly, but powerful positions attract the sickest of psychos. We have seen power abused for sex in Hollywood, and for greed on Wall Street. When an actor or banker is called out for abuses, we recognize their names and society can deal with them accordingly. In this chapter, and this book, we have seen terrible, sick abuses protected by the vestige of the officer's badge or judge's bench.

At the end of 2017, as Hollywood and Media psychos are being revealed, the courage to declare "#metoo" is spreading to victims within the Justice system. In December 2017, Appellate Judge Alex Kozinski of the Ninth Circuit Court of Appeals was hit with accusations of sexual misconduct spanning three decades. In all, fifteen women, students and colleagues among them, came forward to disclose sexual misbehavior including unwanted physical touching, displays of porn and invitations by Kozinski to have sex. In response to the allegations, Judge Kozinski announced his retirement. For thirty years of psycho behavior and harassing women, Kozinski gets to retire into the sunset, and the rest of us get to pay for it, as his final official F**ck You.

But Hollywood seems way ahead of us these days in terms of revealing its psychopaths. As our constitutional rights slip away, psychopaths in the justice system enjoy an unprecedented amount of power. In California, people are illegally arrested and jailed every day, they receive sentences based on evidence planted by cops, confessions obtained under coercion, and false accusations from paid snitches. California is a State of Collusion, where we fear criminals as much as the system that should protect us. It is a place where all arrestees are equal, but some arrestees are more equal than others[188].

188 Paraphrasing George Orwell. Original Orwell quote "All animals are equal, but some animals are more equal than others" from his adult fable, "ANIMAL FARM." The phrase is a totalitarian rewrite of the egalitarian "All animals are equal," done after a revolution by animals becomes a harsh dictatorship by the pigs, at an English farm once ruled by equally cruel humans.

ABOUT AUTHOR JOSEPH TULLY

Joseph Tully is one of California's most controversial and successful criminal defense and civil rights lawyers. He helps people defend their liberty and reputation in an irreparably flawed and unjust legal system—the topic of this, his second book, *California: State of Collusion*.

Tully, labelled recently by author and legal icon Norm Pattis a "*Gunslinger Among Paper Pushers*," has a remarkable record for earning Not Guilty jury verdicts in major felony cases in a system where bullying prosecutors are accustomed to intimidating their way to early guilty pleas.

Lawyer Tully founded and leads the San Francisco Bay Area criminal and civil rights law firm Tully & Weiss. His work has included high-stakes felony cases ranging from capital murder, high profile drug trials, and scores of white collar defense charges to sex crimes, firearm offenses, and landmark cases of every sort including a leading California stand-your-ground self defense victory.

Joseph is a go-to legal commentator for media outlets from the *LA Times* to the *NY Post*. His cases and clients have been featured on *60 Minutes* and other in-depth outlets. He informs and engages audiences of every sort on the speaking circuit including a recent keynote at the annual Mensa conference.

Learn more about Joseph Tully at **www.JosephTully.com**

Media queries or to book Joseph to speak at your event:

maggie@elitelawyermanagement.com